D0903362

HEGEL'S CRITIQUE OF THE ENLIGHTENMENT

HEGEL'S CRITIQUE OF THE ENLIGHTENMENT

LEWIS P. HINCHMAN

University Presses of Florida
University of South Florida Press / Tampa
University of Florida Press / Gainesville

Library of Congress Cataloging in Publication Data

Hinchman, Lewis P.
Hegel's critique of the enlightenment.

"A University of Florida/University of South Florida book."
Bibliography: p.
Includes index.
1. Hegel, Georg Wilhelm Friedrich, 1770–1831.
2. Enlightenment. 3. Political science—History.
I. Title.
B2948.H525 1984 320′.01 84-7286
ISBN 0-8130-0784-4

University Presses of Florida is the central agency for scholarly publishing of the State of Florida's university system. Its offices are located at 15 NW 15th Street, Gainesville, FL 32603. Works published by University Presses of Florida are evaluated and selected for publication by a faculty editorial committee of any one of Florida's nine public universities: Florida A&M University (Tallahassee), Florida Atlantic University (Boca Raton), Florida International University (Miami), Florida State University (Tallahassee), University of Central Florida (Orlando), University of Florida (Gainesville), University of North Florida (Jacksonville), University of South Florida (Tampa), University of West Florida (Pensacola).

Copyright © 1984 by the Board of Regents of the State of Florida

Printed in the U.S.A. on acid-free paper

To my wife, Sandra

CONTENTS

PREFACE

ALTHOUGH this book concerns a problem in the history of political philosophy—Hegel's relationship to the Enlightenment—it actually grew out of my aspiration to understand more clearly the contemporary political and philosophical situation. I first discovered Hegel when I was a visiting student in Germany during the late 1960s, a time of intense political crisis and, for many of us, of bitter disappointments. Initially drawn to Hegel's works merely because of their influence on Marx, I gradually came to suspect that Hegel might still shed some light on our modern predicament in his own right, and perhaps just in those matters where Marx did not see so clearly.

Like the men and women of my own generation, Hegel reached maturity in a revolutionary age when, so it seemed to sanguine souls, the old order was tottering. In his time and ours, human beings appeared finally to be on the verge of a breakthrough toward greater freedom and a deeper sense of community. Moreover, the unsettled times of the late eighteenth century spawned a bewildering assortment of movements, philosophies, protests, and personal credos (again reminiscent of the sixties and seventies): the Enlightenment itself and the radical political movements affected by it in diverse ways, movements of romantic nostalgia and poetic renewal, religious awakenings and reactionary coteries, ideologies of egoistic self-affirmation as well as old-fashioned cynicism.

But, again like my generation, Hegel and his age had to come to terms with the disillusionment of seeing those movements of "liberation" either peter out, turn into tyrannical or obscurantist cliques, or unleash the very forces they had fought against. It is easy to see why Hegel mistrusted the venerable assumption that each entity is self-identical and not another thing. He had too many experiences of movements and ideas turning out to be the very opposite of what their proponents had believed and expected them to be.

The great lesson, if that is the right word, that one learns from Hegel is humility and self-criticism. One can readily discern, in his analyses of the "fragmented egos" and "beautiful souls" of his age, implicit criticisms of the various ideologies that have won adherents in our own. He makes us sensitive to the one-sidedness and blindness of these world-views, their tendency to inspire us to act on a flawed understanding of man and his situation. But more important, Hegel helps us see the shortcomings of the Enlightenment (and perhaps through it, of modern "enlightened" positions such as mainstream social science and analytic philosophy). He encourages us to believe that philosophers have the ability, and indeed the responsibility, to bring their critical acumen to bear on the issues and ideologies that dominate the "consciousness" of ordinary people, to encourage rational thought and self-reflection.

My approach to Hegel, then, is designed to illuminate those aspects of his thought which seem the most insightful, thought-provoking, and relevant for our time. Although I have not been uncritical of Hegel, I have most often been guided by his maxim that it is easier to find fault with something than to show its positive and fruitful side. The single exception to this rule of thumb is in chapter eight, where I take issue with Hegel over what seems to me a serious inconsistency in his entire political thought.

Let me acknowledge the influence and help of several people who contributed more than they realize to the completion of this book. First, I am grateful to the members of my dissertation committee at Cornell—Werner Dannhauser (my chairman), Eldon Eisenach, and Myron Rush—for their patience and many helpful contributions when I first embarked on this project and for their encouragement thereafter. Allen Wood, then of Cornell's Philosophy Department, aided me considerably in understanding the *Phenomenology of Mind* and *Philosophy of Right* in seminars he gave on those works. I would further like to emphasize my special indebtedness to two men I have never met but whose books assisted me in innumerable ways: Charles Taylor, author of *Hegel*, and Stanley Rosen, author of *G. W. F. Hegel: An Introduction to the Science of Wisdom*. Professor Taylor and Paul Eisenberg of Indiana University read an earlier draft of this manuscript carefully and made many valuable suggestions toward improving it.

Finally, I should say a word of appreciation to some very good friends—Michael Votichenko, Baylor Johnson, and Thomas Meyer—for our many philosophical discussions which stimulated my interest in this project to begin with and helped to generate the ideas and criticisms necessary to finish it.

In a different category altogether, I want to thank my wife, Sandra, even though words fail to convey what her help has meant to me. Without the hundreds of hours she put into editing and revising this manuscript it could never have been completed. Indeed, the book is really a joint effort, to which she contributed fully as much as I did.

A NOTE ON EDITIONS

FOR THE sake of consistency, I have done virtually all of the translations of passages from German-language works cited in this book. Wherever possible I have also noted parenthetically in the footnotes the page number (and, if appropriate, the paragraph) of the more familiar English translations in which these passages may be found. Exceptions are those cases in which material available in the German text does not appear in the English version. The most important instance of an exception is the third volume of Hegel's *Enzyklopädie der Philosophischen Wissenschaften*, usually called the *Philosophy of Mind* in English. The *Zusätze*, notes taken by Hegel's students from his lectures, are included in my German edition but not in Wallace's translation.

In two cases I have had to cite English translations of books written in German but not available here in the original. One is Hegel's Jena lectures on *Realphilosophie*, and the other is the text (though not the introduction) of Fichte's *Wissenschaftslehre* (*Science of Knowledge*). In these cases references will be made only to the English edition listed in the bibliography.

Foreign words are italicized for the first usage and appear in roman type thereafter.

Finally, the reader should note that the Haldane translation of Hegel's lectures on the *History of Philosophy* does not always correspond, either in content or in the length of the volumes, to the German edition I used. Whenever a passage from one volume of the German work appears in a different volume of the English translation, this discrepancy is pointed out in the footnotes. Otherwise, the reader may assume that the volume number is the same for both editions.

ABBREVIATIONS

Works by Hegel

"Differenzschrift"	"Differenz des Fichteschen und Schellingschen Systems der Philosophie"
Einl. G. Phil.	*Einleitung in die Geschichte der Philosophie*
Enz. 1	*Enzyklopädie der philosophischen Wissenschaften*, vol. 1 (*Logik*)
Enz. 3	*Enzyklopädie der philosophischen Wissenschaften*, vol. 3 (*Philosophie des Geistes*)
G. Phil.	*Geschichte der Philosophie*
"G. W."	"Glauben und Wissen"
Logik	*Wissenschaft der Logik*
"Naturrecht"	"Über die wissenschaftlichen Behandlungsarten des Naturrechts"
P. Gesch.	*Philosophie der Geschichte*
Ph. G.	*Phänomenologie des Geistes*
P. R.	*Grundlinien der Philosophie des Rechts oder Naturrecht und Staatswissenschaft im Grundrisse*
Realphilosophie	*Hegel's Social Philosophy in the Jena Realphilosophie*
"Skeptizismus"	"Verhältnis des Skeptizismus zur Philosophie"

Works by Fichte

Wiss. Ein.	*Erste und Zweite Einleitung in die Wissenschaftslehre*
Sci. Knowl.	*Science of Knowledge*
Voc. Man	*Vocation of Man*

Works by Kant

K. p. V.	*Kritik der praktischen Vernunft*
K. r. V.	*Kritik der reinen Vernunft*

Works by Schelling

"Darstellung"	"Darstellung meines Systems der Philosophie"
"Bruno"	"Bruno oder über das göttliche und natürliche Prinzip der Dinge. Ein Gespräch."

INTRODUCTION

WHAT impels human beings to start thinking philosophically? According to Hegel, they do so because the affective bonds of their polities have begun to unravel. When the "power of unification disappears from the life of man,"[1] political or public existence no longer satisfies him. The pleasures of what Hannah Arendt liked to call "public freedom" yield to the more esoteric attraction of the *vita contemplativa*. Philosophy therefore bespeaks a "rupture in the actual world . . . the demise of a real world."[2] It is the symptom of and consolation for the decline of an integral "ethical life" or *Sittlichkeit*.

But while philosophy in Hegel's sense (here he is thinking especially of Socrates and Plato) involves a loss of something very valuable, it allows us to gain something even more precious. To think philosophically, one must disentangle the self, the "I," from the world. The individual who philosophizes begins to regard himself as separate from and independent of the web of natural and human relationships which had hitherto circumscribed him and yet made him an integral part of the political whole.[3] Philosophy thus marks the emancipation of human self-consciousness from all particularistic norms and perspectives.

If we isolated only this second, emancipatory aspect of philosophy, it would be identical to "enlightenment" in its broadest meaning. While Hegel usually writes of *the* Enlightenment, referring to the eighteenth-century movement we are familiar with, he sometimes mentions an ancient Enlightenment as well.[4] He stretches the connotation of the word because he regards its core content as applicable whenever the self emerges as a distinct element in human history. In this sense, the modern Enlightenment epitomizes and completes a process of enlightenment which began several millennia ago.

Understood in this way, enlightenment contains both cognitive and moral-political dimensions. Or rather, these are merely different features of the very same phenomenon. When I abstract from specific circumstances, isolating my self or my ego from everything else, I simultaneously become an arbiter of the moral-political milieu I left behind. On this point such diverse "enlightened" positions as ancient sophism, Humean skepticism and Kantian moral philosophy all converge. There is nothing absolute about traditional standards of conduct. Rather they must be subjected to scrutiny by the self, now become a sort of absolute in its own right. To position myself "outside" a moral-political community entails also that I place myself "above" it, requiring it to justify its claims on me before the bar of standards that I thereby proclaim superior to or perhaps more "natural" than those of the actual world. Even if I subsequently find a justification for existing laws, gods, and institutions, these will henceforth derive their validity from principles that I have established. And what I have established, I can also change.

Enlightenment understood as the isolation of self-conscious individuality lays the foundations for political freedom in the modern sense. Where the Greek citizen exercised an ethical or "beautiful" freedom that is impossible in modern states (cf. chapters 5 and 8), he could only do so as a Spartan or Athenian, not as a human being possessed of inalienable rights. By dissolving the bonds of specific political communities, enlightened self-consciousness promotes the conception of man as a universal being. He can now base his claim to rights and human dignity on "natural" grounds rather than on the traditional order of a given society: "political freedom, freedom within the state, commences when the individual feels himself to be an individual, when the subject knows himself to be such in his universality, or when the consciousness of personality—the consciousness of having an inherently infinite worth—comes to the fore."[5]

However, enlightenment makes this kind of freedom possible only at the cost of rendering it empty and in a way meaningless. Thought, the very power which enabled the individual to conceive of himself as an individual, simultaneously devalues the codes of conduct that tradition had passed down as unquestioned goods: "All that we recognize as right or duty can be shown by thought to be nugatory, limited, and by no means absolute."[6] Although he is free, the individual now lacks any concrete, certain principles of action. Moreover, Hegel interprets the alienation between enlightened self-consciousness and the ethical life of a community as a rift between human and divine spirit: "as subjective freedom arises and man descends from external actuality into his spirit, there emerges a reflective opposition that contains within itself the negation of actuality. Specifically, this withdrawal from the present already constitutes an opposition of which one aspect is God or the divine and the other is the subject in his particularity."[7] The withdrawal from the present (*Gegenwart*) of a living ethical community is simultaneously withdrawal from the presence of the divine in human affairs.

If philosophy consisted only in this act of separation or abstraction of oneself from an ethical (*sittlich*) or political-religious whole, then philosophy would be essentially identical to enlightenment. But for Hegel true philosophy differentiates itself from enlightenment precisely in attempting to reconstruct, in thought, the wholeness of life that enlightenment has undermined: "Philosophy is . . . the reconciliation of the corruption initiated by thought; this reconciliation occurs in the ideal world, in the world of spirit [*Geist*] to which man flees when the earthly world no longer satisfies him . . . . But this reconciliation concerns only the world of thought, not the earthly world."[8]

The paradoxes of enlightenment take us to the heart of Hegel's philosophical enterprise. Philosophy must try to restore, albeit only on an intellectual plane, a sense of totality and completeness to human life. To accomplish this, Hegel must show us that the isolated self of enlightenment is an untenable construct, both theoretically and practically. He must demonstrate that a true comprehension of the self of enlightenment will cause us to redefine our entire notion of selfhood. Hegel expects we will come to realize that our identity diffuses beyond our immediate self-consciousness as discrete individuals toward the totality of existence. The philosopher in Hegel's sense cannot truly think himself without including in that thought, at least by implication, the whole of nature and culture. In this way, philosophy provides a totality-in-thought to replace the pre-enlightened totality of naïve natural existence symbolized by personal childhood and also by the ancient polis, man's collective childhood. As Hegel expresses it in one of his most moving passages:

> Thinking is spirit's *entry into itself*, and thereby it makes into an *object* what it is *qua* intuitive, collects itself within itself and thus separates itself from itself. This separation is . . . the *first condition* and moment of *self-consciousness* from whose *self-collecting* as *free thought* alone the development of the universe in thought, i.e., philosophy, can emerge. This is precisely what constitutes the infinite labor of spirit, to withdraw into the *night* and *loneliness of self-consciousness* from its *immediate existence*, its *happy, natural life*, and to *reconstruct* in thought the actuality and intuition it had separated from itself solely by virtue of its own strength and power.[9]

Once the "I" has been extricated from the matrix of experience as a distinct "subject" confronting an object, the problems of epistemology become especially urgent. It is only a short step from positing the subject-object dichotomy to doubting whether we can ever know the object as it truly is. Hegel credits Descartes with having revolutionized philosophy by addressing the problem of knowledge on this abstract plane. But he sees that Descartes' philosophy is only the tip of an iceberg. The Frenchman gave only abstract, formal expression to the modern "revolution of subjectivity" which had been proceeding apace in every sphere of life. Therefore, to Hegel, "Cartesian dualism" meant not just a philosophical doctrine but an entire worldview which had to be combatted on all levels:

> Every aspect of living culture as well as philosophy should have to seek antidotes both to Cartesian philosophy, which, in philosophical form, has given expression to the universal, rampant dualism in the culture of the recent world, and to the universal culture of which it is an expression. The noisy political and religious revolutions as well as the quieter transformations of man's public life are generally only variegated façades of this dualism, which is the demise of all the old ways of life.[10]

What disturbed Hegel especially about Descartes' philosophy (as well as Kant's) was its willingness to put the seal of necessity and irrevocability on the estrangement of the self from the world. To Hegel, the rigid separation of mind (*res cogitans*) and world (*res extensa*) was a phenomenon typical only of modernity. He saw no reason to suppose that this modern experience of extreme alienation represented the final condition of all mankind. Still, one could not escape dualism by regressing to more naïve stages of metaphysics (e.g., the Greek). Somehow, the inner logic of the Cartesian position would have to be represented as culminating in its own negation. In effect, this was the philosophical task Hegel set for himself, and the one that informs all his writings.

From this perspective, we can see why all aspects of philosophy are so tightly connected for Hegel. Aesthetic, religious, political and moral issues point toward the more abstract problems of epistemology. And epistemology, as we shall see shortly, is the specifically modern way of dealing with ontological questions. On the other hand, the abstract principles of Hegel's *Logic* do not come into sharp focus until we see them fleshed out in his other works. Logic and history, metaphysics and politics do not just complement each other in Hegel's writings; they are absolutely inseparable. And no other concept shows this more clearly than that of enlightenment.

A complete picture of Hegel's critique of the modern Enlightenment will thus take us from the most abstract realms of logic to a consideration of the French Revolution and the modern state. But to understand Hegel in all these endeavors, we must try to grasp the underlying continuity of his thought, the recurrent pattern which makes it uniquely "Hegelian." The key to such an understanding, I believe, lies in what Hegel calls "the concept." Of course, the concept is not the only crucial term in Hegel's discourse. We also need to know what Hegel means by mind or spirit (Geist), the idea, "subject," and many more. But all these terms are simply variations on a theme. "The concept" lies at the bottom of them all. Since the first two chapters of this study are devoted to explaining Hegel's speculative philosophy, and hence the concept, I will not try to anticipate those arguments here. But I will try to show what Hegel wishes to accomplish and why his project is so important.

Let us return for a moment to Cartesian dualism. According to Descartes, if we doubt (i.e., abstract from) the content of all our experience, we still retain the intuition of an "I think" from which no further abstraction can be made. We are immediately certain of its existence because to deny it would require an "I" to do the denying, thereby involving us in self-contradiction. What is more, we do not know of the res cogitans by means of discursive or syllogistic thinking. We do not say: All beings that think, are; I think; therefore, I am. Rather, thinking and being are inextricably linked without reference to any major premise designating "all beings" of a class. The complement of res cogitans is "extended being," or res extensa, which means simply all the world (including our own bodies) which is *not*-"I" and which therefore cannot be known directly and immediately by introspection. I cannot doubt that I am, but I can doubt that everything else is.

The effect of Descartes' dualism is a reduction of man and his world to their most abstract determinations. If I ask what I am, the only answer seems to be that I am an empty res cogitans, certain of my own existence but of nothing else. Likewise, my world is reduced to nothing but extension, or, to use Hobbes' phrase, "matter in motion," cognizable in terms of mechanical causation. More exactly, if I wish to know what I am there are really two answers available. I am first that which I know myself to be by abstraction from everything else, a res cogitans. But since the res cogitans is an empty "I," the search for a more concrete answer leads me to consider what Descartes called the "passions of the soul" or the mechanics of my own motivations. We thus find ourselves to be dual beings: on the one hand, detached observers, res cogitans, or the contentless "I think" which forms the subject in every case of knowing; and on the other hand, appetitive machines explicable in terms of cause and effect or res extensa. The purpose of the knowledge we acquire of extended beings is, as Descartes frankly expressed it, to render ourselves "the masters and possessors of nature."[11]

Cartesian dualism illuminates the strange paradox of self-knowledge as it is conceived throughout the modern Enlightenment. The "I" is accorded the remarkable power to abstract from everything except itself, to dissolve all its bonds to the world and isolate itself as self-certainty, the *only* certainty. Yet this certainty remains empty. To arrive at any concrete knowledge of myself, I must turn my attention away from myself and toward the world (which includes my empirical existence). But the world or res extensa has already been defined as precisely not what I am. Thus, strictly speaking, knowledge of myself as a part of extended substance is not self-knowledge at all, but rather knowledge of the not-"I."

One solution to this puzzle would be to deny the reality of the "I" and hence of self-knowledge as distinct from the knowledge of nature. This is the course Hume and many other Enlightenment philosophers chose to pursue. It is also, I think, implicit in modern social science. On this theory, we are at bottom "bundles of perceptions"; there is no unifying force in consciousness distinct from our impressions or thoughts. So it follows that self-knowledge, if it is to make any sense, must mean knowledge of man insofar as his behavior (whether individual or collective) follows the same predictable patterns or laws that we observe to have force in nature. The schema or paradigm used to explain human behavior may be crude or highly complex. But all, from simple attraction-aversion psychologies to the subtle and intricate "systems theories" of today, rest on the same assumption: that self-knowledge proceeds by indirection. We first construct a paradigm based upon apparently sound knowledge of nature; in other words, we begin with what we are not; we go outside ourselves. Then, subsequently, we return to ourselves with an allegedly appropriate model in hand.

Drawing on the Kantian tradition (and on Descartes himself), Hegel inverts the typical procedure employed by the Enlightenment—and its offspring, modern science—to acquire knowledge of oneself. Instead of approaching self-knowledge by means of behavior models elicited from the external, natural world or res extensa, Hegel suggests that self-knowledge, knowledge of the "I," provides us with a paradigm for which we find approximations in external reality. Further, those approximations extend from the prebiological natural sphere, which is still mainly mechanical, to the phenomena of life, human interaction, and above all politics and the creations of "absolute spirit," art, philosophy, and religion. In these latter, the model of knowledge, the "I," finds complete expression and self-transparency. From a Hegelian perspective, those phenomena which were least amenable to comprehension by the prototypes of the Enlightenment become the most clearly and easily understood. At the same time, what is sheerly mechanical or automatic becomes for Hegel the least comprehensible because it least resembles the special character of self-knowledge. In Hegel's terms, we know most completely that in which we can "find ourselves."

Clearly, this brief outline of Hegel's approach to the problem of self-knowledge makes sense only if we suppose that the mind can indeed have knowledge of itself, and furthermore that such self-knowledge would furnish a model through which reality could be made comprehensible. Hegel's claim is that his speculative philosophy has found a way to grasp the mind's knowledge of itself not just as an object, but also as a subject (or, more exactly, as subject and object at the same time). What is more, the structure of the "I" defines the intelligibility of all experience. So there is no longer any point in hanging on to the rigid Cartesian dichotomy of res cogitans and res extensa. The concept is present both subjectively and objectively; indeed, it is the ground of the distinction between subject and object. The concept, which will be examined in chapter 2, is Hegel's great discovery. Even if he had never written a line about history, Hegel's discovery of the concept would have assured him of a place in the first rank of philosophers.

The implications of Hegel's new theory are far-reaching and constitute the subject matter of his various works. But I would like to concentrate on just those implications of his discovery which bear on the issues clustered around the modern Enlightenment, particularly those of a political character.

The Enlightenment's ambiguous posture toward the self and self-knowledge shows up especially clearly in liberal political philosophy. By deriving political authority from a contract among individuals, or from utility, liberals put political philosophy on a new footing. Implicit in their argument is the tenet that we need only obey an authority which we ourselves have constituted. At first glance, this doctrine seems like a celebration of the autonomy of the individual against oppressive, irrational traditions. And in a sense it is.

Yet the liberals' individualist, critical premises are conjoined to a theory of human personality which seems to make autonomy meaningless or valueless. Their attack on tradition usually involved the assertion (or veiled suggestion) that existing institutions are "unnatural." To real historical development they contrasted an image of how men would think and act if the pernicious influence of artificial institutions had never been present, or if it could be removed. By thinking away all these supposedly artificial distortions of natural behavior, they arrive at a reductionist, mechanical image of human thought and action. Man appears as a machine or a passionate animal set in motion (aversion or desire) by sense impressions received from without. Like nature generally, man may no longer be thought of as an entelechy. Thus from Hobbes to Helvétius, there can be no *summum bonum.* Man is instead doomed to an endless striving for satisfaction, a chain of desire-gratification-renewed desire which would cease only in death. The "sunlit" side of the Enlightenment—its emphasis on reason and autonomy and its opposition to religious and political tyranny—was inseparable from its dark side, gloomy acquiescence in the knowledge that I am a mere machine propelled onward by inscrutable drives toward an ever-receding *fata morgana* of satisfaction.

In political-philosophical terms, we could regard Hegel's project as the quest to preserve and enhance the "human rights" tradition of the Enlightenment while detaching it from what he saw as its crudely inadequate image of man. For Hegel, we are what we know ourselves to be. If our self-knowledge culminates in a vision of mechanical necessity dominating all nature (ourselves included), we will have failed to become what potentially we could be: genuinely free beings. Our political liberty will be built on a sort of personal unfreedom, our rational society on individual irrationality.

To accomplish his intellectual task, Hegel will have to reshape our thinking about ourselves from the ground up. He must show us that the atomized, desiring self depicted by the Enlightenment is a necessary and yet incomplete representation of man in the modern world. He must explain how a more careful examination of our experience will reveal to us that the "natural" man depicted by liberal theorists is actually the creature of the historical collectivity to which he belongs. Everything about us that is really human, Hegel will argue, arises out of our interaction with society and the state. And it is precisely our individuality, our consciousness of ourselves as separate, isolated beings, which will appear to be the most perfectly "social" and "mediated" self-conception. In this manner, Hegel will try to portray the starting point of the Enlightenment's social philosophy as the result of a long process of civilization and spiritual development. Or, to return to our original theme, Hegel will show that the Cartesian *cogito* represents an artificially arrested, frozen movement of thought, whether considered in its logical, metaphysical manifestation or in its political guise as "natural" man negating all tradition and positing himself as the point of departure for political philosophy.

BEING AND THINKING FROM DESCARTES TO SCHELLING

1

HEGEL's speculative philosophy is notoriously difficult. At first one is inclined to blame its obscurity on Hegel's terminology since all his crucial concepts are defined by reference to one another. But closer inspection usually convinces the reader that Hegel's terminology is in fact very well suited to convey the thoughts which stand behind it. The real problem in interpreting Hegel's work is less semantic than it is conceptual. He forces us to think in new ways that often defy expression in the language of common sense or even of traditional philosophy.

Hegel's system can best be made accessible by examining his central contention: that the "I," the structure of self-consciousness, was the ultimate paradigm for the structure of all reality. Of course, not all of reality would display the presence of this "I"-paradigm in equal measure or with equal clarity. Still, the "I" was to Hegel the horizon of intelligibility for all things in much the same way that geometry or mechanism was for Hobbes and entelechy for Aristotle. All his important concepts can be traced back to it. For instance, he notes that spirit is "*I*, that is *we*, and *we* that is *I*"; and also that "self-consciousness [is the] *concept of spirit*."[1] Similarly, he asserts that "I is the pure concept itself which *qua* concept has achieved empirical existence."[2] And since the absolute idea is the "rational concept,"[3] it too is indirectly grounded in self-consciousness.

However, by identifying the "I" as the paradigm animating Hegel's speculative philosophy, one has exposed a host of new problems. At first glance, the notion that the "I" could be a model for all reality seems puzzling and even nonsensical. How can something so apparently subjective and personal be transformed into the essence of objective reality? In fact, one might be tempted to ask whether the "I" exists at all, whether it is not a pseudo-entity that language has foisted on us and our philosophers.

To resolve these doubts we must form a distinct idea of what Hegel means by the "I." This task in turn is rendered far easier if we can isolate certain pivotal figures in the history of philosophy whose theories of self-consciousness point toward Hegel's own position. Each of the thinkers considered in this chapter—Descartes, Hume, Kant, Fichte, and Schelling—had a profound influence on his immediate successor and each contributed decisively to a rethinking of the problem of the "I" and its relation to the world. By studying them, we can move toward Hegel's speculative philosophy in a series of easily negotiated steps. Moreover, when we examine thinkers such as Kant and Fichte we will in a way be studying Hegel himself. Hegel unfailingly argued that "*truth* . . . is one . . . and so only *one* philosophy can be the true one."[4] The "one philosophy" to which Hegel refers is not his own as distinct from others, but rather the whole of philosophic thought, which constitutes a many-faceted though still unitary truth. Indeed perhaps one of Hegel's most significant contributions to philosophy was his demonstration that it could be regarded as a whole instead of a disconnected series of contradictory opinions. Since the thinkers included in this chapter have all played important parts in the articulation of what Hegel considered this one true philosophy, it is fair to say that they do not only "lead up to" Hegel's own view but in fact form an essential constituent element in it: "The study of the history of philosophy [is the] study of philosophy itself."[5]

Descartes and Hume

In the *History of Philosophy*, Hegel remarks that the philosophy of the modern age begins with the standpoint which the older philosophers had struggled to attain: actual self-consciousness. By this he means that modern philosophers try not only to analyze the objects of knowledge but also to include the philosopher himself in their conception of true knowledge. The modern perspective ushers in a deep distinction between thinking and being, the Cartesian dualism that philosophy must attempt to reconcile: "the interest is then solely to reconcile this opposition, to comprehend reconciliation in its highest form of existence, i.e., in the abstract *opposition of thinking and being*. Their reconciliation must be apprehended. The interest of all philosophies from that time forward has been to attain this unity."[6] Because modern philosophy reaches the "standpoint of absolute consciousness" and thinks the thinker as an integral part of any knowledge, it inevitably raises the question of how, or whether, we can acquire any "objective" knowledge. Hegel argues that the Greeks did not conceive of the wholly abstract opposition of being and thinking: "Spirit and nature, thinking and being are the two infinite aspects of the idea. The idea can only truly emerge when its aspects have been apprehended, each for itself, in their abstraction and totality. Plato conceived them as the bond, as limiting and infinite, as one and many, but not as thinking and being."[7]

According to Hegel, Descartes initiates the philosophy of the modern world by recognizing that "self-consciousness is an essential moment of the true."[8] When Descartes urges us, as part of his new method, to begin by doubting everything, he is by no means trying to revive skepticism. The real significance of Descartes' principle is that it turns thinking into an "absolute beginning."[9] It expresses the essential character of the Enlightenment, the conviction that "man must see for himself, by virtue of his own thinking, whatever is to be established as authoritative and valid in the world."[10] To Hegel, Cartesian radical doubt is important because it permits thinking to abstract from all content and to arrive at the notion of a pure "I."

The aspect of the Cartesian *cogito ergo sum* which especially attracts Hegel's attention is the unity, within the "I," of being and thinking. Indeed, Hegel calls the cogito ergo sum the "principle about which revolves the whole interest of modern philosophy."[11] In Descartes' own self-understanding, the cogito argument simply reveals the existence of one "fact" which I cannot doubt. My existence is absolutely certain because if I doubt it, I cannot doubt that *I* doubt; the "I" which does the doubting apparently cannot itself be an object of doubt without a self-contradiction. But when Hegel reconstructs Descartes' argument, it looks somewhat different: "Descartes is seeking something certain and true in itself. This would be neither simply true, like the object of faith without knowledge, nor would it be the sensuous or even skeptical certainty which lacks truth."[12]

Descartes' explicit version of the ontological proof merely reiterates, in a somewhat misleading way, the premise which he introduced apropos of the "I": "There is given here, in the form of God, no other presentation [*Vorstellung*] but that of *cogito, ergo sum*, . . . being and thinking inseparably connected."[13] The "I" is a sort of being the existence of which requires only that it be thought. Furthermore, an "I" that could not be an object of thought would simply not exist at all. It would be an absurdity. Hegel is suggesting in these lines a radical hypothesis which will be developed more fully later: If we comprehend God's nature, we shall find it to be like that of self-consciousness, provided we understand correctly what the latter is. We must discern the underlying common structure of both God and the "I" in the paradoxical characteristic of self-positing, the unity of "to be" and "to be thought": "The determination of being is in my own 'I'; this connection itself is primary. Thinking as being and being as thinking, that is my certainty, 'I'. . . . What is inseparable is nevertheless different: but identity is not endangered by this difference [*Verschiedenheit*], they are a unity."[14]

But Descartes does not conclude from the identity of thinking and being in consciousness that thinking and being are identical per se. He lapses into the dualism decried by Hegel, because he makes the cogito a merely subjective principle confronted by a world (being) that cannot be known with the immediate certainty given to self-knowledge. To rephrase this idea in Hegel's terms, Descartes has hit upon "certainty itself" (the "I"), since certainty is only a predicate of all other judgments while it is the very essence of the "I."[15] But he has not sufficiently developed his insight to arrive at what Hegel calls truth (*Wahrheit*), that is, a differentiated content which could be an object of knowledge. Although Descartes sees that self-consciousness is a vital part of truth, he has not yet conceived the principle, first encountered in Kant's philosophy, that all knowledge of being is in some sense self-knowledge. Descartes has thus uncovered "the most interesting idea of modern times"[16] without apprehending the full import of his discovery.

Because Descartes understands the cogito as only a subjective principle, knowledge of objective reality becomes problematic. God alone, here introduced as a sort of *deus ex machina*, can guarantee the correctness of our knowledge of the external world (including our own bodies) because it is contrary to His nature to deceive us. In other words, God secures the correspondence of our perceptions and concepts to the world of res extensa of which we lack immediate certainty. To this formulation, Hegel objects that God is taken as a third thing outside of, and different from, res cogitans and res extensa which, as the terms indicate, are themselves understood merely as things. He criticizes the form of Descartes' argument in which there are "two things, thinking [soul] and body . . . [and] God now appears as a third thing outside of both, not as the concept of unity, nor are both members themselves the concept."[17]

Descartes' metaphysics, constructed in terms of separated "things" linked in an inexplicable way, remains open to serious criticism from empiricists like Hume. Hume's objection has the following form: "There are some philosophers, who imagine we are every moment intimately conscious of what we call our SELF; that we feel its existence and its continuance in existence; and are certain, beyond the evidence of a demonstration, both of its perfect identity and simplicity. . . .

"Unluckily all these positive assertions are contrary to that very experience, which is pleaded for them, nor have we any idea of *self*, after the manner it is here explain'd."[18] Hume is clearly denying that the knowledge we believe we have of a self corresponds to any actual entity. But it is important to take note of his terminology. He maintains that we have no idea of a self which is continually in existence, perfectly identical and simple (i.e., uncompounded). These are among the predicates which rationalist metaphysicians ascribed to the self as a means to draw conclusions about the immateriality and immortality of the soul. Hume's presentation continues:

> From what impression cou'd this idea [of the self] be deriv'd? . . . It must be some one impression, that gives rise to every real idea. But self or person is not any one impression, but that to which our several impressions and ideas are suppos'd to have a reference. If any impression gives rise to the idea of self, that impression must continue invariably the same, thro' the whole course of our lives. . . . But there is no impression constant and invariable. For my part, when I enter most intimately into what I call *myself*, I always stumble on some particular perception or other, of heat or cold, light or shade, love or hatred, pain or pleasure. I can never catch *myself* at any time without a perception, and can never observe any thing but the perception. . . . I

> may venture to affirm of . . . mankind, that they are nothing but a bundle or collection of different perceptions.[19]

Hume's argument is thus an obvious, practically inescapable conclusion of a consistent empiricism. Our ideas all arise from sense impressions or relations among them. But there is no single impression corresponding to the "I"; rather, introspection discloses to us a ceaseless flux of differing perceptions. Hence we ourselves are nothing but a flux, "a bundle or collection of differing perceptions." Hume's position is valid only if one takes the self to refer to a thing, res cogitans. And that is not the view held by German idealism. Hume's arguments are relevant to Descartes' conception of the "I," but not to Hegel's.

To demonstrate this point, let us analyze Hume's contention more carefully. He proposes to clarify the nature of the "I" by means of introspection, i.e., by directing his thoughts upon himself in search of a self. This means he has literally split himself asunder. We now have Hume the observer, the seeker, and Hume the observed, the object of the entire investigation. Hume the observer scans his mental activity trying to spot some one impression that would correspond to a self and, naturally, he finds instead only diverse perceptions. In short, Hume qua observer finds in Hume qua observed nothing that would qualify as a self. Why? The answer is at once obvious and perplexing. The "I," when it tries to make itself into an object, cannot discover itself. It "is" only as a subject. Clearly, Hume the observer, the seeker after himself, betrays the "existence" (though this is a poor expression) of an "I" in the very act of denying it. He says: "When *I* enter most intimately into what *I* call myself, *I* always stumble on some particular perception." He does not realize that the "I" that reflects or "looks for" the self is the very self he is seeking, although if that introspecting "I" is made into an object of thought, it too becomes a fleeting perception.

These reflections point to another problem in Hume's reasoning. When he affirms that for the self to validate itself before his inquiry it must provide a single impression of itself, he is making a tacit comparison to our mode of knowing external objects. Hume demands that the self be cognizable in the same way as an object of perception. This is not altogether surprising given the tendency, already evident in Descartes, to treat the "I" as a thing. But one must ask Hume how he can be so sure in advance that the self is knowable in the same way as a dog or a rock (a mere object that is not at the same time a subject).

Hume simply assumes that both the things of perception and the "I" stand on the same plane of cognition, and that whatever does not qualify as a thing is not at all. German idealism will challenge Hume by reversing his priority: self-consciousness will be the ground of knowledge of all other things. Hegel indeed asserts that a complete analysis of the "thing" of perception leads, by way of the categories of force and understanding, to the concept of the "I."[20]

For these reasons, Hume's attempt to overcome Cartesian dualism by denying the possibility of self-knowledge appears to be incomplete. Nevertheless, he has demonstrated that we cannot regard the "I" as an object of perception. Consequently, the question must arise of how exactly we ought to conceive of the "I" if it eludes every attempt to pin it down as a thing. In order to understand how this problem might be solved, it is necessary to survey Kant's doctrine of transcendental apperception and its relation to possible objective knowledge.

Kant

The *Critique of Pure Reason*, in which Kant's theory of self-consciousness finds its fullest expression, was written with two purposes in mind. First, Kant intended to prove that reason (*Vernunft*) is incapable of acquiring knowledge of objects outside our experience. Its legitimate use is restricted to the formulation of the rules governing the operation of the faculty of understanding (*Verstand*). Pure reason, or reason applied beyond the bounds of formal logic, is illicit, since it has led us into unsolvable dilemmas about the traditional objects of metaphysics: God, the cosmos, and the soul.

Kant's second purpose was to refute the skepticism Hume had fostered by demonstrating that causal explanations lack the universality and necessity characteristic of mathematics. Hume maintained that what we take to be necessity of causal connection in fact springs from a habit of associating certain phenomena with others always observed to accompany them. Cause and effect for Hume are concepts we form on the basis of experience. Hence any specific causal link can never enjoy the status of being any more than a probable inference from the past. Because causal inferences are a posteriori, they lack the universality and necessity characteristic of mathematics.

Kant concluded that Hume's destruction of the causality principle would be valid only if that principle were indeed derived from experience. His doubt about this aspect of Hume's argument was the catalyst that triggered a reexamination of the logical status of all categories of the understanding in his *Critique of Pure Reason*. In Kant's view, Hume's arguments undermined not just the principle of causality but the foundations of all objective knowledge, including even mathematics. The objectivity of our knowledge (its universality and necessity) hinged for Kant on the question of whether synthetic judgments—those that add to our understanding of the logical subject rather than simply explicating what is already contained in it—that were also a priori, or not merely induced from experience, were possible. The apriority of synthetic judgments could only be certified if the understanding contributed certain elements to the cognition of an object. This contribution could not take the form of a subjective association of perceptions superadded to a preexisting objective world. Rather, the understanding would have to participate in the very constituting of perceived reality.

Kant discerns a possible rebuttal of Hume's skepticism in the notion of what an object of experience is. Normally we regard the concept "object" as an abstraction from the various concrete things we encounter (be these sensuous like houses or trees, thought constructs like triangles, or even our own selves taken as objects of what Kant calls "inner sense"). But Kant reflects that what we call an object is actually a unity of diverse perceptions, a manifold that must first have been connected so as to constitute one thing about which predications may be made: "Connection does not however reside in the objects, and could not by any means be elicited from them by perceptions; rather it is solely an accomplishment of the understanding which itself is nothing but the faculty of connecting *a priori*."[21] In this sense the concept "object" is the very condition for having any experience at all, not just an abstraction made ex post facto. Not everyone can give a philosophical account of what an object is, but everyone presupposes that he knows what an object is by making any judgment whatsoever. Thus, for Kant, "object" is an a priori construction to which we automatically "assign" the plurality of perceptions we encounter.

What then are the prerequisites of there being objects (and, by extension, experiences) at all? First, the manifold of sense must be intuited as in space and time. Space and time are not concepts, because we do not subsume specific spaces or time intervals under them in the way, for instance, that we subsume different cats under the concept, cat. Space and time are unitary and continuous. We indeed subdivide them into inches, seconds and so on, but we presuppose them as undivided and continuous before undertaking these divisions. Yet the mere intuitions of space and time, although a priori and required for experience, do not in themselves yield knowledge of objects. Crudely put, they allow us to say "now" or "then" and also "here" or "there," but they do not permit us to say what object is out there now.

As suggested above, the ultimate precondition for having an object of experience is unity of the manifold or a connecting of diverse perceptions. But how is unity possible? The condition of the possibility of unity in the object is the unity of self-consciousness or the "synthetic unity of apperception" which Kant describes as follows:

> The "I think" must *be able to* accompany all my presentations; for otherwise something would be presented [*vorgestellt*] in me that could not be thought at all, which means as much as: the presentation would either be impossible or at least nothing for me. That presentation that can be given before all thinking is called *intuition* [that is, the intuitions of space and time; L. H.]. Thus every manifold of intuition has a necessary relation to the "I think," in the same subject in whom the manifold is encountered. This presentation however is an act of *spontaneity*, i.e., it cannot be regarded as belonging to sensibility. I call it *pure apperception* . . . or also *original apperception*, because it is that self-consciousness that can be accompanied by no further presentation since it evokes the presentation "I think" that must be able to accompany all others and is one and the same in every consciousness. I also call the unity of apperception the *transcendental* unity of self-consciousness.[22]

The "I think" referred to by Kant designates our awareness that any given "presentation" is our own. It does not mean that we consciously reflect on experience as our own at every instant. Kant says only that the "I think" must be able to accompany our presentations, not that it actually does so in each case. The "I think" underscores the fact that I can disengage myself from all my specific presentations and regard them as united within my self-consciousness. It does not suggest any uncertainty about my presentations but only the fact that they are mine, that I know that I have them.

Perhaps the best way to illustrate the importance of Kant's transcendental unity of apperception is to employ a metaphor. A mirror and a wax tablet have this much in common with human consciousness: all three duplicate, in some way, that which is given to them from outside themselves. A mirror reflects images, a tablet receives impressions, and the mind has "presentations" of objects. However, only the mind unites this diversity within one consciousness. A mirror and a tablet differ from the mind because they are not aware that these diverse contents are their own. Kant expresses this theme when he says that without the power of consciousness to unify a manifold, "I would have as variegated and diverse a self as I have presentations of which I am conscious."[23]

The relationship between the unity of an object of experience and the transcendental unity of self-consciousness should now be apparent. A unitary object or connected manifold is only possible because of its internal correlate, the unity of consciousness: "The a priori conditions of possible experience as such are simultaneously the conditions for the possibility of the objects of experience."[24] Kant says much the same thing when he writes that "the unity, which the object makes necessary, can be nothing other than the formal unity of consciousness in the synthesis of the manifold into presentations. So we say: we know [*erkennen*] the object when we have effected synthetic unity in the manifold of intuition."[25]

Two corollaries of Kant's argument must be given proper consideration in order for us to realize what he has gained by his insight into the relationship between subjective and objective unity. First, because any object of cognition is, qua unitary object, constituted by the unity of self-consciousness, Kant reasons that our cognition is always of appearances (*phenomena*) and not of things-in-themselves (*noumena*). The "I" of which we are aware when we reflect is also an appearance, essentially different from the "I" of transcendental apperception: "The transcendental unity of apperception is that [unity] through which any manifold given in an intuition is unified into the concept of the object. It is therefore called *objective* and must be distinguished from the *subjective unity* of consciousness which is a *determination of inner sense*."[26]

The "I" of which we become aware when, like Hume, we introspect is a determination of "inner sense" because it is given as an intuition in time. We feel that we persist over time (Hume to the contrary notwithstanding!) such that the "I" of introspection, if we can disentangle it all from our ever-changing inner states, is an object of consciousness. But transcendental apperception is the "I" that observes or introspects, not the "I" that is fixated as object. Hence the former is noumenal, the latter phenomenal.

Second, although we can only have knowledge of appearances, that knowledge is universal and necessary. If the objects of cognition were truly other than we are, i.e., things-in-themselves, then Hume would be right in saying that causality and the other categories were only contingent, subjective "habits" of thought. However, since we constitute the objects themselves, our knowledge of them includes the explication of their objectivity. To know an object means to say what it is. The "what" concerns not just contingent matters of fact such as color and shape, but also certain relationships which belong to the very concept of an object. These are Kant's twelve categories, which serve to transform subjective into objective judgments.

The table of judgments represents the explication of the nature of mind as such, i.e., of the transcendental unity of consciousness. The categories, which correspond to and are derived from the table of judgments, represent the explication of the nature of any object. The subject side—the unity of consciousness and the table of judgments—corresponds exactly to the object side—the object's unity and the categories—because the object is a construct of transcendental apperception and an external manifestation of the structure of consciousness.

The relationship between the transcendental unity of self-consciousness and the (unitary) object provides the answer to the status of our knowledge of nature and its laws: "We ourselves thus import the order and regularity, which we call *nature*, into the phenomena; and we should not be able to find it there, if we, or the nature of mind [*Gemüt*] had not originally put it in."[27] Kant's conviction is that specific natural laws are only special cases of higher laws, and that the chain of increasing generality leads ultimately to the functions of the understanding itself. Hence he calls the understanding "legislation for nature."[28]

Kant seems successfully to have shown how "*subjective conditions of thinking* should have *objective validity*."[29] Subjective conditions of thinking are involved in the constituting of an object; when we apply the categories in a particular cognition, we are only giving an account of the objectification of the mind's own structure. Kant's entire philosophy thus hinges on the mind's capacity to know itself, or at least to recognize that its synthesizing activity is a precondition for any knowledge at all. Kant explicitly acknowledges the absolute importance of his doctrine of self-consciousness when he writes that "the synthetic unity of apperception is the apex on which hinges all employment of the understanding, even all of logic and, accordingly, transcendental philosophy; indeed this faculty is the understanding itself."[30]

For Hegel, Kant's philosophy in some respects has a truly speculative core and thus marks an advance over Cartesian dualism. Hegel had called the unity of being and thinking expressed in Descartes' cogito principle the most interesting idea of modern philosophy. But it was still deficient because it remained a subjective principle. Self-knowledge did not ipso facto imply any knowledge of the world. The task of philosophy as Hegel saw it was to free the unity of being and thinking from its subjective form and transform it into an absolute unity.[31] This unity begins to emerge in Kant as a synthetic unity of apperception which simultaneously constitutes the ground of all objective knowledge. The mind and the world of objects can now be seen to possess a common structure.

Hegel regards the question "how are synthetic judgments a priori possible?" as an indication that Kant has come close to comprehending the true idea of reason.[32] This idea is of course quite different from Kant's "unconditioned synthesis." It is the idea of the absolute identity of the "I" and the world. If one reads Kant from a common sense perspective, it appears that a knowing subject and an independent world of things-in-themselves are simply given as the absolute point of departure for philosophy. Then the subject casts the net of space and time and the categories of the understanding, thereby generating objects which, though only appearances, can be known by means of universal and necessary rules. What interests Hegel in Kant's argument is the question of how the completely heterogeneous, namely the unity of self-consciousness and the manifold of perceptions, could also be seen as identical: "How are synthetic judgments *a priori* possible? This problem expresses nothing other than the idea that in the synthetic judgment subject and predicate, the former particular and the latter universal, the former in the form of being, the latter in the form of thinking—that these heterogeneous elements are at the same time identical *a priori*, i.e., absolutely."[33]

In other words, the Cartesian problem emerges again here. If the "I think" is the only certainty, how can the subject ever acquire reliable knowledge of what is not-"I"? Hegel discerns in Kant's analysis of synthetic judgments a dramatic reformulation of the problem. Subject and object can only be synthesized in an a priori judgment if they are originally identical and only subsequently opposed by the understanding:

> Thus, on account of the expression "synthetic unity," identity can take on the appearance of having presupposed the antithesis and of requiring the antithetical manifold as something independent of it, something existing for itself. Thus identity can be made to seem by nature subsequent to opposition. But that unity is, in Kant, incontrovertibly the absolute, original identity of

> self-consciousness that posits the judgment [*das Urteil*] absolutely or *a priori* out of itself, or rather, as the identity of the subjective and objective, appears in consciousness as judgment; this original unity of apperception is called synthetic precisely on account of its dual aspect, because the opposites are absolutely one in it.[34]

This citation expresses the peculiarly Hegelian "twist" to Kant's theory of pure apperception. The transcendental "I" is not immediately accessible to thought as an object. Yet it is present in every mental activity and, as Kant explained, is the point on which the whole system of transcendental philosophy turns. Both the "I" of "inner sense" and the unitary object are presentations that are possible because of the transcendental unity of self-consciousness. The subject-object dichotomy is thus a necessary manifestation of the unity of self-consciousness but is not that unity itself. On Hegel's reading of Kant, the structure of subject-objectivity is a self-differentiating of the unity of self-consciousness (itself not accessible to us as an object). Transcendental apperception "splits apart" into a knower confronted by a world that seems independent, but is in truth only comprehensible (in terms of the categories and space and time) because it is originally identical with the knower.

We have seen, then, that Kant laid the groundwork for Hegel's own theory of the mind's self-discovery in its experiences of the world. Yet in Hegel's view, Kant never really abandoned Cartesian dualism despite the identity of being and thinking postulated in the cognition of appearances. Kant's theory of our knowledge of appearances cut in two directions. It certified the universality and necessity of our a priori synthetic judgments, providing a counterargument against Humean skepticism. But it also signified that we could not acquire knowledge of things-in-themselves, a reality not subject to the syntheses of transcendental intuition (space and time) and the categories. Any "unconditioned" principle that would be by definition outside of experience either could not be known at all, or would generate "antinomies" as soon as the categories were applied to it.

It is Kant's insistence that pure reason cannot know the unconditioned to which Hegel objects most strenuously. This limitation on reason is closely related to the dualism at the heart of Kant's epistemology. Because being as it is in itself is for Kant originally different from thinking, the only possible knowledge open to us is relative: relative, that is, to the mind's capacity to "legislate" for nature by means of the categories. The only sure knowledge we can have is mathematical and physical, and the latter only insofar as it can be comprehended under the categories of causality, substance, and reciprocity (*Wechselwirkung*). God, the beautiful, purposiveness in organic nature, and even mind, except in its logical function as transcendental apperception, are not amenable to rigorous, scientific study.

Hegel takes issue with Kant's version of Cartesian dualism in his famous introduction to the *Phenomenology of Spirit*. He attacks the entire enterprise of a "critique of reason" as a false application of an instrumentalist epistemology, calling it a "natural notion" that one ought to examine the "tool" of knowledge before embarking upon knowing itself. However, the analogy between cognition and a tool leads unavoidably to skepticism. Whether we picture cognition as an implement that forms its object or as a medium (like a prism) through which the "light of truth" is supposed to reach us, being as it is in itself does not reach us unaltered. Consequently, instrumentalism transforms itself into the conviction that "the entire beginning, acquiring for consciousness whatever is in-itself by means of cognition [*Erkennen*] is absurd in its very concept and that a limit utterly separates cognition and the absolute."[35] Hegel here takes things-in-themselves or an unsynthesized manifold as equivalent to the absolute, the "unconditioned" which reason desires to, but cannot, know. Thus, absolute knowledge would be knowledge of what is simply true and not merely true in relation to the particular cognitive faculties of finite beings.

Hegel recommends that we not accept Kant's mistrust of knowledge for two important reasons. First, the distinction between ourselves and our cognitive faculties suggests that we can observe and analyze cognition from a neutral vantage point which itself would not already be an act of knowing. In other words, a "critique of pure reason" presupposes the application of reason as analyzing and criticizing, to reason as analyzed and criticized. Yet the analyzing reason must itself be analyzed if the whole instrumentalist argument is not to end in a petitio principii. As Hegel says, anyone who tries to examine his cognitive faculty before proceeding to actual cognition is like a man who wants to swim before getting into the water.[36] Furthermore, Kant's instrumentalist approach to knowledge assumes that it makes sense to distinguish things as they truly are from things as they appear to us, while still claiming that we know nothing at all about the noumenal world. This would seem to be a self-contradictory assumption since we cannot say that the two worlds differ unless we know something of the world of things-in-themselves. In Hegel's view, both of these assumptions are open to doubt and, what is more, they constitute a formidable barrier to actual knowledge, a "fear of truth."[37]

Kant's strictures against the use of pure reason to know the unconditioned apply just as much to self-knowledge as to knowledge of what appears to be other than self. On the one hand, Hegel praises Kant for demolishing the *Seelending* of rationalist metaphysics, the "I" taken as a substance with certain attributes (such as simplicity and unalterability). However, he objects to the grounds Kant deploys to support his critique of so-called rational psychology. The predicates traditionally ascribed to the soul are not false simply because they are an attempt by reason to overstep its limits and acquire knowledge of something outside experience. Rather, they are false because "such abstract determinations of the understanding are too vulgar for the soul, and it is something quite different than the merely simple, immutable, etc."[38] Similarly, Hegel agrees with Kant that "'I' is not a sensible thing, something dead and permanent, a soul-thing having a sensible existence."[39] Kant, however, did not draw the proper conclusion from his critique, the conclusion that the "I" might exhibit a mode of being fundamentally different from that characteristic of ordinary objects, yet still be indisputably real. Instead of taking this step, Kant apparently clung to the conviction that what is real must be a "thing" amenable to sense perception.[40] Here one can readily discern a similarity between Kant's refutation of rational psychology and Hume's search for a self. Despite their differences, they concur that if the "I" is to exist, it must be an empirically given thing. It is this tacit equation of being and thing that disturbs Hegel. Certainly, if only things qualify as real, Kant's critique is justified, even though it leaves us with the empty logical subject of transcendental apperception about which nothing at all can be known. But are "thing" and "empty subject" the only alternative conceptions of the "I" or of the mind's knowledge of itself?

In his critique of rational psychology, Kant had referred to the "circular" character of self-thinking: the fact that one cannot think the "I" as object without an "I" as subject to which the object is given. If one attempts to make this subject-"I" into an object, the circle repeats itself. For Kant, this is an "inconvenience" (*Unbequemlichkeit*), "since we must at all times make use of the presentation of it, in order to make any judgment about it."[41] However, he never hit upon the idea that this "inconvenience" might betoken a mode of being or actuality that, in Hegel's words, would be far "richer" than the being of a mere thing. In a revealing passage from the *Logic*, Hegel disputes Kant's remark about the "inconvenient," circular character of the "I":

> [I]t is surely ridiculous to call this nature of self-consciousness an *inconvenience* or a circle as though it were something deficient, just because the "I" thinks itself and cannot be thought without it being the "I" which thinks. This is a relationship in which the eternal nature of self-consciousness and of the concept manifests itself within immediate empirical consciousness. It manifests itself because self-consciousness is precisely the *existing* and thus *empirically perceptible*, pure *concept*, the absolute relation to itself which, as separating judgment [Urteil], makes itself into an object and is solely this—to make itself into a circle by that very act.—A stone does not have that *inconvenience*; when it is thought or when judgments about it are to be made, it does not stand in its own way.[42]

We recall that in Hume, the "I" splits itself apart in an unsuccessful attempt to find itself as an object. Hegel argues in the above quotation, against Kant's empty subject of transcendental apperception, that the "I" is precisely that activity of splitting itself apart into subject and object and seeking itself in the object. Hence it is neither an abstract, isolated "I"-subject as in Kant nor a "thing" or "I"-object of the sort Hume sought in vain and rationalist metaphysicians claimed to have understood.

For Hegel, self-knowledge is different from the knowledge of things since it does not offer a stable, determinate object to our observation. The "I," as observer, can never become objective to itself. It is not a passive thing or res extensa but an activity. Indeed the "I" of self-knowledge exhibits not only a different but also a far more complex and subtle structure than the things we learn of in perception. To use Kant's term, it is a spontaneity or an act of self-creation. Where the things of res extensa simply are what they are, the "I" makes itself into what it is through its inherently active character. For Hegel, the "I" is thus a window to the absolute since it is the concept itself accessible within empirical existence. Specifically, the "I" and the concept share the same structure: self-differentiation. Each can only be thought as an activity of fission, but in such a way that the differentiated entities are implicitly identical. We see this in the "I" since its differentiae, subject and object, both have their origin in the same act of self-differentiation or what Hegel calls self-diremption (*sich-Entzweien*).

Against the backdrop of Hegel's critique of transcendental apperception, another deficiency of Kant's philosophy becomes evident. Because Kant begins with an empty "I"-subject of transcendental apperception, he cannot satisfactorily explain the relationship between the categories and the unity of self-consciousness. "Kant examines them [the categories; L. H.] empirically and does not recognize [erkennen] their necessity. He does not think of positing unity and developing differences out of unity."[43] Here we encounter the notorious Hegelian claim to deduce a conceptual system from pure unity or (in the *Logic*) pure being. Usually, one understands by "deduce" the operation of eliciting from a set of propositions or concepts other propositions implicitly contained in those that are given. Hegel, when he criticizes Kant for not deducing the categories from the pure unity of apperception, obviously cannot have this sort of deduction in mind because nothing at all is "contained" in the pure unity of self-consciousness. From unity understood as *abstract* self-identity, no deduction can be made. Hegel means in the above passage that the unity of apperception must, like the "I" and the concept, be thought of as self-differentiating.

What Hegel himself undertakes is not a deduction in the sense mentioned above but rather a conception of unity based on the model of self-consciousness, or the mind's knowledge of itself as self-differentiating. Fichte forms the connecting link between Kant and Hegel on this score, because he did indeed try to deduce the categories from the unity of self-consciousness or the "I" = "I."

FICHTE

The difference between self-knowledge and the knowledge of things, already present in a rudimentary way in Descartes, becomes explicit and essential for Fichte. We have seen that Kant tends to view being or knowledge of being as identical in some respects to the self or self-knowledge. Fichte proposes to explain experience, or what he calls "presentations accompanied by a feeling of necessity," by showing how it arises out of the very structure of self-consciousness.[44] In his radical formulation, "I am concerned with the complete reversal of the ways of thinking about these points of reflection [i.e., traditional philosophical concepts and modes of thought; L. H.] so that, in all seriousness and not just 'so to speak,' the object would be posited and determined by the cognitive faculty and not the cognitive faculty by the object."[45]

Fichte thus confronts us with what he considers a clear dualism of philosophical method and principle. Either we are "posited and determined" by objects qua passive recipients of sense data, or else the world of experience is somehow determined in and through our "cognitive faculty." To see what Fichte means by the latter alternative, one must bear in mind that he viewed Kant's philosophy as having demonstrated, although not with sufficient clarity, that the object of experience is possible only by virtue of a prior synthesis of transcendental apperception. Hence he regarded at least his early writings as a systematization of Kant's insights: "I have long said . . . that my system is none other than the *Kantian*."[46]

What then are the philosophical principles underlying each dualistic "school"? According to Fichte, we must find a ground that would enable us to explain experience. That ground must be sought not within experience (lest a petitio principii arise) but outside it, and the only method open to us is abstraction. Since we find ourselves in the relation subject-object or knower-known, there are two alternative grounds of experience. We can either abstract from the "thing" of experience, which leaves us with the intellect (in itself), or from ourselves as knowers, which gives us the thing (in itself). Fichte calls the adherents of the first principle "idealists" and those of the second "dogmatists."[47]

Why Fichte chose such polemical designations for these antagonists becomes plain when he identifies dogmatism with what we would call determinism and idealism with freedom and moral responsibility. The idealist, according to Fichte, is capable of the "free act" of abstraction from all specific contents of thought such that the "I" alone becomes an object for him. I hasten to add that Fichte means by an "I-object" neither the "thing" of rational psychology nor an "impression" that would correspond to a self such as Hume sought. Rather, he thinks of it "as 'I' in itself: not as an object of experience, for it is not determinate, but is rather determined solely by me, and is nothing without this determination, and is generally not at all without determination; rather [it is] something sublime and raised above all experience."[48] When Fichte says the "I" is not determinate he means that it lacks the specific given being characteristic of a thing. Like Proteus of mythology, the "I" is infinitely determinable in the sense that it can have any number of objects, yet it must have *some* object, some form, or it is nothing at all. I can "determine" myself as the thinker of any object, including myself *as* thinking it. And in some cases the "state" of myself is determinable solely by the intellect (e.g., as we will see later, in the case of obedience to a moral law). Fichte insists that to form a conception of this infinitely determinable and self-determining "I" is a free act which cannot be demonstrated to someone in the way a geometric proof could, since it requires that each person introspect and understand the significance of his introspection: "That self-consciousness does not obtrude, and does not come of itself; one must really act freely, and then abstract from the object and attend solely to oneself. . . . In a word, this self-consciousness cannot be demonstrated to anyone; each person must produce it in himself by his own freedom."[49]

Fichte concludes that neither dogmatism nor idealism can refute its opponent, the former because it must ultimately have recourse to an unprovable thing-in-itself, the latter because it cannot compel the dogmatist to perform the above-described free act of self-consciousness. The absence of a final arbiter in this dispute led Fichte to the notorious position that the philosophy one chooses is a matter of interest or even character. In Fichte's harsh judgment, "What sort of philosophy one chooses thus depends upon what sort of person one is: for a philosophical system is not a dead household object which we can lay aside or take hold of just as it pleases us; rather it is animated by the soul of the man who has it. A character indolent by nature or rendered weak and stunted by intellectual servitude, learned luxury and vanity will never elevate himself to idealism."[50]

Fichte's pronouncement seems to undermine the very basis of truth: intersubjectivity. He seems to have reduced philosophy in the end to an existential choice or psychological inclination. Yet the verdict should not be quite so severe once one weighs in Fichte's unyielding commitment to discursive truth *within* a chosen philosophical framework. Hegel was obviously influenced by Fichte on this issue, although he could never accept Fichte's strict either-or because it was an outgrowth of the very dualism or alienation that had to be overcome by speculative reason. As we have observed, there is only one philosophy for Hegel, of which empiricism (Fichte's "dogmatism") is a moment. However, Hegel never considered such "dogmatism" genuine philosophizing. In fact, he echoes Fichte when he remarks that "If the given matter of intuition and the manifold of presentation is taken as the real *vis-à-vis* the concept and what is thought, this is a viewpoint which one must have dismissed not only as the *condition for philosophizing*; even in religion, it is presupposed that one has dismissed it."[51]

In constructing his system of idealism, Fichte begins with a step that had a profound impact on Hegel's conception of philosophic method. There is a "double series" of mental acts that underlies Fichte's entire science of knowledge, "that of the 'I' which the philosopher observes, and that of the observations of the philosopher himself."[52] This double series roughly parallels what we noted earlier in Hume: the split, within introspection, between a subject-"I" and a putative object-"I" which is to be sought. However, for Fichte the subject-"I" encompasses both observation by the student of idealism of his own mental acts and the observation of his procedure by the philosopher. The object-"I" consists in the observed mental acts which the philosopher bids his readers to perform. The situation is similar to any case in which one person asks another to perform some act (e.g., holding his breath) and to observe that act and its results (e.g., dizziness). Both the requester and the performer stand on the same level of observation. However, the student does not yet know what the consequences of his deed will be, nor how to interpret it, while the philosopher, or commander of the act, does know these things because he has presumably already performed the act and analyzed it.

The purpose of this mental experiment is to show how the "I" can be construed as the ground of all experience and how an objective world arises through the very fact of self-consciousness. For this reason the first postulate of the doctrine of science is, "Think yourself, construct the concept of yourself; and note how you do it."[53] Immediately the peculiar quality of the "I" begins to emerge. If I ask you to perform a physical act, that act can be observed in a detached fashion, even though it occurs in your own body, because you differentiate that act from your own consciousness of it. It is an object for you. But in thinking oneself, the observation of that act and the self-thinking itself are one and the same. As Fichte expresses it, "The intellect, as such, watches itself; and this self-seeing extends immediately to everything that it is, and in this *immediate* unification of being and of seeing consists the nature of the intellect. What is in it, and what it is as such, it is *for itself*; and only insofar as it is what is for itself, is it this as intellect."[54] To put it another way, the "I"-subject of introspection is actually constituted in and through the act of introspecting. I am what I know myself to be.

In this concept of the intellect is already the embryo of Hegel's concept of spirit. Hegel writes: "Spirit is essentially only what it knows of itself."[55] This definition of spirit is practically a paraphrase of Fichte. But there is a serious objection to this line of reasoning which Fichte must confront before he can establish the doctrine of science on a firm footing. We have seen that the "I" as observed by us is actually this very self-observing, an activity of returning-into-oneself or making oneself into an object. Does this not presuppose that the "I" is already there? One can only return from "B" to "A" provided that "A" is already present. Fichte replies to this objection: "By no means. Not until this act, and solely by means of it, through an act upon an act itself, which determinate act is preceded by no act at all, does the 'I' become for itself *originally*. It is only there previously *for the philosopher*, as a fact, because the latter has already undergone the entire experience."[56] In a later essay clarifying the *Science of Knowledge*, Fichte enlarges on this explanation: "you must think of your present self-positing, elevated to clear consciousness, as preceded by another such positing which occurred without clear consciousness to which the present [clear consciousness] relates itself and by which it is conditioned."[57]

In other words, the return-into-self of the "I" does not presuppose any substratum called an "I" that is already in existence. It is the tendency of language to make us think in terms of substances to which attributes adhere that leads us to conceive of the "I" as "already there." Hence Fichte steers a course between the entirely empty "I"-subject of Kant, which can never be thought, and the "I"-object or "impression," which Hume sought in vain, by regarding the "I" as a pure act: "'*I*' and *action returning-into-itself* [are] completely identical concepts."[58] One must understand the "I" neither as pure subject nor as pure object but as subject-object, or rather the activity of returning-into-itself through which subject and object arise: "I am subject and object: and this *subject-objectivity*, this return of knowledge upon itself, is what I mean by the term 'I' when I deliberately attach a definite meaning to it."[59]

To shed some light on this idea we may recall the discussion of Kant's transcendental apperception. Kant says that the "I think" must be able to accompany all my presentations. There is no object for us without our being aware that we are aware of it. I cannot have an object of consciousness without distinguishing myself from that object and yet simultaneously being related to it as a subject. This is one of the fundamental insights of all German idealism. Fichte and Kant claim that self-consciousness is the precondition of all consciousness, not, of course, in the sense that we are self-conscious at time "A" and then conscious of an object other than we are at time "B." Rather, consciousness and self-consciousness are simultaneously present.

Fichte calls the knowledge we have of this "I" intellectual intuition an intuition which we (as philosophers) find in ourselves if we observe what we do when we think ourselves. This intuition, as we saw earlier, cannot be demonstrated but only grasped by introspection. Fichte explains it in the following way:

> Certainly however it can be demonstrated to anyone in the experience he himself concedes he has had, that this intellectual intuition occurs in every moment of his consciousness. I cannot take a step, move either hand or foot, without the intellectual intuition of my self-consciousness in these actions; only by this intuition do I know that *I* do it, only by means of it do I distinguish my action, and in it myself, from the pre-given object of the action. Anyone who ascribes an activity to himself makes reference to this intuition. In it is the source of life, and without it is death.[60]

The intuition of the "I" is now called by Fichte a "*self-positing, as* positing (anything objective, which can also be I myself as a mere object)."[61] He means that the "I" arises or is posited only in conjunction with an object (myself or something else) that arises at the same time. Although I can only conceive of myself within the framework of subject-objectivity, as an "I" posited as opposed to some object, I must conceive of subject and object as originally identical: "Any possible consciousness, as the objective correlate of a subject, presupposes an immediate consciousness in which subjective and objective are *utterly one*. . . . One will always seek in vain for a bond between subject and object if one has not grasped them *equally originally in a unification*."[62]

To take the case of Hume's "search" for a self, his diremption into observer and observed presupposes a higher unity in which these terms are identical; for how could Hume "split himself apart" if he (qua subject and object, respectively) were not originally one? This immediate intuition of unity (intellectual intuition) is the precondition for all discursive thought, yet it itself is not capable of discursive analysis, since we should have to think it as object (for a subject) to explicate it and hence destroy its original unity. That Fichte took this intellectual intuition to be unthinkable emerges plainly in his "popular" work, *The Vocation of Man*, in which a "spirit" holds a dialogue with him and reveals the essentials of the *Science of Knowledge*. After Fichte terms the "I" a subject-object, the following conversation ensues:

Spirit: "Canst thou then comprehend the possibility of thy becoming conscious of this identity, which is neither subject nor object, but which lies at the foundation of both, and out of which both arise?"

I: "By no means. It is the condition of all my consciousness, that the conscious being, and what he is conscious of, appear distinct and separate. . . . In the very act of recognizing myself, I recognize myself as subject and object, both however being immediately bound up with each other."

Spirit: "Canst thou become conscious of the moment in which *this inconceivable one separated itself into these two*?"

I: "How can I, since my consciousness first becomes possible in and through their separation—since it is my consciousness itself that thus separates them? Beyond consciousness itself there is not consciousness."

Spirit: "It is this separation, then, that thou necessarily recognizest in becoming conscious of thyself? In this thy very being consists."[63]

The conception of the "I" analyzed here gives Fichte the key to a deduction of the categories. He begins with the principle of identity (A = A) and inquires what entitles us to employ this principle. It soon emerges that the identification of the two A's in A = A is based on an original act of self-positing, "I" = "I," the subject-objectivity of consciousness described above. Again it must be emphasized that this self-positing, this absolute "I," is not opposed to anything. As Fichte analyzes it, it has not yet bifurcated into subject and object: "The absolute self of the first principle is not *something* (it has, and can have, no predicate)."[64] Clearly Fichte has only reinterpreted the Kantian tenet that empirical identity, the unity of an object, must have its origin in the unity of transcendental apperception.

Fichte calls his second principle, not-A ≠ A, the principle of opposition. He derives this principle, too, from a primordial act of consciousness: "Every opposite, so far as it is so, is so absolutely, by virtue of an act of the self, and for no other reason. Opposition in general is posited absolutely by the self."[65] Of course, the content (A) of not-A ≠ A is the same in both position and opposition. The A and not-A of not-A ≠ A must each be self-identical in order to be thought at all, so that the formula could just as well read: (not-A = not-A) ≠ (A = A). But according to Fichte, the form of negation, difference, or opposition can never be derived from identity or self-sameness. Just as in the case of identity, the logical principle of opposition has its analogue in an act of consciousness, namely: not-"I" ≠ "I." Any distinction between one thing and another rests upon the original distinction between myself and what I am not.

Fichte seems to be arguing that, in positing difference (not-"I") or the world, the absolute "I" also posits itself as a finite, empirical "I" confronted with an object which it is not. As in the case of Hume's introspection, we have here an unthinkable unity which splits itself apart into subject and object in order to think itself. To identify ourselves as "I" or to think ourselves we must differentiate ourselves into knower and known. In this way, an object (not-"I") is distinguished from the "I" but is also identical with it since both subject and object stem from a primordial act of self-diremption. This is Fichte's third principle, ground. In the absolute "I" (or through its diremption) are posited a divisible "I" opposed to a divisible not-"I," each of which limits the other. Fichte maintains that there must be an activity in the human mind which limits the "I" and not-"I," such that in every subject-object relation there is a shifting border (labeled "X" by Fichte, the product of the limiting act, "Y") between the subjective and objective components. Thus we have an original unthinkable identity of "I" = "I" which then posits a not-"I" confronted by a (finite) "I": "The self is to be equated with, and yet opposed to itself. But in regard to consciousness it is equal to itself, for consciousness is one: but in this consciousness the absolute self is posited as indivisible; whereas the self to which the not-self is opposed is posited as divisible. Hence, insofar as there is a not-self opposed to it, the self is itself in opposition to the absolute self."[66]

Fichte thought he had demonstrated that the three categories of quality—reality, negation, and limitation—are explicitly grounded in the activity of the "I." But has he really accomplished his goal of explaining experience by reference to a principle which is outside experience? He has indeed located identity and difference, reality and negation, subject and object, within the absolute self. However, a dualism remains insofar as each of the elements within these conceptual pairs appears to have arisen by a separate act of the absolute "I." Self-consciousness and consciousness of the not-"I" are not conceived as identical acts: "How the self is able to distinguish something from itself, can be deduced from no higher ground of possibility anywhere, for that distinction itself lies at the very base of all derivation and grounding."[67] In Hegel, by contrast, the act of distinguishing is at the same time an identifying, such that identity and difference are not two separate forms.

Before we consider the deficiencies of Fichte's doctrine of science as understood by Hegel, we should take special note of what Fichte has contributed to Hegel's philosophy. As was mentioned earlier, Fichte conceived of the doctrine of science as a dual series in which the philosopher bids us to perform certain mental acts. We thus have the primary series of the acts themselves and the secondary series of the philosopher's interpretation. The unique feature of this double series is that the first series is not static, but rather is self-developing:

> What [the science of knowledge; L. H.] makes into the object of its thinking is not a dead concept which would only behave passively toward the investigation of it, and which is made into something only because the science of knowledge thinks about it. Rather it is living and active, generating cognitions out of itself by its own activity so that the philosopher need merely observe it. His business in the matter is nothing more than starting this animate object upon a course of purposive activity, watching its activity, conceiving it and comprehending it as one.[68]

Here we have arrived at the blueprint for Hegel's conception of philosophic method. He writes in the *Logic* that philosophy cannot borrow its method from subordinate sciences such as mathematics: "Rather it can only be *the nature of the content, setting itself in motion*, which provides the subject matter of philosophic cognition. It is this content's own reflection which then posits and originates the specific character [*Bestimmung*] of philosophy."[69] He expresses the same conviction even more forcefully in the *Encyclopedia*: "Our thinking, moved by the concept, remains thoroughly immanent in the object which is likewise moved by the concept; we only watch, as it were, the proper self-development of the object and do not alter it by interpolating our subjective presentations and notions."[70]

Furthermore, we have ascertained that the "I," as an act of returning-into-itself, is both observer and observed. It only is what it is for-itself. Hence the first series of mental acts (or the development of the concept in Hegel) eventually transforms itself into the standpoint of the philosopher, that is, the second series of mental acts that "sets in motion" and observes the first series. This is roughly the structure of

Hegel's *Phenomenology* in which the first series consists of the successive forms of appearing consciousness and the second series in the philosophic "we." The philosopher, represented by the observing "we," merely preserves the continuity of the experience undergone by appearing consciousness.

Fichte has also furnished Hegel with an explicit doctrine of self-knowledge as tantamount to knowledge of the object. Of course, the same principle may be elicited from Kant's writings, but there it is beclouded by the notion that reason cannot legitimately be employed to know things-in-themselves. In Fichte, the principle is quite explicit: "in that which we call knowledge and observation of outward things we at all times recognise and observe ourselves only; and . . . in all our consciousness we know of nothing whatever but of ourselves and of our own determinate states."[71]

Yet there is a profound ambiguity in Fichte's program since this identity of thinking and being is bought at the price of reducing the world to a negative of the self, literally a not-"I" with no further content than this mere "not." How can there ever be a unity of being and thinking if identity and difference are posited by two separate acts without any formal continuity or identity between them? Fichte formulates his own dilemma: "The truly supreme problem which embraces all others is, how can the self operate directly on the not-self, or the not-self on the self, when both are held to be utterly opposed to each other?"[72]

His solution is practical rather than theoretical: "Since there is no way of reconciling the not-self with the self, *let there be* no not-self at all!"[73] Thus, what began as an attempt to give the ultimate ground for "presentations accompanied by a feeling of necessity" transforms itself into the dictum that there shall be no such presentations or that the "I" should stand alone in the world. Here we encounter one of the critical parts of our discussion. Cartesian dualism has become self-aware in a double sense. First, the conquest of nature, announced by Descartes as philosophy's goal in the *Discourse on Method*, finds its most extreme expression in Fichte's definition of the external world as "infinite shock" (*unendlicher Anstoss*). We posit it, says Fichte, simply as an obstacle which we can then overcome on our way to true autonomy. Second, we see in Fichte's philosophy the moral-religious counterpart of Cartesianism, the Protestant idea that salvation (liberation) is attained only by the repression of our *inner* nature through strict obedience to the moral law.

For Hegel, the ethical dualism of Fichte is inseparable from his theoretical dualism: "'I' = 'I' is the absolute principle of speculation, but this identity is not demonstrated by the system; the objective 'I' is not equivalent to the subjective 'I,' both remain absolutely opposed to each other. The 'I' does not find itself in its appearance or its positing; in order to find itself as 'I,' it must annihilate its appearance. The essence of the 'I' and its positing do not coincide: *'I' does not become objective to itself.*"[74] Self-knowledge, the foundation of Fichte's entire system, is only partial because the "I" cannot find itself in the world or is not objective to itself.

Two steps are required to transform Fichte's partially speculative, but still dualistic, philosophy into absolute idealism. First, identity and difference, or position and negation, must be viewed as identical in their difference. Fichte does not conceive "positing, pure activity of the 'I,' and opposition . . . as the same."[75] This amounts to saying that being and nothingness are still separated in Fichte, not thought together as the same. A correct understanding of the relationship between "I" and not-"I" would not represent them as products of two different acts that are then conjoined by means of a border between them. Rather the limit as an activity (a *negative* activity, since it posits "I" and not-"I" as being each what it is only by virtue of *not* being the other) would simultaneously posit the "I" and not-"I" as what they are. But in that case, "I" and not-"I" would no longer be in simple opposition. The one, since it would only be by not being the other, would be essentially identical to its opposite. The absolute "I" would then be a negative activity which, by limiting "I" and not-"I," would also create them as specific, determinate entities. This brings us close to what for Hegel is the second deficiency in Fichte's system.

We have seen that the absolute self is an "unthinkable one," that which the "I" is "before" it differentiates itself into subject and object. If it is entirely indifferent to its being a subject *or* object (since it is both and neither as the activity which generates them), then why should we think of it as subjective at all? Hegel advances this conclusion by arguing, "To obtain transcendental intuition in its pure formlessness, one would have to abstract from its character as something subjective; speculation would have to remove this form from its subjective principle to elevate it to the true identity of subject and object. . . . It remains [in Fichte; L. H.] a subjective subject = object, for which appearance is absolutely alien and which never reaches the point of intuiting itself in appearance."[76]

The route from Descartes through Fichte has ended in a paradoxical conclusion. We began with the premise that self-consciousness, the mind's knowledge of itself, is a cognitive principle *sui generis* different from the knowledge of things. But we also found that, even in Descartes' cogito ergo sum, there is an implicit identity of self-knowledge and being. In Kant and Fichte we have discovered that self-knowledge or self-consciousness provides the key to knowledge of at least the essential structure of being. Finally, having arrived at the highest principle of self-knowledge—intellectual intuition—we discover that self-knowledge is not really self-knowledge at all. Rather, it is the intuition of a principle beyond the self which, as negative activity, is responsible for the very subject-object structure with which we began and which lies at the heart of modern (Cartesian) dualism. It remains only to sketch out how Schelling drew this conclusion in order to complete the transition from the modern philosophy of self-consciousness to Hegel's absolute idealism.

Schelling and Spinoza

The first principle of Schelling's philosophy (at least of his early works, which contributed directly to Hegel's own position) is "absolute reason" or "reason insofar as it is thought as the total indifference of subjective and objective."[77] By "indifference" Schelling means a reason which is neither the reason of man qua thinker nor a logos of being (ontology), but which expresses itself as both. He tells us that to arrive at this idea of reason we must reflect upon "that which, in philosophy, takes up a position between subjective and objective and that obviously must behave indifferently toward both. . . . In order to think [reason] absolutely, abstraction must be made from the thinker."[78]

We recall that Fichte offered only two alternatives for explaining experience. One can either abstract from the object and arrive at a pure "I" as the ground of unity of objects (as transcendental apperception) or abstract from the subject to arrive at a thing-in-itself which produces consciousness by some unarticulated principle of causality. Here Schelling suggests that we must abstract from both knower and known, both subjective and objective unity. But this seems like preposterous advice because it would be tantamount to thinking nothing: a pure identity which, lacking anything to limit or determine it, would also be a pure nothing. This is Schelling's posture indeed, when he calls this absolute reason or highest unity "the holy abyss . . . from which everything emerges and into which everything returns."[79] Hegel concurs with him, to a certain degree, when he writes: "For philosophy the first thing . . . is to know [erkennen] *absolute* nothingness."[80]

Reason, as neither subjective nor objective, becomes for Schelling the "true-in-itself" which falls into the point of indifference between subjective and objective. To understand this we should remember Fichte's third principle, that of ground, whereby a divisible not-"I" and a divisible "I" are held apart by a shifting boundary. Schelling realizes that this limit or point of indifference is exactly what makes the subjective and objective be what they are. Rather than a third principle which defines a relationship between two already posited entities, he wishes to think the limit as the image of an absolute unity which appears *to us* only in the differentiation of subject and object. Another way to state the same idea would be to consider the thought of unity itself. You cannot think it without simultaneously thinking nonunity, difference, or opposition. Yet to think unity and opposition together requires the thought of a higher unity in which both would be contained. If we then try to think this higher unity in the same way, it too will demand the thought of nonunity and so on ad infinitum. Clearly, the only way to avoid an infinite regress is to think the higher unity as that which appears only in and through the positing of a limit between the original unity and the nonunity which defines it. This is the same perplexity which Fichte encountered in trying to think the "I-subject" without an infinite regress. As we said, he solved it by arguing simply: There *is* consciousness; hence, there is a unity that is subject-object, or, better, that articulates itself in the complex subject-object but that in itself is not thinkable, only accessible as "intellectual intuition." Schelling expresses this idea in this passage:

> To begin with, then, I praise that as the *prius* which precedes all else, since, apart from it, only two cases are possible: either unity which has opposition standing opposed to it is to be posited as the first thing; in that case, however, it is itself posited with an opposite; or else the opposites [are posited], in which case, however, they are thought without unity, which is impossible. For whatever is opposed is so truly and in a real way only by being posited within one and the same [unity].[81]

Schelling provides us with an example that may help to render this theme more transparent. There are, he says, two senses of "higher unity." One may be seen in cases of "relative opposition" in which two things are combined to form a third that is a unity of the first two (such as hydrogen and oxygen in water). Here the higher unity is an empirically existing thing that is different from its subaltern parts. The second case occurs when an "absolute opposition" is present, for instance, between a person and the image he casts in a mirror. This opposition is absolute in the sense that it cannot be unified in any third thing. Yet the identity we perceive between the original and the image is complete. The absolute identity is what makes them be the same.[82]

Schelling concludes that, viewed from the standpoint of absolute reason, everything is one; there is simply no difference in the world. That there seem to be differences (as, for example, between being and thinking) occurs because of "reflection," the fact that we isolate some finite entity from the absolute totality of which it is a part: "There is therefore nothing in itself outside of totality, and if something is regarded as outside totality, this only happens by virtue of an arbitrary separation from the whole performed by reflection. In itself [i.e., from the perspective of absolute reason; L. H.] this does not take place since all that is, is one, and is absolute identity itself within the totality."[83] Furthermore, Schelling does not accept Fichte's division of all philosophies into dogmatism and idealism. Since subject and object (roughly, man and nature) are the differentiae of absolute identity, a transcendental philosophy which begins with the "I" and a philosophy of nature which begins with pure objectivity should reach the same conclusions.

This leads us to consider briefly the position of Spinoza. I did not discuss his theory earlier because he does not begin with self-consciousness but rather with a substance that has two attributes, being and thinking. But, in Schelling, the doctrine of self-consciousness has become a doctrine of absolute reason that is no longer subjective at all. In fact, Schelling essentially is a Spinozist, as he himself admits: "Thus, true philosophy consists in the proof that absolute identity [the infinite] has not emerged from itself and that everything which is, insofar as it is, is infinity itself, a proposition which only Spinoza among all previous philosophers has known, even though he did not present a complete proof of it."[84]

Consequently, as far as Hegel is concerned, Spinoza and Schelling share many of the same philosophical defects, to which he alludes in the preface to the *Phenomenology*: "To regard any existent as it is in the *absolute* here consists in nothing but saying of it that one has indeed now spoken of it as a something; in the absolute however, the A = A, there is no such thing, rather everything is one in it. This one knowledge, that everything is the same in the absolute . . . or passing off one's absolute as the night in which, so to speak, all cows are black, is the naïvety of empty knowledge."[85] Similarly, in Spinoza we find that specific, differentiated entities are merely absorbed into substance (the equivalent of Schelling's absolute identity) like matter into the "black hole" of modern astronomy: "All differentiations and determinations of things and of consciousness only return into the one of substance; thus, one can say, everything is only thrown into this abyss of destruction in the Spinozist system."[86]

Despite its seeming emptiness, Schelling's conception of absolute unity did point the way toward Hegel's own system and the reconstruction, in thought, of ethical wholeness. The position of absolute unity or identity must be retained, for it is the only means of overcoming Cartesian dualism. But it must be possible for this absolute unity to differentiate and determine itself like Fichte's self-developing object (the "I") of the first series of mental acts. Only from the perspective of this task do Hegel's key philosophical terms—spirit, subject, the concept, the *Idee*—become wholly intelligible. To these we now direct our attention.

HEGEL'S SPECULATIVE PHILOSOPHY

2

HEGEL's own position emerged gradually as he emancipated himself from Schelling's influence. At first powerfully attracted to Schelling's absolute idealism, Hegel began, in his Jena period (1801–7), to appreciate the price philosophy would have to pay for such an amorphous absolute as Schelling professed to have discovered. If the distinctions we characteristically make between subject and object, man and nature, divine and human prove to be mere illusions—as Schelling flatly said they were—would philosophy not willy-nilly relinquish any claim to achieve rational knowledge about concrete problems?

Hegel's originality, strongly evident in the *Phenomenology of Mind* (1807), did not actually consist in his absolute idealism, since Schelling had already broken that ground. Rather, Hegel found a way to conceive of the absolute such that it would only manifest itself to human consciousness (and hence only exist at all!) within the dualistic terms mapped out by Descartes, Kant, and Fichte. Hegel's guiding idea can be simply expressed as follows: Human beings began, in modern times, to experience themselves and their world in dualistic categories. This was not by any means a "mistake" (as it must seem from Schelling's absolute standpoint); it reflected the actual situation in which people found themselves in the wake of the breakdown of ethical life and the "revolution of subjectivity" evident in many spheres of modern culture. If philosophy was to retain the notion of an absolute, it would have to be shown that this absolute required, for its very being and appearing, the sort of dualistic, "alienated" world whose typical expression was the Enlightenment. In this manner, philosophy could become a science describing the various guises in which the absolute appeared and pointing out their manifold connections and relationships. One would still "see the whole" in Schelling's sense of grasping the infinite in finite entities; yet the whole would be an articulated series of definite forms, each vitally necessary to the self-defining of the absolute.

In this chapter, we shall see in a more precise way how Hegel worked toward the same insight from two directions, firstly by "finitizing" Schelling's absolute and secondly by transforming the structure of the "I" (as described by Fichte) into a model or paradigm of general applicability to other phenomena. In the remainder of this work, we shall then review in detail how Hegel gathered together the diverse strands of Enlightenment thought and culture into a coherent picture.

The Deficiencies of Schelling's Absolute

The first clue to Hegel's revision of Schelling is his opposition to the "virtuoso" character of the knowledge of the absolute, intellectual or transcendental intuition. From Hegel's discussion in the "Differenzschrift" of 1801, we learn that he still considered Schelling's version of intellectual intuition as "the absolute principle, the sole real ground and stable standpoint of philosophy."[1] But by 1807, the year in which the *Phenomenology* first appeared, he had broken with Schelling in the sense that the concept rather than intellectual intuition had become the animating principle of his thought. Schelling, who read only the preface to that work, quickly realized that Hegel had repudiated intuition as a philosophical first principle. In the last letter he wrote to Hegel, Schelling remarked: "So I admit that I have not yet grasped your meaning when you oppose the concept to intuition."[2]

Schelling's puzzlement is not surprising. In Kant, Fichte, and Schelling himself there is complete unanimity about the inaccessibility of transcendental or absolute identity to thought. Since this sort of identity is logically prior to all subject-object relationships and since one cannot conceive of anything which cannot be an object of one's consciousness, one cannot form a concept of absolute identity. Hence it must be an intuition. In this sense Schelling's absolute closely resembles the idea of the good in Plato, which is constitutive of all specific goods but must ultimately be apprehended by the "eye of the mind" rather than by an abstract concept.

Yet if this absolute is only an intuition, it remains by definition inaccessible to discursive analysis. If one does not have the intuition of absolute identity, the philosophy on which it is based seems to be an arbitrary construct and not truly scientific in the sense of being intersubjectively verifiable. It appears as a "virtuoso" performance in which philosophers have the gift of intuition while the rest of us must continue to view the world as a bundle of dualisms. This deficiency of intellectual intuition, which troubled Hegel, finds clear expression in his *Logic*. He rejects the suggestion that the *Logic* should begin with the "I," because the proper conception of the "I" would already presuppose that one had performed the "absolute act" of abstraction from all empirical consciousness.

Hegel's program for correcting this "arbitrary standpoint"[3] of Schelling's philosophy has two complementary aspects. First, the movement from ordinary to absolute consciousness (i.e., to the absolute as identity of subject and object) must itself be capable of scientific treatment. It must be shown that there is a necessary line of development for any consciousness toward absolute knowledge. Of the "subjective postulate" of intellectual intuition, Hegel remarks: "In order that it might be demonstrated as a true demand [*wahrhafte Forderung*], the progress of the concrete 'I' from immediate consciousness to pure knowledge would have to be shown and presented as occurring in the 'I' itself, by virtue of its own necessity."[4] This is, of course, the requirement that the *Phenomenology* is intended to fulfill. But that program cannot be put into effect if Schelling's version of the absolute, the mere repetition of absolute identity, is taken as fundamental. According to Hegel, Schelling's absolute cannot provide anything more than the semblance of an expansion (*Ausbreitung*) of knowledge since it does not contain any genuine internal development:

> When this expansion is scrutinized more closely, it proves not to have come about because one and the same [entity] took on diverse forms; rather it is the formless repetition of one and the same thing that has only been applied *ab extra* to diverse material. . . . The idea, which is certainly true for itself, does not in fact ever go beyond the beginning. . . . This is as little the fulfill-

ment of what has been demanded as arbitrary notions about the content would be; namely, the wealth whose source lies within it and the self-determining difference of forms.[5]

We may summarize Hegel's objections by asserting that Schelling has indeed demonstrated how a complete analysis of self-consciousness will lead to the absolute; however, he has not shown why the absolute necessarily appears as a series of finite relationships. This demonstration constitutes the core of Hegel's *Logic*, *Phenomenology*, and even the *Philosophy of Right*.

The "I" and the Concept

To understand Hegel's unique position within the German Idealist tradition, we must briefly return to Fichte's attempt to analyze the structure of self-consciousness. We saw that he regarded position and negation (A = A and A ≠ not-A) as two separate acts of the absolute "I." But he never makes clear exactly why or how difference can emerge from a pure identity ("I" = "I"). The answer, for Hegel, is that pure identity is simultaneously nothingness. Fichte's "inconceivable one," which I can never think because thinking requires that I split myself apart into subject and object, is what Hegel calls pure negative activity. It sets the limit "between" determinate entities by virtue of Spinoza's maxim that all determination is negation. In other words, "I" and not-"I" arise through the very same negative activity which determines each as what it is. When I try to think this "I" as it is "before" it splits apart into subject and object, I thereby split it (i.e., myself) into subject and object. This defeats my attempt to think it as a third thing "behind" them. But I can now think it as the activity of negation through which subject and object are de*term*ined (i.e., given limits and hence specific being). Thus, paradoxically, the "I" reveals itself to me in the same movement by which it is concealed. As Hegel puts it, "To appear and to split into two [sich-Entzweien] is one and the same thing."[6] Or, in the words of Stanley Rosen, to understand Hegel's doctrine of the absolute one must "distinguish between form and the *process of formation*":[7] "the Absolute is not a 'thing,' whether in the sense of subject or object. The Absolute is the formation-process of subjects and objects."[8]

If negative activity qua determining posits subject and object as the limit through which the one is not the other, then each is at the same time precisely its other. This is because the same negation that distinguishes them also relates them: "'I' as this absolute negativity is implicitly identity in other-being; 'I' is itself and overreaches the object as something *implicitly* sublated [*an sich aufgehobenes*]; it is *one side* of the relationship and the *whole* relationship;—*the light* which manifests itself and other things too."[9] The "I" is one side of the relation and the whole relation in the sense that as a self confronting a not-self, it is limited, finite, empirical "I." But it is also the absolute as the negative activity that posits the difference between "I" and not-"I," dividing and identifying them at the same time.

In the final chapter of the *Phenomenology*, Hegel concisely formulates his conception of the "I" as negative activity: the "I" "has a *content* which it distinguishes from itself; for it is pure negativity or self-dirempting [sich-Entzweien]; it is *consciousness*. This content in its difference is itself the 'I,' for the content is the movement of self-sublation, or the same pure negativity as the 'I.' 'I' is introreflected in the content as something differentiated from it; the content is only *comprehended* if the 'I' is with itself [*bei sich*] in its other-being."[10] Hegel's reinterpretation of Schelling's absolute as negative activity suggests a solution to the arbitrariness of "intellectual intuition." If the absolute is only conceivable as the implicit identity-in-difference of subject and object, then what the "I" is, is inseparable from what the object is. The content is only comprehended (*begriffen*) when the "I" is "with itself" in its other-being: "Thus, the 'I' is only manifest to itself insofar as its other becomes manifest in the form of something independent of the 'I.'"[11] In other words, the path to the absolute is not a leap into the abyss of pure identity, as in Schelling, but the long process through which the "I" comes to comprehend itself in its other. In Fichte's terms, the "I" need be only "set in motion" in order to begin the voyage toward the absolute as we philosophers look on. But the unity of subject and object makes sense only from the standpoint of an absolute conceived (like Schelling's) as "indifferent" to its manifestations as subject or object. The "I" could discover itself only in its other if both "I" and other constitute the determination-by-negation of the absolute.

The interpretation of the absolute as negative activity also provides a transition from Schelling's "intellectual intuition" to Hegel's "concept." The traditional opposition of concept and intuition parallels the distinction between abstract universality and the particulars that supplied the universal with "instantiations" or cases of application. Modern philosophers from Descartes through Fichte came to regard the thinking subject as the source of universals that were synthesized with the particulars of intuition. The difference, for example, between Hume and Kant hinged on whether universal categories such as cause and effect ought to be viewed as impositions of subjective habits of thought upon a manifold of singular sensations, or whether these categories were "already" in the objects as the very conditions for experience.

But provided that the German idealists can demonstrate that the subject-object structure of experience is only possible if this dichotomy is a manifestation of the absolute, then the universal does not have to be "applied" to the particular or the latter "subsumed" under the former. Rather, the universal is self-particularizing in exactly the same way in which the absolute differentiates itself within the subject-object structure. Actually these are only different expressions for the same movement. The universal is just as much in re as it is a subjective activity, or, to reintroduce an earlier distinction, thinking and being are essentially identical: "'I,' the subject of consciousness, is thinking; logically, the object receives further specification by virtue of *what is identical in subject and object*, their absolute nexus, that which makes the object the object of the subject."[12] Thus, since thinking qua subjective activity involves the use of concepts or universals, it is essentially the comprehension of the object as itself universal. It is in this sense that Hegel describes the "I" as a "melting-pot," a "fire," and as "crushing" reality, since the "I" as thinker finds itself in the object by means of its universalizing activity: "Thinking as activity is thus the universal-in-*action*, and more precisely the self-activating universal, since the deed, what has been produced, is precisely the universal."[13]

It is crucial to realize that the "universal in action" that we experience as a subjective operation on an independent object is really the activity of the absolute manifesting itself to itself through our thinking.[14] Hence—and I take this proposition to be the core of Hegel's entire philosophy—a complete knowledge of the object will culminate in a knowledge of the formation-process by which subjects and objects appear at all. And since that formation-process finds its proximate expression in the self-differentiating activity of the "I," complete knowledge of the object is also knowledge by the "I" of itself qua negative activity or universal-in-action.

It is in this sense that the "I" is a theoretical paradigm something like the watch of seventeenth-century philosophy, the organic body of medieval theologians, or the servo-mechanism of modern sociology. Furthermore, the "I" as paradigm is itself nothing but *the concept*. If we know what the "I" is, then we also know what the concept is: "The concept, having blossomed forth in the sort of existence [*Existenz*] that is itself free, is nothing other than the 'I' or pure self-consciousness. Indeed I *have* concepts; but 'I' is the pure concept itself, which has attained existence [*Dasein*] as concept."[15] One could thus assert that the concept is incomprehensible without the "I" as a model accessible to our own self-consciousness: "The self-related universal exists nowhere but in the 'I.'"[16]

To summarize, Hegel's solution to the formalism and lack of diversity in Schelling's absolute is the concept, but not understood as an empty abstraction requiring singulars to "fill it up." He does speak of "the thought" (*der Gedanke*) as a universal in the traditional sense, but immediately adds that it is essentially an aspect of the concept which is "concrete" or self-developing: "the thought is nothing empty and abstract; rather it is determining; or the thought is essentially concrete. We call this concrete thought the concept."[17]

Hegel elaborates on the distinction between concept as abstractly universal and self-differentiating. In ordinary usage, "concept" designates what is common to a number of particulars. But, says Hegel, "the universal of the concept is not merely a common feature in respect to which the particular has an independent existence. Rather, the universal is self-particularizing [specifying] and remains with itself [bei sich] in its other in undimmed clarity."[18]

For Hegel, the concept is the essence not only of all thought but of being itself. He underscores its absolute importance in a highly metaphorical passage which, despite its apparently mystical overtones, brings together all the logical relationships included in the concept:

> [T]he absolute concept may be called the simple essence of life, the soul of the world or the universal blood which is omnipresent and neither interrupted nor clouded by any difference. Rather it is itself all differences as well as their having-been-absorbed [*ihr Aufgehobensein*]; hence it pulsates within itself without moving, trembles inwardly without losing its tranquility. It is *self-identical*, for the differences are tautological: they are differences which are none. This self-identical essence thus relates itself [*bezieht sich*] only to itself; *to itself*. This "itself" is then an other toward which the relation points, so that *self*-relating is really *self-dirempting*, or that self-identity is precisely inner difference. The dirempted moments are thus in-and-for-themselves, each the opposite of an other,—such that when we speak of the one, the other is already contained in the expression. . . . What

> is *self-identical dirempts itself*—this means as much as to say: it supersedes [*aufhebt*] itself as something already dirempted, it supersedes itself *qua* other-being.[19]

This cryptic-sounding passage is quite comprehensible if one recalls what has been said about the "I" as a paradigm of the concept. The self-differentiating "I" is here said by Hegel to be the "soul of the world," "the essence of life," because self-knowledge and knowledge of being converge in one and the same concept. It is active in that none of its moments (namely, the unity that only *is* as differentiated, the differentiated entities themselves, and their identity as different) can be thought in isolation from the others. It is a *perpetuum mobile* because it is internally unstable. But it is also "tranquil" when thought of as a self-enclosed totality, just as the "I" of self-consciousness remains identical to itself in differentiating itself into subject and object.

Yet this "concept of the concept" suggests that the formalism of Schelling's absolute is only partially remedied. Hegel has reinterpreted absolute identity (the "A=A") as inconceivable apart from the negative activity that separates it and makes it discursively accessible to us. This gives us a framework within which knowledge can be more than the mere absorption of everything into an abyss of absolute identity. The very expression "concept" (as opposed to "intellectual intuition") suggests that knowledge rests on intersubjectivity instead of a subjective capacity which only some people possess. Yet if the knowledge of whatever is, is ultimately knowledge of the concept by the concept, it would seem that Hegel too must pronounce all cognition to be an endless repetition of the same pattern. This is in some sense true, but otherwise most misleading because Hegel's concept of the concept also involves the preservation and enrichment of content, or the development of the abstract toward the concrete.

Toward a Systematic Science

In the preface to the *Phenomenology of Spirit*, which he intended as an introduction to his entire system, Hegel describes his principle of philosophical truth as follows: "In my view everything . . . depends upon conceiving and expressing the true not only as *substance* but just as much as *subject*."[20] The development of substance into subject is the theme of all Hegel's works from the *Logic* to the *Philosophy of Right*. His remark suggests that substance, roughly equivalent to the absolute identity of Spinoza and Schelling, is not an alternative notion to subject. Rather, Hegel's subject is a developed and articulated substance, an absolute identity enriched by the explicit inclusion of difference or otherness. Hegel does not reject Spinoza and Schelling; he simply attempts to transform their intuited absolute into a discursively accessible principle.[21]

Hegel links the emergence of subject from substance to the proposition that "knowledge is only actual and can only be presented as science or as system."[22] These two arguments are essentially the same because substance means an absolute identity (Schelling's A = A) that has not articulated itself, a mere "original" or "immediate" identity. Substance emerges or "posits itself" only by means of the negative activity that is at its very core, the continuous diremption into a series of dualisms each of which manifests that negative activity more completely. The series of these forms is a system or science. As Hegel asserts, "the true is the whole; the whole however is only the entity completing itself through its development."[23]

Hegel's point can best be discerned in his theory of language. If we begin with the words "God," "state," "society," "man," we are, in Hegel's view, uttering empty names with no significance. Only the addition of the predicates provides the "what," the determinacy of a name. But the nature of our language implies that the sentence subject is in fact really a substance, something that has being apart from its predications, which are thus accidents. The activity of predication seems to belong to a thinker separated from both the sentence subject (in truth a substance) and the predicates, such that the addition of predicates appears to be the external act of a detached mind. Even to say that the absolute *is* subject presupposes that the absolute is somehow "already there," and that we, as detached minds, must find a predication (here, "subject") that expresses what it is. Hegel contends that substance cannot really become subject unless predication is understood as the (negative) activity of substance in which it dirempts itself or mediates itself with itself.

We must now inquire what the character of this mediation is. According to Hegel, "mediation is nothing but self-sameness that moves of its own accord, or it is introreflection, the moment of the 'I' that is for-itself, pure negativity."[24] The "I"-paradigm proves to be the prototype for the identity-in-difference that characterizes the development from substance to subject. Thus the program of Hegel's systematic science in all its forms consists in the mind's study of its self-activity: "For the true is actual only as system; or the principle that substance exists essentially as subject finds expression in the notion that the absolute is spirit. . . . The spiritual alone is the *actual*; it is essence or being-in-itself,—the *determinate* or that which stands in *relation*, *other-being* and *being-for-itself*—but it remains within itself in this determinateness and self-externality. . . . Spirit knowing itself as spirit in this developed form is science."[25]

The task and meaning of systematic science is the demonstration of how abstract or original identity (substance) can be mediated through a series of finite relationships so as finally to become a subject. What is required for this to happen is the gradual evolution to a new concept of identity that would include negation, otherness and mediation within itself. Here the paradigm of the "I" plays a central role. The identity of human self-consciousness, Fichte's "I" = "I," has proven to be literally unthinkable apart from its self-differentiation into a series of finite subject-object relationships. My thoughts, actions, and experiences are all other than I am (i.e., I can abstract from them and return into myself); yet they are also paradoxically what I am. I must distinguish myself from them to be conscious at all, but I must also acknowledge them as the constitutive elements of my personal identity if the latter is not to be contentless abstraction.

The perfect identity-in-difference of the "I" and its other is the *telos* of Hegel's *Logic* and the true experiential referent of the concept and subject as philosophical terms. The *Logic* must be understood as a movement in which an original pattern of identity, difference, and restoration of identity is retained throughout. Yet we must also see how these basic elements are defined in a progressively more adequate way—adequate, that is, to express the highest form of identity-in-difference which we encounter in the "I." In the course of this movement we will begin with supposedly self-subsistent entities to which relationship (i.e., negation or otherness) is external and accidental. In due course it will be shown that the entities or *relata* in a relationship are in fact only constituted as what they are by their relationship. As Hegel puts it, "the rational is relationship itself."[26] This emphasis on relationship rather than on the relata as self-subsistent entities is already familiar to us. We know that the absolute, and its finite representative, the "I," is not a thing but an activity which separates and identifies its relata. The task of the *Logic* is to make this premise explicit, thereby permitting thought to think itself in the element of abstract logical categories.

The skeletal groundwork of the *Logic* consists of three moments: the abstractly rational (*verständig*), the dialectical or negative and mediating, and the speculative or positive-rational (*vernünftig*). These correspond exactly to the three moments of the concept or of self-consciousness. The abstract-rational moment approximates the bifurcation of the absolute into subject and object or the self-differentiation of the concept into specific, determinate identities, except that these entities are now frozen, fixed as stable, finite monads (to borrow an expression from Stanley Rosen), abstracted from the negative activity through which they emerge and persist. The viewpoint of the understanding and of ordinary logic which prevails in the isolation of determinate entities characterizes nearly all of modern philosophy and the Enlightenment.

The dialectical moment of logic is intended to dissolve the barrier betwen categories or entities held to be rigidly exclusive of one another. Taking our earlier discussion of the concept as an example, we may observe that the negative activity that separates determinate entities (the activity by means of which A and not-A are each specified as not the other) also tacitly identifies them, since each is what it is (i.e., is determinate or finite) by virtue of a limit that is in fact its other. Were the other removed, each A and not-A would expand out into a vapor of absolute nothing since it would lack a determination or negation which sets bounds to it and makes it be something in particular.

The third moment, the speculative, only designates the *totality of the process* whereby stable entities are posited and separated, then dissolve into each other. Hegel avers, in agreement with Schelling, that "the absolute . . . is . . . the identity of identity and non-identity; within it, opposition and oneness are simultaneously present."[27] The speculative, then, makes manifest what dialectic already contains. If A and not-A (identity and nonidentity) are identical by being different, then the speculative moment merely "gathers up" this result into a concept of totality in which we move from an "ineffable one" which differentiates itself, annuls its differentiae, and returns into a new unity that is totality in the literal sense, since there is nothing "outside" it. To illustrate, we can examine the infamous dialectic of finite and infinite in the *Logic*.[28]

When we start with a finite "something" (*etwas*) and ask what it is, we are driven to its other, which delimits and determines it. But the other is other by reason of its opposition to something. Hence we bounce back and forth from a finite something to a finite other, thereby falling into an infinite regress or what Hegel calls a "bad infinity." However, this infinity only *is* by virtue of its *not* being the finite. Hence it is self-contradictory because it is supposed to lack limit (in-*fin*-ite), which it precisely has insofar as it is contraposed to the finite that is its limit. If we seek a new infinite that lies beyond both the finite and the old infinite, we are no better off, since we arrive only at a new opposition of our broader infinite versus the old infinite (now part of the finite). The speculative resolution of this dilemma is to conceive the infinite as the movement through which each is driven to its other, is posited as identical to it, and becomes therefore a unity of itself and its other (or of identity and nonidentity).

This solution is obviously the same as what we have come across in the "I" and the concept. Indeed, Hegel remarks: "Self-consciousness is thus the proximate example of the presence of infinity."[29] We think of the unity of differentiated entities as the activity through which they are posited, which is not itself an entity but which reveals itself in the activity of separating and unifying. But the absolute that we conceive as the totality of this movement (here the "true" infinite) is actually a result that includes its moments. As soon as we detach it from the movement by which it manifested itself, it becomes itself a stable entity that stands in opposition to otherness. This is the insight we achieved when we observed what happens when we try to think the "I" as an object. It then becomes an object *for* a subject (in this case, the "I") and is thus not revealed as the focal point of all objects but rather as a thing, a fleeting perception, or what have you. We were driven finally to depict it as a subject-object, as Fichte argued. It is this characteristic of the speculative as a result or totality that allows it to accumulate content.[30]

To understand more specifically how an originally abstract principle can accumulate content and thus become more concrete, we must consider some of the more crucial phases of development in the *Logic*. Hegel begins the *Logic* not with the specific being of any given entity but with pure being as such. It quickly becomes apparent that pure being is indistinguishable from nothing (*Nichts*), since to be is to be determinate, a condition that is absent in a notion of pure being. We can indeed say that pure being is *not* nothing, thereby giving it a determination, but the "not" indicates that being only *is* what it is through the negativity separating it from nothing.

Yet being and nothing are not simply identical. To equate them requires at the same time that we differentiate them or think them as not the same, otherwise there could not be two terms in the equation. Hegel expresses the identity-in-difference of being and nothing in two distinct forms. On the one hand, it is *becoming* which signifies only the instability of being and nothing, respectively. It is not so much a new notion as it is a description of our paradoxical attempts to think being and nothing as stable, separate forms. Or it is, like the "true" infinite, the activity of the absolute which differentiates and identifies being and nothing in a ceaseless oscillation. Hegel calls becoming the "first concrete thought" or the first *concept*, insofar as being and nothing previously were mere abstractions.[31] By "abstraction" he means that being and nothing were each posed as selfsame, stable thoughts, each having been defined as *not* the other. Becoming is the concept (*in ovo*) because it expresses the unity-in-difference of being and nothing, not as a "third thing" outside them, but as the activity through which each "turns into" its other.

Becoming appears to create an impasse for the further development of the *Logic*, since it only expresses an oscillation. The solution is to posit a being which includes negation in its very notion: namely, determinate being or Dasein. A Dasein is distinguished from other-being by its quality. The empty notions of pure being and nothing are replaced by the more specific idea of a something that is not another thing. Here negation is conceived as a barrier separating one thing from another and thus integral to the definition of determinate being.

The final term in Hegel's dialectic of quality is *being-for-itself* (*Fürsichsein*), which proves to be the "concept" of being and determinate being. Being-for-itself exemplifies the fundamental leitmotiv of both the *Logic* and Hegel's thought as a whole, because it is thc cmbryonic form of self-consciousness. It is the explicit exclusion of otherness from itself, regarded as an activity, or "polemical, negative behavior toward the limiting other."[32] Furthermore, "In the 'I' we have the proximate example of being-for-itself. As existing, we know ourselves first of all to be distinct from all else that exists and also related to it. Furthermore, however, we know that this whole breadth of existence culminates, as it were, in the simple form of being-for-itself. When we say: 'I,' this is the expression of infinite and, simultaneously, of negative self-relation."[33]

So far the problem of the *Logic* has been to find a means of thinking being such that it does not immediately collapse into its other. In other words, we must think anything at all as selfsame and stable; yet it *is* only so because of the negation that gives it determinacy. Hence we need a model of being which can be self-identical by virtue of its negating activity. In being and Dasein, negation simply "happened to" being as though it were not an integral part of it. Here, in being-for-itself, we find the thought of a being that actively negates. Being-for-itself "is self-relation by virtue of the negation of other-being. When I say I am for myself, I not only *am*; rather I negate in myself all that is other, I exclude it from myself insofar as it appears external."[34] Being-for-itself is thus also a negation of negation since the determination of otherness (which I negate) was itself already an instance of negation. To phrase this in the more familiar terms of the "I"-paradigm, the "I" is essentially a return-into-itself out of its relationship to other-being. To say "I" means to distinguish oneself from everything else. To be (as "I") and to negate or return-into-oneself are the same. As Fichte so strongly emphasized, to be an "I" is to be for oneself, to know oneself as not another thing. The "I" is not a thing, not a determinate being; instead it is pure negative activity.[35]

Being-for-itself thus reveals Hegel's most fundamental philosophic insight. Every instance of the speculative principle is a case of the concept that, as we saw, follows the pattern of the "I." Even becoming, as abstract as it is, demonstrates the concept. However, not every case of speculative unity exhibits the concept as self-aware in the same degree. The seeming anthropomorphism of Hegel's *Logic* suggests that the contradictions of philosophic thought can be resolved only if the philosophic subject or thinker is included in the definition of the problems. The internal development of the *Logic* expands knowledge by introducing new categories, but also intensifies it by arranging those categories in such a way that they manifest the structure of mind to itself in a progressively more adequate form. Eventually, this revealing will culminate in the explicit acknowledgment that the concept is "thought thinking itself," or that it knows itself *as* knowing.

The essential character of all development in Hegel's philosophy requires, then, that the thinker to whom an object is given shed his "detached" attitude toward it and recognize that his increasingly more adequate cognition of the object is simultaneously an ever more concrete development of self-knowledge. This implies that the "I" or self-consciousness must ultimately make itself its own object in order to be completely transparent to itself: "essentially, the concept can only be grasped as such by mind [Geist]. The concept is not just the mind's property, but rather its pure self."[36]

We now have the means of understanding Hegel's unusual theory of *truth*. As a starting point, he takes the traditional "correspondence" theory, the view that truth designates a correspondence between our notion of a thing and the thing itself. But he subdivides this principle of truth into "correctness," which expresses the essentially commonsensical theory of correspondence, and truth proper, which concerns philosophical truth alone. Truth, according to Hegel, means "correspondence of a content to itself." He adds that, in logic, "thought determinations are considered with a view to how far they are capable of grasping the true."[37] The various categories are true (progressively) to the extent that they express the nature of self-consciousness or mind to itself. "Correctness" differs from truth because it presupposes a thinker, himself not the object of thought, who compares the notion of a thing with the thing itself to see whether the former corresponds to the latter. In this operation, the mind never becomes transparent to itself because it does not make explicit to itself the status of the categories (identity and difference, similarity and dissimilarity) by means of which it judges and compares. The "detached" observer does not see that he himself is the ground of those categories, or the negative activity which separates and identifies them. The thinking activity must become objective to itself if truth in Hegel's sense is to be attained: "That the form of thinking is the absolute form and that truth, as it is in-and-for-itself, appears in the form of thinking, this is the claim of philosophy *per se*."[38]

Nevertheless, being-for-itself is by no means the final category even of the first division of the *Logic* (the doctrine of being). Being-for-itself points beyond itself toward more concrete categories in which the nature of self-conscious activity finds clearer expression. In the second great division of the *Logic*, the doctrine of essence, Hegel introduces a series of thought-determinations that are characteristic of *reflection*: "The standpoint of essence is generally the standpoint of reflection."[39] In ordinary usage, "reflection" refers to light thrown back from its rectilinear course by certain kinds of surfaces, so that we have the same object duplicated, once as immediate and once as reflected or "posited." And, according to Hegel, we have roughly the same meaning in mind when we say that we reflect on a matter in the sense of thinking it over. We wish to see the matter on two levels: first as it immediately appears to us, and then as it "really" is after we have found grounds, causes, or motives to explain it. The standpoint of reflection is thus one that divides being into an essence and its appearances. Moreover, reflection characteristically works with relative notions such as cause and effect, force and its manifestations, wholes and parts, which explicitly require their complements if we are to grasp the full significance of statements in which they are used. Hegel often calls these relative terms "introreflected" to emphasize that they impel us to see being in a double way, once as immediate and once as mediated.

Recalling the basic problem of the *Logic*—the search for a way to think being as including negation within itself—it is easy to see that "essence" represents a dramatic advance over against the flatness of being. First, when we refer to the essence of something, we have in mind (so Hegel believes) a highly complex thought structure. The essence, say, of Renaissance painting is at first glance that which is distinctive and characteristic of works of art in that period, after one has subtracted the idiosyncratic styles and mannerisms of individual artists. But such an essence obviously has no independent existence apart from those artists' works. And none of those works is, as such, the "essence" of Renaissance art; each is *not* what the essence is. On the other hand, the essence transcends its appearances. Hegel would say that it is "indifferent" to its determinate embodiments. If we should discover a whole set of unknown da Vinci works, these would embody the essence of Renaissance art just as much as those works we already have. In no sense is the whole (essence) equivalent to an enumeration of its known parts. In fact, we often judge the parts (the works of art) against the whole (the essence of Renaissance painting) to determine their quality, authenticity, or what have you. Hegel construes essence, then, as an entire *movement* that includes what is immediately at hand, the separation of this immediacy into the appearance/essence dichotomy, and the recognition that each of these terms only is what it is by its contrast and relation to the other. He calls this a "movement of reflection," a "self-related negation."[40]

Hegel's point is that we arrive at essence by abstraction from the immediate data of experience, and that this abstraction constitutes a negation of such data or the postulating of them as dependent, contingent, or derivative. However, we must not exclude the activity of abstraction from its result, the essence. The activity of abstraction is just as much a "return-into-itself" of being, because being and thinking have the same structure. Again we find that the deepening of knowledge in the *Logic* depends on including the activity of the thinker ever more explicitly within the categories of thought.

Moreover, the sphere of essence differs markedly from mere immediate being because its categories are no longer treated as independent existents separated from other-being by a barrier. For example, positive and negative or ground and grounded, typical categories of essence, plainly require each other in order to be at all, whereas we can speak of a unit, a something, a qualitatively defined existent without explicit reference to any complementary category. Hegel illuminates this difference by contrasting becoming in the sphere of being with the movement of reflection within essence. "Becoming" referred to the oscillation between being, originally defined as absolutely different from nothing, to nothing and back again. The movement of reflection, however, Hegel calls "the movement of nothing to nothing and thereby back to itself."[41] By this Hegel means that the correlative terms of essence are nothing in themselves and explicitly point toward their respective complements, which in turn are likewise nothing in themselves.

The sphere of essence or reflection yields in turn to the logical category of the concept and its concrete form, die Idee. The transition depends on the internal instability of the categories of "actuality": substance, cause, and reciprocity. In effect, Hegel is criticizing Spinoza (and, by indirection, Schelling) for attempting to interpret the absolute as a substance with attributes, or as a cause of the world.

Spinoza's substance appeared within the sphere of essence as the only category that would permit us to resolve the paradox implicit in such reflective terms as whole and parts, force and its manifestations, inner and outer. All these categories Hegel interprets as progressively more discerning attempts to define the absolute, or to reveal how one could think of it as self-identical in its manifestations. In substance, we have an "absolute" identity because, as Hegel says, "each of its [the absolute's; L. H.] parts [is] itself the whole, or each determinate entity [*Bestimmtheit*] is the totality. That is, to be determinate at all is a sheerly transparent seeming [*Schein*] in which each difference disappears as soon as it is posited."[42] This passage echoes Schelling's argument that there is only absolute identity and that whatever is, is "in" the absolute or A = A.

As we have seen, the substance category is deficient because it displays no internal development, no progressive intensification of self-consciousness or self-knowledge. The attributes of substance (thought and extension) are unconnected to the substance whose attributes they are. Human subjectivity is swallowed up in what Hegel calls the dark, formless abyss of substance, which devours all determinate content.[43]

In order for substance to be transformed into the concept, human self-consciousness must be understood as the self-knowledge of the absolute. In Spinoza's system, human knowledge is only mathematical and quantitative knowledge of nature, as was the case in Descartes. But Hegel insists upon a self-knowledge which is not merely empty self-certainty (the cogito) but also the accumulation of a concrete content which reveals the absolute *within* self-consciousness. The absolute reveals itself to itself in our self-knowledge. Thus, the concept differs from substance (or Hegel from Spinoza), because it includes human self-consciousness as an integral, indispensable element of the absolute. In Spinoza, man cannot genuinely discover himself in the experience of the world, whether of nature or of human things, because all of res extensa is understood as a causal nexus in which human actions are strictly determined. And since self-consciousness is essentially a negation of negation, a self-awareness mediated through our knowledge of other-being, we can discover ourselves for Spinoza only as determined, as ensnared in a web of necessity. Thus the transition from substance to the concept is for Hegel a transition from necessity to *freedom.*[44]

In the "Differenzschrift," Hegel provides his clearest explanation of the relationship between necessity and freedom:

> Every system is a system of *freedom* and *necessity* at the same time. . . . freedom is the character of the absolute when it is posited as an "inside." Thus, even though it is posited in a limited form, in specific points of the objective totality, it remains what it is, something unlimited. As "inside," it is regarded as opposed to its being, i.e., it is potentially able to relinquish its being and take on a different phenomenal state. Necessity is the character of the absolute to the extent that it is regarded as "outer," as an objective totality.[45]

When the absolute is posited as "inward," as taking on limited or determinate form, it exists above all as human self-consciousness. The "I" is the proximate example of infinity because it remains identical to itself in all its determinate states and relationships. It is essentially the capacity to abstract from any determinate being. But this negativity is accessible only as an inner phenomenon, as the essential character of self-knowledge. Viewed from the outside or as a mere object, human actions can equally well appear as necessitated, as part of a system of determinism. Hegel is here vindicating self-knowledge as an aspect of the absolute that is of higher significance than the necessity that characterized Spinoza's absolute qua substance.

However, this pure negativity, which we also discovered in being-for-itself, is only one dimension of freedom: "The substance of spirit is freedom, i.e., not being dependent on another, or self-relatedness. Spirit is the actualized concept that is for itself, has itself as an object. . . . However, spirit's freedom is not merely independence of the other which has been attained outside the other; rather, freedom is such independence attained in the other."[46] In the *Logic*, this same idea emerges in Hegel's discussion of "reciprocity" (Wechselwirkung), the final term of the system of actuality or substance. In reciprocity we have two independent substances acting upon each other in a nexus of mutual causation. Hobbes' state of nature provides a fine political example of reciprocity because each man is driven to violence by the fear of violent death he may suffer at the hands of the other, even though the violence of the other is itself only an effect of his dread of the first man. Reciprocity collapses because the implicit identity of the seemingly independent substances becomes actual; that is, each is implicitly its other and the whole relation within the concept:

> [The concept], the totality which has resulted from reciprocity, is the unity of *both* of the *substances* present in reciprocity, but in such a way that each of them is from now on free. Their identity is no longer blind, or *inward*; instead each is essentially determined as seeming [Schein] or as a moment of reflection, such that it has immediately collapsed into its other or its posited-being. Each contains its posited-being *within itself* and is thus posited as sheerly self-identical in its other.[47]

The paradigm of reflection, the movement "from nothing to nothing and back to itself," finds complete expression in the movement from the pure negativity of one "I" to that of the other and back to itself, such that the identity of one person is entirely constituted through his recognition *as* a person, a free being, by all others. The causal reciprocity of Hobbes and Spinoza yields to the mutual recognition of Hegel's concept, each person knowing himself as an individual only through the entire society which recognizes him as such. I am free because the other is no longer an independent, alien substance but another "I" and hence identical to me. I become transparent to myself or "find" myself in the other. Freedom is not simply "given" as though all men were separate substances or atoms; rather it is achieved by elevating ourselves to insight into the essential ethical unity of all men. Individuation is thus the complement of socialization. Through the nexus of mutual recognition, the contingency of the individual in Spinoza's system becomes genuine freedom:

> [F]reedom presupposes necessity and absorbs it into itself [*enthält dieselbe als aufgehoben in sich*]. The ethical man is aware of the content of his actions as something necessary and valid in-and-for-itself. Rather than suffering any diminution of his freedom for this reason, a man's consciousness of the necessity of his acts gives his freedom genuine actuality and content, as distin-

guished from caprice [*Willkür*], which is a merely potential freedom still devoid of content.[48]

We have again reached the concept, not by way of an analysis of self-consciousness, but by studying the self-development of logical categories, especially "substance." Nevertheless, we have found that the *Logic* also treats self-consciousness as the core of the concept by showing that logical development leads us eventually to freedom or interiority. The attempt to think being as self-identical and excluding nonbeing has generated a series of contradictions, each of which exhibited speculative unity but in progressively more adequate forms. In the logical concept, we have speculative unity in its developed form as identity-in-difference. To express this, Hegel uses the terms "universal," "particular," and "singular," which he explicitly identifies as equivalent to a moment in the self-positing of the "I." The following passage on the moments of the concept ties together many of the strands of my argument:

> "I" . . . is *first of all* this pure self-relating unity, but not immediately, rather only by abstracting from all determinateness and content and returning into the limitless identity with itself. Thus it is *universality*. . . . *Second*, "I" is, as self-relating negativity, immediately also *singularity*, *absolute determinateness*, which opposes itself to the other and excludes it. It is *individual* personality. That absolute *universality* which is just as immediately absolute individuation [*Vereinzelung*] . . . constitutes equally the nature of the "*I*" and the *concept*.[49]

The particular (*das Besondere*) constitutes a middle term in both "I" and concept. Reverting to the "I"-paradigm, we could say that the universal is the "I" before its self-diremption into subject and object. What Fichte called an "inconceivable one" or subject-object and what was for Schelling an absolute identity no longer subjective in nature, is now found to be the universal. But clearly the "I" or the universal is *nothing* unless it differentiates itself by means of a determination through negation into subject and object. These its differentiae constitute the particular. From the viewpoint of the *Logic*, the universal (as a moment of the absolute) can dirempt itself into other dual terms not immediately or obviously related to self-consciousness (i.e., the categories of being and essence hitherto discussed). The concept is indifferent to its manifestation as being or thinking. These differentiae that are, in the "I"-paradigm, finite subject and object are thus specifications (Besonderungen) of the universal. Singularity designates the "I" which is a specific individual conscious of himself as at the same time universal or as the negative activity actualizing itself as subject and object. Thus singularity, like the true infinite, denotes the resolution of the opposition between universal and particular as the "formation process" through which they arise.

The concept is now explicit to itself in the *Logic*, but it must still undergo further development in order to become the *idea*. According to Hegel, the deficiency of the concept in its immediate form is that it lacks objectivity. To become the idea, it must articulate the unity of itself and of actuality: "the idea is the concept insofar as the latter has been realized. To realize itself, it must determine itself, and this determination is nothing other than itself . . . the idea is the fulfilled concept, fulfilling itself with itself. . . . Reason [equivalent to the idea; L. H.] is the concept giving itself reality."[50]

The course of development of the concept may be briefly summarized. In its initial forms as the universal, particular, and singular, it is subjective, in the sense of representing the mind's activity to itself within the element of formal logic. The concept, in its first subjective form, now concerns itself with judgments and syllogisms rather than with categories intended primarily to explain the external world. However, Hegel diverges from traditional logic by arranging first forms of judgment then types of syllogisms in an ascending order. These eventually culminate in a notion of the concept as *objectivity*. As objectivity, the concept develops from mechanism and chemism to teleology, in which its true nature as self-relating activity emerges. The telos of objectivity is the permitting of mind to discover itself as the concept in the world. Even though the concept is now equally present as subjectivity and objectivity, these aspects of it are not of equal significance. This is because only self-consciousness knows that it is the concept: "in the *negative* unity of the idea the infinite overreaches the finite, thinking overreaches being, and the subjective, the objective."[51] Hence, nature is not mere extension as it was for Descartes and Spinoza. But neither can self-consciousness discover itself with perfect transparency in nature.

If the idea is completely present in a specific thing or institution, then we may assert that it is "true" in the Hegelian sense that its actuality corresponds to its concept. A true house must not be ramshackle or unheated, and a true state cannot, for example, be a mere federation like the Holy Roman Empire.[52] The idea thus resembles the Greek conception of excellence or virtue (*aretē*) since it establishes an immanent standard of judgment for each thing. However, the idea is not what Hegel derides as a mere "ought," an ideal arbitrarily conceived and employed to discredit all actual institutions: "Thus [the idea] is not to be regarded as a goal to be approached, but which would itself always remain a sort of *beyond*; instead, anything actual only *is*, insofar as it has the *idea* within itself and expresses it."[53]

This immanence of the idea is the basis for Hegel's much decried proposition that the actual is rational and the rational, actual. With a proper grasp of Hegel's speculative philosophy, it is not hard to see that his argument represents a tautology. "Rational" or "reason" means the same as the idea: "The idea can be conceived . . . as *reason* (this is the genuine philosophical significance of *reason*)."[54] So Hegel is simply saying that the idea is actual, which is its definition (the unity of the concept and its actuality). This does not mean that every existent corresponds to its concept or exhibits the idea perfectly: "that sort of reality which does not correspond to the concept is mere *phenomenon* [*Erscheinung*], something subjective, contingent, arbitrary, which is not the truth."[55] He concedes that anyone can find circumstances that are not what they should be and require reform, but denies that such matters are of interest to philosophy, which deals with essential reality, not with what is contingent.[56]

In the *Logic*, the idea is the most complete and highly developed form in which Hegel's subject appears. But the idea, which Hegel, following Aristotle, defines as "thought thinking itself,"[57] is more a Greek than a Christian principle: "The Greek world developed thought as far as the idea; the Christian or Germanic world has apprehended the thought of spirit. Idea and spirit are the distinguishing features."[58] Logic is not the final expression of the absolute because its native element is pure thinking. As such it does not encompass and penetrate the world as it is actually experienced by finite human beings. The Greek philosophers turned away from the transitory phenomena of experience in order to contemplate the idea in its purity. But in their turn to contemplation, they contributed to the estrangement of man from the political and religious world he inhabited. Eventually this radical break between being and thinking would culminate in the "unhappy consciousness" of the Christian world and the alienation characteristic of modern culture.

The fragmentation of man's ethical life called for a new philosophical principle capable of defining his altered situation and ultimately of reconciling him with it. This is the role that Hegel assigns to spirit.

When we say that the idea is "thought thinking itself," we do not designate who does the thinking. If the idea is ascribed to God, or identified with His being, then God is at best an impersonal activity. But Geist is explicitly intended to include human spirit as one of its aspects. The ghostly "essential forms" (*Wesenheiten*) of the *Logic* are brought down to earth and fleshed out in the field of human aesthetic, political, religious, and moral experience. Hegel's philosophy of spirit thus concurs with the Enlightenment in according unprecedented importance to the "here and now" without, however, reducing the latter to mechanically understood nature or atomistic sense impressions.

SPIRIT

First and most obviously, spirit or mind is the "I": "If we examine spirit more closely, we find that its first and simplest determination is to be 'I.'"[59] It is the essential character of the "I" to be a finite subject or individual person, that is, to be a subject confronted by an object which appears to be other than the self. Dualism, fragmentation, and alienation are inherent in the very concept of spirit. Substance cannot develop toward spirit without self-differentiation: "the other, the negative, contradiction, diremption thus belong to the nature of spirit. The possibility of pain is inherent in diremption."[60] Furthermore, the dualism inherent in the structure of consciousness means that the "I" must labor ceaselessly in both a theoretical and practical sense to articulate itself: "Thus, spirit is internally at odds with itself; it must overcome itself as its own true nemesis; development, in nature a tranquil emergence, is a harsh, endless struggle against itself. What spirit wishes is to attain its own concept; but it conceals this from itself. It prides itself on its own self-alienation and revels in it. Development is . . . the hard unwilling labor against itself."[61]

But just as dualism inheres in the "I" as its essential condition of being (what is called "intentionality" in modern philosophy), so too does it have the capacity to assimilate other-being or return into itself. Hegel calls spirit "that which produces itself, pure activity, supersession [*Aufheben*] of the opposition between subjective and objective which spirit itself presupposed."[62] Or again: "Spirit is essentially the result of its own activity; its activity is to transcend immediacy, negate it, and return into itself."[63] Thus, the whole movement—self-diremption into subject and object, assimilation of the object or other-being and return into pure self-identity that characterizes spirit—is essentially the same as what we found to be the nature of the concept, being-for-itself, the true infinite, the idea, and every other speculative term in Hegel.

In the realm of spirit, the preservation of content takes on an explicit form because we are dealing with a self that undergoes the experience of fragmentation and becomes increasingly manifest to itself in the series of subject-object complexes. The "first series" of mental acts that we observe can accumulate content precisely because the "I" does preserve itself intact throughout its differentiations; spirit "acquires its truth only by finding itself within absolute fragmentation [*Zerrissenheit*]."[64] This is what Hegel means when he asserts that spirit is only what it knows itself to be.[65] Any specific instance of the subject-object dichotomy (for example, the Newtonian scientist who conceives the universe as a force manifesting itself) indeed reveals spirit to itself or discloses to me what I am. Yet the "pure negativity" of the "I" allows me to differentiate myself from that specific actualization of spirit's activity and acknowledge it as an incomplete definition of what spirit truly is (in this case, because the Newtonian scientist has not yet made his "detached attitude" into an object of critical analysis). These successive realizations of spirit within the subject-object dichotomy constitute what Hegel calls "Schein," seeming or appearance. For this reason, the *Phenomenology* is a science of "appearing consciousness." Furthermore, these appearances, when fully articulated, exhaust the essence of spirit as it is in and for itself. This is because spirit—like the "I," which is its finite, immediate form—is nothing apart from its manifestation or self-knowledge: "The determinateness of spirit is therefore *manifestation*. Spirit is not just any determinateness or content, whose expression or externality would be only formally distinguished from it; spirit does not manifest *something*, rather its determinacy and content is this manifesting itself."[66]

The second aspect of spirit that must be clarified is its *universality*, its character as "an 'I' that is we, and a we that is 'I.'" It is especially important to examine carefully Hegel's meaning here because his political philosophy stands or falls with the assertion of the universality of spirit given in the very nature of self-consciousness: "When we say 'I,' we mean something singular to be sure; but since everybody is 'I,' we end up saying something quite universal. The universality of the 'I' enables it to abstract from everything, even from its own life."[67] Hegel's argument is quite brief and apparently superficial. To say that I can abstract from everything does not mean that I am unable to refer to my distinctly personal self when I say "I." But if we return to

Fichte's argument concerning the universality of self-consciousness, Hegel's point becomes clearer. Fichte argued that I must distinguish myself, as subject, from everything else (as an object of consciousness) in order subsequently to differentiate myself as a specific person from other specific persons. Thus, the "pure" self appears as a precondition for the empirical, personal self. When Hegel says that I intend to refer to myself as singular, but, because everyone else says "I," I name only something universal, he seems to have Fichte's view in mind. Both consider consciousness essentially the act of self-identification through differentiation from all else. The "I" is therefore for Hegel, as well as his predecessors as far back as Kant, a "pure" or "transcendental" self as a condition for being empirical and personal.

Yet Hegel does not entirely share his predecessors' theories of self-consciousness, because they detach individual, empirical consciousness so radically from the transcendental "I." In the doctrines of Kant and Fichte there seems to be no difference among various transcendental selves. They constitute "one person" synthesizing the manifold of experience in the same way. By contrast, Hegel discovers the true beginnings of spirit in *mutual recognition*, where I do "find myself" in the other, but only as a distinctive self: "spirit is . . . this absolute substance, which is unity within the perfect freedom and independence of its opposition, namely of diverse self-consciousness, each existing for-itself."[68]

The universality of spirit is not the undifferentiated unity of transcendental apperception but the unity-in-difference of independent, empirical human beings who must discover or indeed produce the nexus of mutual recognition as a political or ethical community.

> In universal spirit, each thus is certain of himself, certain he will find nothing in existing reality but himself; he is as certain of the other as of himself.—I intuit in all the others that they are just the same independent beings as I am, since they are for-themselves; I intuit free unity with the others in them in such a way that such unity comes into being as much on my account as through the others,—they exist as me, I as they.
>
> Thus, reason is in truth actualized in a free people.[69]

One cannot understand the universality of spirit either as a "group mind" or as detached from finite human beings, designating their merely external similarity or identity, in the way that suburban tract houses are alike: "The universality of spirit must not be conceived merely as a set of common characteristics [*nicht als blosse Gemeinschaft-*

lichkeit]; instead it is penetrating unity in the sense of unity with itself in the determination of itself and in the determination of the other."[70]

The third definition Hegel gives of spirit is freedom: "the *essence* of spirit is . . . , formally speaking, *freedom*, the absolute negativity of the concept with itself."[71] But freedom, like spirit's universality, has several facets. To be free in Hegel's sense means first of all to be able to abstract from all else, even one's own existence, which is essentially the definition of the "I."

The negativity of self-consciousness represents Hegel's version of Greek autarchy: freedom is "not being dependent upon another."[72] But self-sufficiency does not mean a "flight" from otherness. Hegel consistently rejects any interpretation of spirit's freedom that would put a premium on withdrawal from the world, whether in the form of Stoic imperturbability, monastic seclusion, or the pietistic inwardness of romantic "beautiful souls." Rather, he understands self-sufficiency to include the labor involved in spirit's assimilation of other-being. Above all, freedom is coterminous with the recognition of oneself in other people, which is of course the same as spirit's universality: "*true* freedom [consists] in the identity of myself with the other . . . thus I am truly free only when the other is free as well and is recognized as free by me."[73]

The *Phenomenology of Mind* and *Philosophy of Right* become more lucid works if one constantly bears these words in mind. The isolated individual, whether as a liberal "natural man" or Fichtean ego, is not truly free for Hegel. As long as freedom is defined solely as protection of individual rights or as a victory over nature and inclination, it will always remain, Hegel thinks, a defective and perhaps even contradictory idea. As we can already discern in embryo here, Hegel will try to weld together freedom and community into a single concept, not only rhetorically, but in his analysis of what it means to be a self.

The definition of spirit as freedom discloses still another of its dimensions. Because neither the pure self-consciousness of subjectivity nor the mutual recognition essential to spirit are present in their fully articulated form in the primitive modes of human existence, spirit's freedom must be a *historical* accomplishment:

> [T]he essence of spirit . . . [is] its deed. . . . More precisely, its deed is to *know itself*; I am, but immediately I am only a living organism; as spirit I am only insofar as I know myself. . . . However, consciousness essentially implies that I am *for myself*, an *object* to myself. With this absolute judgment [Urteil], distinguish-

> ing myself from myself, spirit gives itself existence [Dasein], posits itself as self-external. . . . One mode of this externality, however, is *time*.[74]

An example Hegel often uses to illustrate the historic transition from substance to subject also illustrates the development of spirit as freedom, since "subject" is equivalent to spirit. He claims that the category of substance predominates in the Orient because subjectivity, individuality, and personality have not yet emerged except as "negations" of substantial unity. He means that the Orient is still what sociologists would call a "traditional" society in which individual choice and judgment are powerfully restricted by the incubus of ancestral custom. As Hegel pictures him, the religious or philosophical Oriental desires above all to annihilate his individual self-consciousness, to "submerge" himself in the void (substance in its negative connotation). He thereby intends to eradicate even the inchoate differentiation of substance and subject: "The affirmative is merely substance; the individual is what lacks substance, the accidental. Political freedom, right, ethical life [Sittlichkeit], pure consciousness, and thinking are not present in what is accidental. That such relationships might emerge requires that the subject posit itself as consciousness contraposed to substance and thus exist as recognized."[75]

It is fundamental to realize that, for Hegel, a break with ancestral custom and tradition—enlightenment—is essential in the "deepening" of substance to subject. As we saw in the introduction, the rupture with substantial ethical unity is the precondition for all philosophy. Now we can also see that it is the very essence of freedom or Geist. Hegel's reconstruction of wholeness in thought can never take the conservative course of simply revivifying tradition. To attempt to restore the dominance of the ancestral would be, from Hegel's perspective, not merely inexpedient or inadvisable but illogical, if the "I" is incorporated into logic as concept.

The impossibility of reconciling man with himself or with ethical unity through a return to substance illuminates the fifth and most encompassing definition of spirit, that it is God: "the divine [should] in general be conceived as spirit."[76]

The knowledge of God as spirit requires that He have within Himself individual personality or "negativity."[77] Differently expressed, "God may only be termed spirit insofar as He is known as *mediating Himself with himself* internally. Only in this way is He *concrete*, animate, and spirit."[78] Hegel is here repeating, in a theological context, his argument in the *Logic* that being must come to include negativity within itself as its essential moment. God is not grasped as a self unless He is understood according to the model of self-consciousness that is negativity or self-mediation.

Hegel enlarges on the definition of spirit as God by means of two propositions: "(a) God is only God, insofar as He knows Himself. (b) His self-knowledge is furthermore His self-consciousness in man and the knowledge *of* God by man which proceeds to man's self-knowledge *in* God."[79] In other words, God as spirit is not separated from the world: "There is only *one* spirit, the universal, divine spirit."[80] The *one* spirit has existence or determinate being through human self-consciousness. Indeed, Hegel considers the essential teaching of Christianity to be the revelation that human and divine spirit are the same: "the divine nature is the same as the human, and this unity is intuited."[81] The consciousness of God in religious faith is in truth the intuition of God by himself in the human spirit, or equally the intuition of each individual of his own inherent divinity: "the subjective spirit that harkens to divine spirit is itself this divine spirit. That is the truly fundamental determination of spirit's behavior toward itself."[82]

The definition of Geist as divine spirit sheds additional light on all the other dimensions of spirit and makes the whole course of the *Phenomenology* more intelligible. To begin with, Hegel's criticism of the substance category proves to have profound theological significance. To conceive God as substance means that one has not understood the divine nature as self-consciousness or as a person. I have already noted that Spinozistic substance reflects, for Hegel, the category of necessity; it shows that Spinoza has not grasped human spirit, self-consciousness, or freedom. Now we can see that his failure adequately to portray human spirit implies equally that he has not understood divine spirit. This conclusion follows from Hegel's argument that God is only what He knows Himself to be, and that His self-knowledge occurs only in and through finite, human spirit. Consequently, the entire movement of the *Phenomenology* must be taken to represent not only the elevation of human spirit to full self-consciousness, but just as much the development of divine substance toward genuine personality. To use the categories of the *Logic*, God as the universal must particularize Himself within the (finite) subject-object relationship in order to become "intensified" into self-consciousness as the singular.

Hegel's conception of spirit also suggests the outlines of a solution to the problem I raised in the introduction. Spirit, in order to actualize its nature as freedom, had to break with the "substantial" world of the ancestral; indeed, this breach, which signals the onset of enlightenment, actually makes spirit become what it is *an sich*. The reconciliation promised by philosophy must thus include enlightenment or free self-consciousness not only as the path of liberation for human spirit, but also as the process by which God first becomes what He is—i.e., intensifies the substantial into subjectivity. We can now interpret the dualisms of enlightenment, the fragmentation of ethical, political, and religious life, as the movement of God toward self-knowledge by way of His "alienation" within the subject-object dichotomies of finite mind. God as spirit is essentially what we saw the absolute to be: the pure negativity which manifests itself within the differentiations of human knowledge, such that He eventually grasps that pure negativity as His very essence. God is therefore something like a tracker following footprints in the snow and eventually coming to realize that the footprints are his own.

The double movement of the *Phenomenology*—man's ascent toward universality and free self-consciousness, and God's descent from abstract substance to human subjectivity—is effectively captured in a passage from the preface to that work:

> [T]he disparity that occurs in consciousness between the "I" and the substance that is its object is the difference of substance, its *negative* as such. It can be regarded as the deficiency of both, but is in fact their soul or the motive force within each of them. . . . Now if this negation at first appears as a disparity [*Ungleichheit*] of the "I" to the object, it is really just as much the disparity of substance to itself. What seems to take place outside it, to be an activity directed against substance, is its own doing; and it proves to be subject in its very essence. To the extent that this is completely demonstrated, spirit has equated [*gleich gemacht*] its existence and its essence. . . . Being is absolutely mediated; it is substantial content which is just as immediately the property of the "I," self-like [*selbstisch*] or the concept. With this the phenomenology of spirit is concluded.[83]

At the beginning of this essay, I contended that a radical reinterpretation of self-knowledge, the cogito of Descartes, lay at the heart of Hegel's entire philosophical enterprise. Our discussion of spirit has disclosed that all human knowledge is self-knowledge because it is the activity of divine spirit revealing itself to itself as subject, self, or concept within human consciousness. This is a profoundly important step because it conditions Hegel's attitude toward the Enlightenment and his expectations that its dualisms provide the key for the reconciliation promised by philosophy. Hegel is now in a position to interpret the most diverse and even antagonistic intellectual and spiritual developments—the Lutheran Reformation, modern natural science and empiricism, the French Enlightenment and Revolution, German Romanticism, and even the modern liberal state—as different aspects of a single movement from substance to subject. Hegel's critique of the Enlightenment is designed to elicit and clarify their inner affinity, which is the progressively more adequate knowledge of spirit by itself as self-consciousness. That critique must go beyond the forms of speculative thinking we have considered so far and enter the "matter at hand" (*die Sache selbst*) if we are to be convinced that Hegel's speculative philosophy really can overcome, in thought, the fragmentation of modern culture.

THE METAPHYSICS OF EXPERIENCE

3

THUS FAR we have moved through the rather rarefied air of metaphysical speculation, reconstructing the tortuous ways in which Hegel appropriated and also criticized the principles of his predecessors. The crucial idea—to reiterate—is Hegel's discovery of the precise nature of self-consciousness and his transformation of this discovery into a sort of paradigm for grasping other complex relationships.

Hegel understood his discovery to be a resolution of a philosophic puzzle that had been implicit in metaphysics from Descartes to Fichte. Philosophers have tried to make the "I" an autonomous and independent substance, or an unconditioned and absolute starting point for all further speculation. Yet the "I" is empty. It gets all determinate content from outside itself. So when philosophers have tried to explain what it means to be a self, they have had recourse to straightforwardly naturalistic accounts (e.g., Descartes and Locke), or else to "parallel worlds" theories (e.g., Kant).

Hegel's "concept of the concept" is meant to show that the elements of man's being—"I" as negation of other-being (being-for-itself) and as participant in definite subject-object relationships—are inextricably linked to one another. I cannot know who I am outside of the concrete relationships within which my identity is manifested. On the other hand, being a self means negating all these relationships and standing outside of and above them. For Hegel, these possibilities—inner retreat and engagement, ironic detachment and earnest pursuit of truth, as well as their many other permutations—defined the situation of the modern Enlightenment. Comprehending the Enlightenment, and thus incidentally becoming truly enlightened oneself, would mean demonstrating the concealed identity of these dichotomous and diverse attempts at self-definition, piecing together a whole picture of the self.

When we descend from the heights of metaphysics to survey the intellectual struggles of modernity as Hegel saw them, the identity-in-difference of the participants' viewpoints is invariably what he wishes to bring to light. The two most important manifestations of the dichotomous, fragmented ego of modernity were reformed religion and the scientific study of nature (including man taken as an integral part of nature). True to his project, Hegel will try to show why the painful estrangement and struggle of these forces represents a necessary intensification of spirit's quest for self-knowledge. The first aspect opens up the inwardness of man's spiritual life to a deepening and enriching experience; the second changes the world of sense into an object of rational inquiry where man can discover much more order and harmony than he would have previously suspected. As Hegel notes, "Spirit now dwells and moves about in its own proper sphere; in part this is the natural and finite world, in part the inner world, above all that of the Christian religion."[1]

For the present we shall confine ourselves mostly to Hegel's account of spirit's struggle to master "the natural and finite world." Here we shall confront directly what has all along been implicit: Hegel's critique of the Enlightenment's philosophic premises, chiefly its commitment to sense experience, scientific method, and/or mathematics as the touchstones of truth. Still it is wise to recall that we are isolating only one horn of the Cartesian dilemma when we examine the difficulties (as Hegel sees them) of empiricism. Both aspects of that dualism are equally one-sided and abstract. On one hand, the Protestant (and his philosophical apologists such as Kant, Jacobi, and Fichte) insists that only faith (or, for the Kantian, respect for the moral law) can render one's actions truly good. The chief concerns of religion shift from dogma and ecclesiastical hierarchy to the nature of a person's inner life. In its extreme form of pietism, modern Christianity degenerates into a species of narcissism that posits a complete divorce between the inner self, reduced to the empty "I" = "I," and the world. The modern Enlightenment, at least in its English and French variants, suffers from the opposite failing. Rather than retreating from the world into the self, the man of the Enlightenment turns all his attention to the natural and social environment. There he expects to find everything organized according to rational principles and, if such is not the case, he will change the world to make it conform to reason. To Hegel, the man of the Enlightenment has admirable intentions but is doomed to failure. In effect, he wishes to discover himself in the world since reason is the quintessence of human spirit. But he cannot do so because he does not know himself and hence lacks a correct (i.e., speculative) concept of reason.

The theoretical credo of the modern Enlightenment can be summarized fairly easily. First, the source of all our knowledge is experience (empiricism). Second, our experience will inevitably reveal rational principles at work, or at least it can be made to conform to reason (rationalism). On the surface, Hegel does not appear to take issue with either tenet. His *Phenomenology* is a study of the experience undergone by consciousness, and he consistently affirms the rationality of the actual. However, he regards the concepts of experience and reason employed by most Enlightenment thinkers as woefully inadequate. In general, the *Aufklärer* have only produced what Hegel calls philosophies of the understanding or reflection.

Experience, Understanding, and Reflection

The isolation of the understanding as a faculty distinct from reason may be traced back at least to Kant's *Critique of Pure Reason*. There Kant defines the understanding as a capacity for rules and categories insofar as these are applied to an object of experience. Reason, on the other hand, aims at an "unconditioned synthesis" in which the categories are applied to what cannot, by its very nature, become an object of experience.

Both Schelling and Hegel seize upon Kant's distinction, but they reserve the term "reason" for speculative identity. They hold the understanding to be a faculty concerned exclusively with finite determinations: "finitude is the most stubborn category of the understanding."[2] The understanding is at once the mental capacity for separating and differentiating and the faculty which works by the principle of identity. Hegel argues that "The capacity to separate the concrete into abstract determinate qualities must be esteemed as the infinite power of the understanding."[3] Or again: "The activity of separating is the power and labor of the understanding, the most marvelous and greatest, indeed the absolute power."[4] But he also remarks that "the principle [of the understanding; L. H.] is identity, simple self-relation."[5] The understanding works by fixing some aspect or quality of its object as self-identical and thereby different from all its other aspects.

These citations should dispel the widely held belief that Hegel scorned "mere" understanding for the sake of a higher reason which could dispense with the labor of finite thought. Hegel notes that we can never develop any definite or determinate thoughts, either in the realm of theory or of practice, unless the understanding exercises its power to abstract and to set artificial lines of demarcation in the fluid reality of sense perception.[6] The understanding functions whenever we analyze anything, since to analyze means to dissect a whole into parts that, taken by themselves, are merely abstract or "unactual." Even when I analyze an apple into redness, tartness, and roundness, I am abstracting out qualities that have no independent existence. This capacity to analyze a concrete totality is the amazing power of the understanding and of thinking generally.[7] Accordingly, Hegel insists that understanding is a moment of reason rather than a separate faculty or mode of cognition.[8]

In Hegel's various writings, the understanding is only hazily and imperfectly distinguished from common sense (*der gemeine Menschenverstand*) below it and reflection above it. Generally, Hegel assumes that ordinary thinking operates on the level of presentations, or the mental images of objects. The understanding turns isolated presentations into thoughts (Gedanken) by classifying and ordering them according to more general categories.[9]

But if the understanding differs from ordinary consciousness in its attempts to categorize and explain its presentations, then it trespasses on the turf of reflection. Indeed, Hegel often speaks of the reflective understanding which is "the understanding which abstracts and thereby separates . . . and does not advance beyond these separated elements."[10] However, Hegel occasionally describes reflection with much the same deep respect that he reserves for the "miraculous power" of the understanding to divide and identify: "reflecting is an activity which separates," or "reflection [is] absolute separation."[11] And because to be is to be something determinate, reflection is also "the faculty of being and limitation."[12] To confound matters completely, Hegel remarks that the reflective understanding, when it has turned against reason, behaves as common sense (gemeiner Menschenverstand).

The difficulty one encounters in making sharp distinctions among common sense, understanding, and reflection indicates not that Hegel was a muddled thinker, but that he was profoundly aware of the continuity between ordinary consciousness and science. To Hegel, science and the grounds, explanations, and models it works with in its capacity as understanding or reflection signify an extension of common sense principles, not their reversal.

In sum, the real significance of empiricism is not its epistemology, which Hegel held in low esteem, but its conviction that experience is amenable to rational explanation. Even though the empirical sciences claim to begin with raw experience, "What they essentially intend and produce are *laws*, general propositions, *a theory*; *thoughts* about what is present at hand."[13] As we know, Hegel hopes to push empiricism beyond itself and toward a speculative reconciliation. The presence of thought in the empirical sciences (as laws and explanations) makes them potentially philosophical, if only the limitations of reflection and the understanding could be made explicit in them. "The empirical sciences do not rest content with the perception of singular data in the phenomena; instead, they prepare these for philosophical consideration by thinking them through, i.e., discovering general determinations, genera and laws within them."[14]

This should not be taken to imply that the understanding or empirical investigations come to incorrect conclusions about their proper objects, which are finite. Philosophy must rather show that empiricism, since it is a construct of the understanding, cannot adequately grasp the traditional concerns of metaphysics (freedom, mind, spirit) "because these objects immediately present themselves as infinite in respect to their content."[15] But in addition, it must be demonstrated that empiricism leads beyond itself toward knowledge of these "absolute objects." Otherwise, knowledge of being (as a series of finite objects) could never culminate in self-knowledge, and Cartesian dualism could not be overcome. At the same time, the absolute must include the finite thinking of empirical understanding, or knowledge of it would amount to a virtuoso act of intellectual intuition not accessible to whomever is willing to use his mental faculties.[16]

The Reductionism of Empiricist Metaphysics

For Hegel, the power and vitality of empiricism had a twofold source. First, it redirected man's attention to the world and made it possible for him to feel at home there after the long exodus of medieval otherworldliness. The rediscovery of the natural world also affirmed the value of the senses and of their testimony in determining the truth.[17] But this renewed trust in the evidence of the senses also prompted many individuals to put more credence in their own experience than in any dogmatic authority, a development which Hegel welcomed: "The principle of *experience* contains the infinitely important determination that man himself must be mentally or emotionally involved [*dabei*] if he is to accept some content and hold it to be true. More specifically he must find such a content to be in accord with or united to his own self-certainty."[18]

So far, Hegel's evaluation of empiricism dovetails reasonably well with what the empiricists themselves might have claimed. But Hegel also ascribes virtues to the empiricists that they almost certainly did not possess. He praises them for demonstrating that the actual is rational: "There is contained in empiricism this great principle, that what is true must be in reality and accessible to perception. . . . Like empiricism, philosophy knows [erkennt] only what *is*; it knows nothing of what merely *ought* to be and therefore *does not exist*."[19] This is a serious misrepresentation of the empiricists' intentions. While they did claim to discover natural laws or principles of utility in experience, they surely meant these to be employed as standards for judging the religious and political institutions of their time. Radical *philosophes* such as Helvétius and La Mettrie could never have accepted Hegel's suggestion that empiricism implies "the reconciliation of self-consciousness with reason that is in being, with actuality,"[20] even though such men were uncompromising empiricists. For the most part, Hegel saw little merit in empiricism's self-interpretation, its "uncomprehended" form. Emil Fackenheim, in his study of religion in Hegel's thought, distinguished between comprehended and uncomprehended Christianity, i.e., roughly between Christianity as viewed from Hegel's speculative vantage point and as understood by Christians themselves.[21] The same distinction can be applied here to empiricism first as a moment of Hegel's *one* philosophy that is essentially a speculative reconciliation and then to empiricism as its proponents understood it.

Of all the empiricists it is Locke to whom Hegel devoted the most attention because he found in the Englishman's epistemology all the fundamental propositions that were further developed but never repudiated even by later empiricists like Hume and the French philosophes: "A wide-ranging culture [*Bildung*] begins with Locke, which, although it has assumed different forms, has remained the same in principle."[22] And again: "Lockean philosophy is highly esteemed. On the whole it is still the philosophy of the English and the French, and even, in a certain sense, now of the Germans."[23]

In Hegel's view, Locke has misperceived the purpose of philosophical thinking, because he has shifted the focus of concern from the truth of ideas to their genesis. Locke does not ask whether a given category (e.g., perception, causality, substance) is true in and of itself; rather, he asks how it arises in our minds. His answer, that our complex ideas are formed by abstraction from sense experience, Hegel calls "trivial."[24] Hegel's theory of truth, as we have seen, concerns the correspondence of a thought content to itself. Hegel always asks whether a given category is internally consistent or whether it exhibits contradictions which drive it beyond itself. This means that each category is examined according to whether it retains its identity in its differentiation or includes pure negative activity within it as its essential nature, as in the concept or the "I." Locke, because he asks only how we come to know such categories and ignores their truth, misses the point of philosophizing: "In this sole concern with derivation and psychological origins, the sole obligation of philosophy—to determine whether these thoughts and relationships possess truth in-and-for-themselves—has been overlooked."[25]

Hegel does not dispute that elementary sense experience is temporally prior to the formation of more abstract or complex categories.[26] But he characterizes this as a mere account of "what happens," whereas philosophy is supposed to reconstruct events in thought and thereby comprehend them: "Philosophy is not supposed to be an account of what happens; rather it should be a knowledge of what is *true* in events. Furthermore it is supposed to comprehend, within the true, what appears to be a mere occurrence when it is recounted."[27]

The source of the quarrel between Hegel and Locke is the status of universals and, by extension, of thought as the "universal in action." Hegel assails the arguments of Locke, and especially of Hume, that would have transformed the universal into a secondary, subjective addition to sense data. As Hegel expresses it, Locke thought of "immediate actuality [as] the real and true."[28] True to his Kantian heritage, Hegel adopts a quite different position. What is true in experience are the universals: laws, relationships, categories, and uniformities. Experience would be impossible without them. Hence they are not subjective additions to experience but its objective core.[29] Thought, as the universal in action, does indeed disengage the universal from contingent sense data. And in this sense one could say that thought alters what is immediately given in perception. But it does so only to elicit various logical relationships which constitute a higher-level actuality than immediate sense data: "Reflection [*Nachdenken*] *alters* the manner in which the content exists in sensation, intuition, and presentation.

Thus it is only by means of an alteration that the *true* nature of an object comes to consciousness."[30] And from this Hegel concludes that "This indispensable basis, the concept, the universal, which is thought . . . itself, cannot be regarded *only* as an indifferent form, superficially grafted onto a content [*an einem Inhalte*]."[31] In short, even though the universal is a product of thought, it is nevertheless objective: without its presence in being, there would simply be nothing there to experience. As Hegel expresses it, speculative philosophy readily admits the empiricist principle that there is nothing in the intellect that will not also have been in the senses,[32] but just as decisively asserts that there is nothing in sense that was not also in the intellect.

The inability of Locke and other empiricists to conceive correctly the relationship between universals and sense experience blinds them to the essential character of all philosophical thinking. On the one hand, they take sense particulars to be real and independent of mental activity. Yet in order to say anything about sense experience they must use the categories of the understanding, dissecting and analyzing the concretum of sense experience. This procedure has two consequences. First, the empiricists do not realize that the products of analysis—abstract thoughts like force and law or, in political philosophy, natural rights and passions—transform the concrete totality of experience precisely because they are so abstract. Hegel asserts that this form of analytic cognition is the standpoint of "Locke and all empiricists."[33] Second, he argues that these empiricists deceive themselves into believing that they have depicted things as they really are, when in fact they are doing just the opposite.

Hegel argues that the empiricists strip away from reality whatever seems to them contingent, so that the result of their analyses is a pure *abstraction* even though they attempt to pass their abstractions off as "real." This is the character of virtually all liberal political philosophy, especially of its depiction of natural men, natural laws, etc. Hegel characterizes this sort of procedure as the first, obvious notion that would occur to ordinary Verstand. One simply peels off the layers of history, custom, etc. just as though these were the skins of an onion in order to find out what is true and necessary: "If one thinks away everything that might even remotely be regarded as particular or evanescent, such as what pertains to particular mores, history, culture or even the state, then all that remains is man imagined as in the state of nature or else the pure abstraction of man with only his essential possibilities left. One can now discover what is necessary in man merely by looking at this *abstract* image."[34]

In Hegel's estimation, then, the empiricists have missed the point of their own discovery. They have managed to winnow out of the historically contingent societies around them a notion of man, pure and simple, to whom they can then ascribe certain fundamental or "natural" rights. But because their own rhetoric has so often stressed the importance of firsthand experience as against pure reason and argument from authority, they assume that their natural man is a datum of experience, obvious to anyone, rather than a construct of the understanding.

Hegel levels the same charge against empiricism when it is employed as a philosophy of modern science. However important firsthand observation might be to scientific inquiry, it will not make sense unless it is pursued in the context of what we today might call a scientific paradigm. The very quest for universal principles in nature and society would, Hegel thinks, necessarily commit a consistent empiricist to some metaphysical (i.e., nonexperiential) vision of reality:

> The fundamental deception in scientific empiricism is always this: it makes use of metaphysical categories such as matter and force, not to speak of one, many, universality, infinite, etc. And, using these categories as guidelines, it makes further *inferences*, thereby presupposing and applying the forms of inference, all the while not knowing that it contains and practices metaphysics itself, and makes use of these categories and their syntheses in a completely uncritical, unconscious fashion.[35]

Hegel's objection, I think, reflects a deeper concern that the unacknowledged metaphysics implicit in empiricism might impoverish and flatten out the reality of man and nature, robbing it of the qualitative gradations that betoken higher and more spiritual forms of life. But we must emphasize yet again that Hegel assigns a very important place to the analytic procedures of the understanding. Since Hegel considers self-knowledge the mind's most vital project, he cannot disparage the necessary condition of analyzing immediate, concrete totalities into abstract (because detached) parts which are amenable to rational cognition. Accordingly, we find him defending, however reluctantly, the highly unromantic abstractions of Verstand even though the latter does violence to the concreteness of the object it analyzes: "Empiricism, in analyzing objects, falls into error when it supposes that it leaves these objects as they are, since it does indeed transform the concrete into something abstract. In this way it also happens that the living is killed, for only the concrete, the one, is animate. Nevertheless, that separation must occur if we are to comprehend, and spirit itself is internal separation."[36] Indeed, Hegel believes that the true nature of things consists in the universal, which is a thought. The analytic procedure of empiricism thus strikes out upon the right road toward knowledge, but proceeds only half way. Having reduced the manifold of history, nature, spirit, and politics to simple abstract determinations like pleasure and pain or attraction and aversion, empiricism now calls a halt and pronounces this abstraction to be the nature of reality itself. Hegel protests vehemently against this "misunderstanding that takes the *natural* principle or the *beginning*, the point of departure in natural development or in the history of the self-cultivating [*sich bildend*] individual, to be the *true* and the *first thing* in respect to the concept."[37]

Hegel's attack on the abstract thought of the understanding recalls once again the deepest ambiguities which he discerned in the Enlightenment itself. On the one hand, the men of the Enlightenment could employ understanding in the service of principles which Hegel undeniably accepts: rational inquiry against superstition, individual conviction against mere authority, the rights of man against monarchical despotism. But the "negative" power of analytic thought also made it very difficult for the Enlightenment to provide an alternative vision of man, society, and even nature which would adequately describe the "spiritual" relationships and ideas that concerned Hegel so much, such as religion, family life, art, community, and solidarity, even philosophy. Hegel wanted the Enlightenment to put back together the whole which it had disassembled, perhaps an impossible demand for it: "[T]he main thing is that the separated elements must be reunited."[38]

Hegel does not reflect as often as one might expect on the reasons behind this apparent "blind spot" in the Enlightenment. Why should philosophers as perspicacious as Descartes, Locke or Hume not have seen these flaws in their own thought, if indeed they truly are flaws? In trying to reconstruct Hegel's critique of the Enlightenment, I found only one passage that really starts to provide a clue. Like Jürgen Habermas in our own day, Hegel seems to believe that the philosophic emphasis of the Enlightenment on reduction of the rich totality of life to simple, abstract categories suggests an unacknowledged "cognitive interest" of its exponents. They reason as far as they need to in order to demonstrate how some phenomena might, in principle, be predicted and controlled. To understand something means, for the Enlightenment, to show what factors produced it. If we can imitate those same factors, replacing natural agency by human agency, then we ought to be able to produce the same results. Behind what Hegel takes to be the cognitive interest in control lurks the deeper imperative of sheer physical survival. The mind, together with its apparatus of categories, would seem to be an instrument at the disposal of our bodily needs. As Hobbes suggested in *Leviathan*, reason imitates nature in creating a sovereign for the sake of the survival of those who submit to it. This cognitive interest would then partially explain why the empiricists (again using the term in Hegel's sweeping sense) tend to reduce the manifold of experience to ever-simpler determinations. These ideas are, I think, clearly spelled out in the following passage, where Hegel summarizes critically the views of Köppen, a disciple of Jacobi and of the latter's mentor, David Hume:

> We can comprehend space, consciousness . . . , and the objective world only in terms of analytical units; we can only break them down into component parts. In this way a boundless field (i.e., open-ended and lacking totality) is opened up for our investigation, which we are compelled to cultivate for the sake of our *physical* survival *alone*. Those things whose mechanism we have discovered can also be produced by us if the means themselves are *in our hands*. In this manner, what we construct *at least in our imagination* we can comprehend; and what we cannot construct, we also cannot comprehend. The cognitive process of understanding is a ceaseless equating that we call connecting and that is a continual diminution and simplification of the manifold, to the point, if such were possible, of its complete elimination and annihilation.[39]

Hegel's argument against this analytic procedure is a *reductio ad absurdum*. To flatten down the diverse content of concrete experience to some simple determination by discovering a quality of "sameness" in everything ultimately impoverishes experience toward the vanishing point. For example, to argue as Helvétius did that all behavior can be explained on the basis of pleasure and pain means that we merely repeat, apropos of any human action, the same thing over and over, i.e., that the person sought pleasure or avoided pain. Moreover, according to Hegel there is no arbitrary stopping point on the path of abstract empiricism. Some empiricists "find" aggression to be the natural impulse in man and reduce all behavior to it; others find sociability, still others benevolence. Yet as Hegel points out: "First of all empiricism, in this process of separation, lacks any criterion at all for establishing the dividing line between the contingent and necessary; that is, empiricism cannot say what, in the chaos of the state of nature or in the abstraction of a human being, should be omitted and what retained as a permanent feature."[40]

In other words, these empiricists have not driven abstraction "to the point of absolute, negative unity";[41] rather, they have only extinguished a great number of particularities and determinations. In Hegel's view, it was Kant and especially Fichte who showed us that a complete analysis of human activity and the world, a relentless process of abstraction, leads us to conceive human beings as pure negativity, the "I" that excludes from itself every determination. Human beings as empiricists portray them are indeed abstract atoms, reduced to some primitive impulse of motivation. Yet the abstractness which characterizes them seems to come from "outside," from the empirical scientist who strips away "inessential" determinations such as history or custom. From Hegel's perspective, however, they have not come to see that this abstraction is the very activity of thinking, the nature of the "I." The abstract atoms of empirical analysis are each instances of pure negative activity, stripping themselves of contingency and accidentality. Thus when the analytic procedure of empiricism is pushed to the limit it yields nothing but pure identity (the identity of self-consciousness) that is just as much nothing at all or pure negativity.

Empiricism fails not because it thinks and thereby separates the concrete whole into abstract thought determinations, but because it does not carry thought far enough. If it had, it would have discovered not primitive abstractions like pain and pleasure, aggression or force, but the concept: "Abstracting thought must . . . not be regarded merely as the putting-to-one-side of sensuous material, which would not thereby suffer any diminution of its reality. Rather, abstracting thought is the reduction and absorption [Aufheben] of this material, *qua* mere phenomenon, into its *essential* being that in turn manifests itself only in the concept."[42]

Enlightenment empiricism stood halfway between the concrete immediacy of ethical life and the concrete-in-thought of philosophy. It distorted reality by reducing it to primitive abstractions, yet could not overcome that abstractness because it did not grasp the concept, or pure negative activity. For this reason Hegel prefers even nonsystematic empiricism that merely collects data and descriptions to the abstract empiricism of modern theorists of natural right.[43] Even an undigested mass of empirical data, suggests Hegel, gives a more accurate representation of a concrete whole than a theory that stretches the whole out on the Procrustean bed of some lifeless, abstract model.

Hegel believes that his own theory is free from the reductionist bias of empiricism because its heart and soul is the concept, the only "paradigm" of reality that is not abstract and lifeless, but rather a "pulsebeat" or an eternal self-differentiation and return-into-itself. In all of Hegel's works, the primitive, abstract or simple indeed marks the beginning, but "the *abstract is the untrue*."[44] The more articulated, developed, and concrete is not an illusion behind which lurks the primitive (as in Hobbes where striving after power for the sake of security underlies every aspect of state and society). Instead, these simple abstractions mark only the beginning of philosophical thought, not its completion: "[T]he *beginning* is the *least* formed, the least developed and internally defined; it is rather the poorest, the most abstract."[45]

The reductionistic tendency of empiricism becomes especially evident in its attempt to explain the mind's activity in terms of natural processes. By contrast, Hegel's own philosophy stands or falls with the assertion that the mind can have knowledge of itself that is not mediated through biological or mechanical models. This, in turn, amounts to the assertion that we have not understood Geist by tracing the origins of mental activity back to chemical processes in the brain, the influence of "conditioning" upon our thought processes, or the evolutionary development of mental capacities in man's struggle to adapt to his environment. Hegel asserts the independence of mind from nature in an uncompromising way: "[T]he emergence of spirit from nature [should] not be thought of as though nature were the absolutely immediate, the first thing and originally positing activity, while spirit for its part would only be posited by nature. Rather, nature is posited by spirit and the latter is absolutely primary. Spirit as it exists in-and-for-itself is not the mere result of nature, but is in truth its own result. . . . Spirit does not emerge from nature in a natural fashion."[46]

The reasons for Hegel's position should be clear by now: if mind is portrayed as an extension (albeit highly refined and complex) of res extensa, then its specific character as negative activity has not been understood. His own version of a philosophy of mind consequently depicts the liberation of the "I" from inner and outer nature through its own activity. Hegel never abandoned Fichte's insight into the self-producing character of the "I" and reasserts it in his doctrine of consciousness:

> The being-for-itself of free universality is a higher form of the awakening of the soul to *selfhood* [*zum Ich*], or to abstract universality insofar as it is for abstract universality. In this way, it is *thinking* and *subject* for-itself and more precisely it is the subject

> of a judgment in which the "I" excludes from itself the natural totality of its determinations as an object, a world *external to it*, at the same time relating itself to this external object in such a way that it is immediately introreflected in it or is *conscious*.[47]

The act of self-identification in which I posit myself by excluding everything else from myself as not-"I" has no precise analogue in nature. Hence, it is incomprehensible so long as one adopts the attitude of empiricism and observes the mind from the outside, excluding from consideration the very activity by means of which subject and object arose in the first place: "The self-relating universal exists nowhere outside the 'I.' In *external nature*, . . . the universal . . . does not reach *actual being-for-itself*."[48] Empiricism tends to reduce mind to nature insofar as it insists upon finding a causal relation between the two. Mind cannot have caused nature since nature existed long before human consciousness. So the only alternative is to assert that nature caused mind, or that mind arose as the result of a causal chain in which nature was gradually modified so as to produce the brain. But, according to Hegel, it is the causal relation itself that must be called into question. He sees no reason to assume its absoluteness, particularly when one is trying to comprehend the mind: "The assumption made about speculative philosophy, that the causal relationship is especially predominant in it, is fundamentally wrong. For the causal relationship is in fact entirely excluded from it."[49] Instead, mind or the "I" is a *causa sui* in which "*producer and product are equated*."[50]

Here again, the natural world may be prior in time, but if we ask *what* it is we must ultimately have recourse to universals like force, law, and species to provide an answer. Thus the empiricist is put in the position of asserting that mind is reducible to (or caused by) something that, when he attempts to explain or describe it, turns out to be a thought determination or category. Hegel's contention is that if the empiricist took his criterion of experience seriously, it would lead him to reject as insufficient the unacknowledged metaphysical categories through which he had hitherto interpreted experience. The path of experience thus leads away from the formulations of ordinary empiricism and toward the concept.

Empiricism Comprehended

Empiricism hardly counts as philosophy at all for Hegel because of the self-deception inherent in its attempt to repudiate metaphysics while covertly practicing it. Therefore, to demonstrate that the principle of experience really does lead beyond itself toward a speculative reconciliation, Hegel must take it out of the hands of Locke and its other apologists. In the early chapters of the *Phenomenology*, he sets up a "naïve" consciousness which adopts a more or less instinctively empirical attitude without being committed to any full-blown empiricist philosophy.

This consciousness appears twice in the *Phenomenology*, once as understanding and once as "observing reason." The former still regards its object as other than itself, thereby preserving a distinction between being and thinking, while the latter is "the certainty of consciousness that it is all reality."[51] But both adopt the detached attitude toward their objects which is typical of empirical investigation. Moreover, both employ categories of reflection, i.e., relational notions in which the world is duplicated. It is seen once as immediate and then again as pointing beyond itself to a more essential reality which grounds or explains it. And just as in the *Logic*, the perplexities occasioned by these categories of reflection lead to the discovery or "positing" of the concept. But in the *Phenomenology*, the concept takes on the explicit form of self-consciousness, the "I." In other words, Hegel takes the position characteristic of German idealism since Kant: that an adequate analysis of the objects of experience will reveal the presence of the self within them.

The chapter entitled "Force and Understanding" is preceded by two shorter sections in which Hegel shows the inadequacies of "sense certainty" and "perception." "Sense certainty" is an attitude that claims that the entire world of sense experience is immediately accessible to us, and that we do not need laws, theories, or universals to explain it. In describing the world, this consciousness has recourse to demonstrative pronouns or vague adverbs like "this," "here," and "now." But such words themselves are universals, and the most empty ones at that, since they are entirely indifferent to their content. For "perception," which is a category of reflection, experience consists of a manifold of "things," each distinct from all others and identical to itself in spite of the diversity of its properties. Here the subject is implicated more directly in the process of knowing. It is an obvious step (one taken in different ways by both Locke and Kant) to differentiate the thing as it is in-itself from the thing as it is for-us. But once we declare that there is a gulf between essence and appearance, we must admit that we cannot obtain certain knowledge of the former. Appearances may deceive us. On a more general level, the understanding splits the sensuous concrete into various abstractions (as here into one-many, thing-properties, being-for-itself and being-for-another), but cannot reconstruct the concrete-in-thought that would be equivalent to penetrating the façade of deception to attain the essential core of things. Consequently, the gulf between essence and seeming that is also the dualism of subject and object can (indeed must) widen to the point where the necessary connection between the moments is no longer visible.

In "force," the understanding has found a superior category, one which more closely approximates the concept. Force is an activity that remains identical to itself throughout all its manifestations. Moreover, force only is, insofar as it expresses itself. Gravitational force, for example, shows itself in a relationship among countless objects, but it is entirely itself in each of these manifestations and indeed would be nothing at all apart from them.

This demonstrates that the understanding, in employing the category of force, acknowledges that empirical investigation is not so much concerned with sense data as it is with the theories that explain those data. The scientist regards things in toto as appearances explicable in terms of hypothetical entities which are not themselves accessible to perception. Thus, the theoretical constructs of the scientist constitute a supersensuous realm of laws which is the "inside of" or the "ground behind" the phenomenal world. For Hegel, this attempt to explain the world as it appears to us by a supersensible world different from the world of appearances is characteristic of modern "reflective" culture. But once we take this approach, we are forced to concede that the supersensible might be the inverse of what it appears to be. For instance, Descartes' evil demon might have fooled him into believing that he had a body, or that a chair was in his room and not a table. The inverted world is a nearly ineluctable consequence of the divorce between being and thinking characteristic of Cartesian dualism. Once the distinction between things as they are for-us and as they are for-themselves has been accepted as a genuine limitation on knowledge, then the inverted world becomes at least conceivable. Hegel does not want to say that things ultimately are (or are not) the inverse of what we perceive them to be. He simply wants to draw our attention to a significant difference between modern and ancient thought. For the philosophic tradition from Plato through Aquinas, it seemed self-evident that there was an objective order of things that could be reproduced or reflected in the mental picture that we construct of the cosmos. But from Descartes to Fichte, i.e., in a very significant strand of the Enlightenment, it was not at all clear that any cosmic order existed that could be neatly distinguished from our mental image of it. As a result, any appeal to the experience we have of the world may encounter the objection that all such experience is simply an externalized version of the order of our own thoughts, indeed that the "real" world may not be anything like what we experience it to be.

Hegel proceeds to show how the dialectic of law and the inverted world leads us to the concept. But empiricism has not yet spoken its last word in the *Phenomenology*. It reappears in a more concrete form as "observing reason." Reason is the comprehended phase of scientific investigation. It stands upon the plane of Kant's transcendental apperception, and it is intersubjective in character: its conclusions are intended to be valid for every self, because the manifold of experience is synthesized according to a priori rules anchored in the structure of self-consciousness as such. Consequently, reason adopts the Kantian category as its principle of experience and interprets the category as "essential being [Wesenheit] or simple *unity* of what exists solely as thinking activity; or reason is this: that self-consciousness and being are the *same* essence."[52] However, Hegel is quick to point out that reason has only the naïve certainty that it is all of reality. It is indeed idealism, but not the systematic idealism of Kant and Fichte; rather, reason simply takes an idealistic attitude toward the world.

Reason begins by observing external nature, planting the ensign of its sovereignty on all its heights and depths. Unlike the understanding that confined itself to the Newtonian universe of law and force, observing reason must try to come to grips with the phenomenon of organic life. Its downfall is that it uses mechanistic categories like efficient causality and reciprocity that cannot do justice to even the simplest behavior of organisms. Like Kant, Hegel thought that teleological explanations had an important place in biology, a belief that nowadays few would endorse. Still, we should not fail to appreciate the genuine insights in Hegel's argument. Old-fashioned mechanistic explanations frequently pictured organisms as entirely passive, responding like machines to external pressures and forces in predictable ways. Rejecting this, Hegel insisted on ascribing the "purposes" of self-preservation, reproduction, etc. to animals.[53] In partial agreement with Hegel, modern biological research has demonstrated both the crucial role of genetic inheritance and mutation in shaping an organism's behavior as well as the myriad adaptations, behavioral and morphological, that organisms have developed to survive in diverse environments. Our view of biological organisms may still be mechanistic, but it certainly portrays living creatures as much more complex machines—more active, adaptive, and environment-shaping—than the mechanistic theories of Hegel's time.

A related problem, one perhaps more directly relevant to political theory, concerns whether specifically human behavior can be understood by reference to a mechanistic paradigm. We have already noted that the deepest ambiguity of the Enlightenment surfaces in this very issue. Even though the Enlightenment begins, for Hegel, in Descartes' discovery of the cogito and hence of the distinctive character of spirit or mind, it soon gives rise to an almost antithetical current of thought, typified by Hobbes, Helvétius, La Mettrie, Hume, and others, which comes close to denying self-consciousness, or else treats it as an epiphenomenon of man's biological nature. For Hegel, then, it seemed that the Enlightenment, even in its most ingenious representatives such as Kant, tended to make mechanism its highest constitutive category. In so doing it rendered unattainable the telos of mind to become transparent to itself, since inorganic or mechanically controlled nature never fully approximates the form of the concept or the "subject."

Among reason's strategies for observing the human mind or spirit are what Hegel calls "psychological laws." At first, reason had attempted to fathom the mind by enumerating a series of logical laws that supposedly govern our mental processes. But it was forced to concede that the mind is not just a "bag" of disconnected laws. Instead it is a unity modeled on the *Logic*'s being-for-itself. We recall that being-for-itself refers to an identity constituted by the active, explicit negation of otherness, a definition Hegel resuscitates to delineate the field of psychology. The object of psychology is "the active consciousness that is for-itself in such a way that it annuls [aufhebt] other-being and has its actuality in this intuition of itself as negativity."[54] Hegel believes that the for-itself is an appropriate category for empirical psychology since it investigates the relationship between behavior and external influences.

This broad definition of empirical psychology encompasses practically everything that today would be the province of the behavioral sciences. Hegel's psychology considers the various faculties and inclinations which determine the behavior of the individual toward his environment. But it also deals with what today we would call social roles and socialization, the process whereby the individual conforms to the pregiven habits, mores, values, and ways of thinking of the society in which he lives. Hegel insists that neither form of behaviorism does justice to the unique character of human self-consciousness: negative activity.

The brand of psychology which isolates various faculties and inclinations to explain behavior is compelled to acknowledge some sort of unity in consciousness. After all, it is *one* person, the individual, that psychology wishes to describe. So it tends to picture the mind as a "bag"[55] in which the various faculties coexist, a metaphor somewhat reminiscent of Hume's "stage" across which diverse impressions parade. Having abstracted out these faculties, psychology now tries to use them to explain the behavior of an individual person. But these explanations are, as Hegel says, even more uninteresting than enumerating the species of insects or mosses.[56] Such explanations usually amount to little more than ascertaining that Jones did such and such because he has more common sense or a greater inclination than Smith. In short, the behavior is simply introreflected into a faculty or inclination that is almost identical to the behavior.

Such a covertly tautological explanation of behavior by reference to various faculties and inclinations is only one of the pitfalls of empirical psychology. Hegel takes up another problem with explicit reference to what he terms "pragmatic historiography." The pragmatic historian (in our time he would be the Freudian or the psychohistorian) makes use of the reflective distinction of interior and exterior to reduce historical deeds to certain subjective, private motivations characteristic of the person's "inner" life: it is "frequently the case that certain people, in judging others who have accomplished something right and excellent, make use of the untrue distinction between interior and exterior so they can claim that such accomplishments are only external, and that these actors were really interested in something quite different—the satisfaction of their vanity or of other reprehensible passions."[57]

Hegel insists on the contrary that "man is nothing but the series of his deeds,"[58] a phrase which could have been culled from the writings of Sartre or other existentialists. But his concerns are actually more characteristic of Nietzsche. He fears that the reductionism inherent in the inner-outer category of pragmatic historiography will efface the distinction between acts which really are undertaken for private gain or other particularistic ends, and the *res gestae* of world-historical individuals who have sacrificed private contentment for the sake of genuinely universal purposes. The approach of the pragmatic historian bespeaks "the attitude of envy"[59] reminiscent of Nietzsche's *ressentiment*, which intends "to divest of its nimbus everything which has hitherto been celebrated and praised, and to reduce it to the level of vulgar mediocrity in respect to its origin and actual significance."[60]

But Hegel, unlike Nietzsche, does not propose to become a psychologist himself to combat the corrosive effects of empirical psychology. Rather, he considers the results of pragmatic historiography the outcome of a "category mistake," namely the application of a distinction between interior and exterior, which, when fully analyzed, proves contradictory whether taken in its identity or in its difference aspect. The significance of the remainder of Hegel's section on reason will be to undermine the interior-exterior category and with it the whole attitude of observation.

First, however, Hegel must come to grips with the "sociological" aspect of empirical psychology, specifically its attempt to explain behavior on the basis of external influences. Here we have an exterior, the mores and customs of a society, and an interior, the person's motives now pictured as a sort of "black box" such that a complete explanation would demonstrate the identity of the individual and the society:

> If the exterior [i.e., society; L. H.] were constituted, in-and-for-itself, just as it appears in each individual case [*an der Individualität*], then individuality would have been comprehended by reference to its exterior. We would have a double gallery of images, of which one would be the reflected appearance of the other. One set would be the gallery of complete determinateness and circumscription by external circumstances, the other would be the same things, but now transposed into the mode in which they exist within the conscious being. The former would be the surface of a sphere, the latter, its center representing [vorstellen] the surface within itself.[61]

Hegel's objections to this sort of behavioral explanation display his (essentially Kantian) demand that the rational should be universal and necessary. One cannot normally hope for anything more than probabilities or high correlations between circumstances and individual behavior in social science. But for Hegel a finding that 70 percent of all Roman Catholics vote for the Democratic party would not constitute a genuinely rational relationship. He points out that "Individuality . . . is just this: that the individual is the *universal both* merging in a tranquil fashion with the universal *at hand*, the mores, customs, habits, etc. and conforming to them, *and also* reacting to them in a contrary way and inverting them. . . . *What* is supposed to influence the individual, and *what sort of* influence it is supposed to have—these questions actually have the same meaning—depends therefore only upon the individual."[62]

In other words, the societal circumstances that condition individual behavior are not simply "out there" independent of the individual; they only exist *for him* insofar as they interact with his own subjectivity to form a peculiarly individual world. Thus a sociologist confronted with two people exposed to a Catholic upbringing who react to it in opposite ways must concede that their individual personalities and idiosyncrasies must have predisposed them to act in the ways they did. What began as an explanation of individual behavior by reference to external circumstances ends in the avowal that the influence of such circumstances on the individual can be understood only by reference to the individual himself.[63]

The modern social scientist would probably make two replies to Hegel's objections. First, he would insist that correlations and probabilities do indeed help us explain the behavior of large numbers of persons even though they do not provide us with anything like necessary connections in individual cases. Second, he would likely argue that if we know all the determining factors of an individual's life as well as their relative importance and priority, we could explain the individual's behavior completely. Here the social scientist parts company with Hegel. Hegel considers negative activity to be the essential feature of mind. He would regard the social scientist's model of behavior as inadequate because it depicts the self as a passive recipient of influences rather than as the activity of negating or transforming them. Moreover, Hegel repudiates the very notion of causality which the social scientist, as a protagonist of the understanding, necessarily presupposes: "[In] *relationships of physical-organic and spiritual life* . . . what we call a cause does prove to have a different content than the effect. *But* this is only the case *because* what affects a living being is independently determined, altered, and transformed by it, i.e., *because the living being does not permit the cause to have its effect*. . . . It is the nature of spirit . . . *not to admit anything originally other into itself*."[64] Here again we find that the quarrel between Hegel and the empiricist tradition has little to do with the relative value of experience as a source of knowledge. Rather it is a question of which logical categories most faithfully express the various dimensions and levels of what we in fact experience. If, says Hegel, causality cannot illuminate the nature of human consciousness, then it must be deemed inapplicable and a higher category, the concept, must supplement it.

But observing reason does not abandon its attempt to find a reductionist explanation for mind. Where psychological or sociological explanations fall short, it descends to yet more primitive levels of analysis. In physiognomy and phrenology it depicts the exterior of mind—facial features and skull formation—as the key to its interior. From an earlier discussion we recall that reason had proclaimed itself to be all of reality and set out to ransack the world of experience to prove its point. In a way it does discover itself in these most crass of pseudosciences, but only by a reductionism so absurd that it must call into question its whole enterprise and begin to see the incommensurability of the "I" to any determination of mere being.

Reason thus abandons both the category of being and observation as its guiding epistemological principles. From now on it will be spirit, human self-consciousness inhabiting a human world. Its object will no longer be nature, or even the mind understood as an extension of nature, but another self-consciousness that it recognizes as itself (that is, as an "I") and that in turn recognizes it as a self. "Thus, the object to which it is positively related is a self-consciousness; the object is in the form of thinghood, i.e., it is *independent*; but [consciousness] has the certainty that this independent object is not alien to it. Thus it knows it is implicitly recognized by the other self-consciousness; it is *spirit* which has the certainty of its unity with itself in the duplication of its self-consciousness and in the independence of both."[65]

Reason, like the understanding, returns from its mediation through experience to the concept which is self-consciousness. But the self-consciousness to which understanding penetrated was singular and appetitive. Now reason discovers that the truth of experience is intersubjectivity. Reason (or spirit) cannot be expressed in terms of being or simple self-identity. It must make itself into what it is. But to comprehend the self-producing nature of spirit means essentially to think the "I," for only it is truly for-itself. We thus have a reason for which reason itself (the "I") is the object, the intersubjectivity of mutual recognition.

The collapse of observing reason leads us directly into the sphere of human *praxis*, society, the state, and religion. Reason sees that its observational attitude was essentially a form of alienation. Self-consciousness externalized itself both by seeking itself in the experience of external things (res extensa) and by adopting the detached attitude of scientific investigation in which it abstracted from its practical relations to others. The attitude of modern science is thus seen to be quite literally artificial, a form of self-discipline in which I make myself into what I am. For this reason, scientific empiricism must be considered a variant form of the Bildung (self-formation or culture) that Hegel takes to be the characteristic attitude of the Enlightenment.

In a wider sense, modern scientific empiricism is self-alienated because it assumes the absolute validity of reflection or reflective understanding. It attempts to fathom itself indirectly and asymptotically by observing an infinite (in the "bad" Hegelian sense) series of finite forms: "When reason has burrowed through all the viscera of things and opened up every artery in them in the hope that reason itself will bound forth to meet it, such good fortune will not be its lot."[66] Instead, reason or spirit conceals the absolute (and here itself) from itself in the endless multiplication of finite, "observed" entities:

> The power of limitation, the understanding, attaches to the edifice it has constructed between man and the absolute everything that man considers sacred and valuable. Then it buttresses its edifice with all the powers of nature and talent, and extends it into infinity. In it, one can find the complete totality of limitations, but not the absolute itself. The absolute, now lost in the parts, drives the understanding onward toward the infinite development of multiplicity, while the latter, because it endeavors to extend itself toward the absolute but just reproduces itself endlessly, only mocks itself.[67]

In the end, empiricism is both symptom and weapon of the culture of reflection that paradoxically asserts both the absolute validity of stable, self-identical forms as fixated by the understanding and the absolute power of the self over any fixed determination (as the skepticism and even nihilism of the Enlightenment). The "truth" of empiricism is the "I," and specifically the cultured self of the Enlightenment and French Revolution that adopts empiricism as a means to demolish all authority and tradition. To that world of self-made (in the philosophical sense) individuals we now turn.

POLITICAL POWER AND PERSONAL FRAGMENTATION: THE CULTURE OF EARLY MODERN EUROPE

4

IMPORTANT as the principle of experience may have been in revolutionizing the study of nature, its significance for human affairs preoccupied Hegel even more. The man of the Enlightenment adopts the same strategy toward the investigation of political and social life that he had toward the world of res extensa generally. He expects that the study of society will yield uniform patterns just as the physical universe had done. Like the scientist of "observing reason," the Aufklärer expects to find rationality behind the contingencies of human affairs. But when applied to political life, the search for rational or "natural" laws has two important consequences: first, such natural laws tend to be extremely abstract and reductionistic; and second, they function as an "ought" or nonactual standard for existing institutions. Thus the Enlightenment's emphasis on independent and critical thought, summed up in the watchword "experience," set the stage for a clash between premodern, authoritarian and traditional institutions and the newly proclaimed rational or natural standards of right.

In principle, as we shall see, Hegel approves of the proclamation of the rights of man. Like most progressive thinkers of his time, Hegel had a deep antipathy for corruption, arbitrary government, and officially sanctioned cruelty. But he had another agenda as well. The objective world was the stage upon which man, as historical actor, discovered and understood himself. As long as reason had not penetrated and reformed society, human beings could not attain full self-consciousness. The image of human freedom would remain clouded by particularistic, preenlightened forms of life, and man would not truly find and actualize himself as the citizen of a rational state.

On the other hand, Hegel sensed a certain ominous one-sidedness in the Enlightenment's political program. The search for rational and transsubjective standards of justice in the form of natural laws resurrects the dialectic of interior and exterior. The latter, what Hegel often calls positive law, draws its legitimacy from the "interior," the abstract rational principles of human associaton now deemed natural. But it is only a small step to assert (as Hume eventually did) that the interior of things—natural law—is not objectively present in experience. "Natural" law is not really natural at all. It is a convention whose obligatoriness rests solely on our habit of obedience and its usefulness to our subjective ends. In the political sphere as well as in the metaphysical, empirical reflection tends toward skepticism or even nihilism: "Since perception is supposed to remain the basis for whatever we hold to be true, universality and necessity appear as something *illegitimate*, as a subjective contingency, a mere habit whose content can be constituted in any number of ways. An important consequence of this is that legal and ethical determinations as well as the content of religion appear to be contingent and to have lost their objectivity and inner truth when considered in this empirical way."[1]

The Enlightenment culminates in the "desperate conclusion that our knowledge is something merely subjective."[2] To combat this corrosive skepticism and restore the integrity of man's political and ethical life, Hegel must prove to the proponents of the Enlightenment that they are not enlightened enough. He must show them that their dualistic assumptions and adherence to the dogmas of the understanding are self-contradictory and self-defeating. We have already seen how he conducts this argument on a theoretical level. Now we will examine Hegel's contention that the practice of the Enlightenment leads to a hopeless impasse unless it transforms itself into speculative philosophy.

To appreciate Hegel's argument we must bear in mind that the consciousness of the *Phenomenology* has now explicitly reached the level of spirit. The diverse figures we encounter are now regarded as defining and embodying a single spirit that is, however, inwardly fragmented.

The earlier forms of consciousness, typical of the "detached" attitude of scientific empiricism, experienced the instability of the understanding's self-identical forms. But they did not apply that insight to the "I" itself, the source of the principle of identity and the understanding's rigid abstractions. Yet when the phrenologists claimed that spirit is a thing, they unwittingly laid bare an important truth: that spirit must objectify itself to know itself. It must become alien to itself rather than retaining the stable self-identity typical of scientific thinking:

> Consciousness knows and comprehends nothing that is not in its experience, for what is in experience is only spiritual substance, and this, more exactly, as *object* of itself. Spirit, however, becomes object, for it is this movement, to become *an other to itself*, i.e., *object of itself*, and then to annul [aufheben] this other-being. And experience is just the designation for this movement in which the immediate, the nonexperienced, i.e., the abstract, whether of sensuous experience or of the simple as it is grasped by thought, alienates itself and then returns to itself from this alienation. Only then is the immediate and abstract presented in its actuality and truth as well as becoming the property of consciousness.[3]

As we have stressed, the self has no definite or determinate core. What it is only comes to light in the series of subject-object relationships within which experience unfolds, both historically and on a personal level. One could say, as Hegel does, that a person must become "alienated" from himself in order to know himself; that is, he must literally plunge into the human and natural world, apparently alien and "other," in order to discover therein what he really is. The introspective narcissist may believe that he is plumbing the depths of his soul. But he overlooks the enormous extent to which his personality and thought have been formed by the historically transmitted patterns of life beyond his subjectivity.

But Hegel wishes to press the issue of alienation toward a higher stage of development. If it is true that all experience is alienation, then we must come to feel and experience that alienation for what it is. We must, in other words, become aware that what we are in some sense depends upon what we are recognized and seen to be by others. Furthermore, we must feel keenly the perhaps unbridgeable gulf between the self we present in everyday life and the inner awareness accessible to no one but ourselves. In Hegel's language, spirit cannot simply be self-alienated. It must know itself as such.

Of course, the empiricist forms of consciousness in the *Phenomenology* have certainly gotten a glimpse of the alienated character of experience in the inversion (*Verkehrung*) of their own theoretical expectations. But it is modern culture, the human world rather than the world of scientific investigation, that reveals the complete personal fragmentation that the theoretical attitudes only point toward. The contradictory, "inverted" character that empiricism discovered in the objects only served to drive consciousness back upon itself, into the seemingly unassailable self-identity of the Cartesian cogito. But according to Hegel, the fragmentation of modern culture is so complete that it attacks even the "I," providing the historical, cultural precondition for speculative philosophy.[4]

The Demise of Ethical Life

To grasp the meaning of fragmentation in our modern world, we must first form an acquaintance with its "other," the ethical life or Sittlichkeit that for Hegel was best exemplified in classical Greece. The ethical man is one who carries out his duty not because it coincides with an abstract principle of justice or morality, but rather because it *is* his duty. To reflect upon duty destroys its ethical character. This turns an abstract, universal principle into the "interior" of concrete duties, the source of their obligatory character. Moreover, when I reflect upon my duty, I put myself outside and above it as the "absolute" point from which specific duties are compared to an abstract principle of justice: "[T]he true [ethical life] of the ancient world has as its principle that each man should abide in his duty. An Athenian citizen did what was expected of him, so to speak, instinctively. If I reflect upon the object of my action, I must be aware that my will has been superadded to it."[5] Hegel refers to ethical life as a "second nature,"[6] suggesting that the ancient citizen adjusted himself to the prevailing mores and institutions almost as though these were natural conditions of existence that he simply had to accept as inevitable. "For the subject, ethical substance, its law and powers . . . possess as object the character of being—in the highest sense of autarchy—an absolute, infinitely more solid authority and power than the being of nature."[7]

Hegel's treatment of ethical life in the polis constitutes the first section on spirit in the *Phenomenology* and is entitled "true spirit." By contrast, the last section on spirit is called "spirit certain of itself," and gives an account of the German Enlightenment as exemplified primarily by the moral theories of Kant and Fichte. Our acquaintance with speculative terminology should alert us to the character of the development we will witness in this long treatment of spirit. The Greek world is "true" spirit; this means it contains the absolute content without absolute form, i.e., without the for-itself or the "I." We recall from the earlier discussion of Descartes that the cogito is equivalent to self-certainty, the pure "I" or transcendental apperception which lacked all content. In the context of spirit, Hegel is suggesting that the modern Enlightenment in its political form (France) and moral form (Germany) has still not gone beyond the "certainty" of Cartesian dualism. Thus, spirit can attain certainty and truth—the absolute content knowing itself as such—only if the *truth* of Greek ethical life and the *certainty* of modern Enlightenment can be comprehended as aspects of the same self-differentiating "one." This comprehension would be equivalent to a reconstruction of ethical wholeness, which is Hegel's philosophical project, but only in thought. Greek ethical life or "true spirit" embodies a certain absoluteness of content, a complete interpenetration of the individual and his world, which we cannot recapture in practice.

To see why this is so, we must examine Hegel's account of ethical life in the ancient world more closely. "True spirit" appears as the culmination of a long series of forms of appearing consciousness, all embodying different attitudes of *reason*. These various "reasonable" consciousnesses have a single attitude in common. They are convinced that the individual can "actualize" himself or be a world unto himself without having completely assimilated the sociocultural milieu within which he exists. Whether he is intent on reforming society, making it more virtuous, assisting in realizing larger social purposes, or making judgments about the prevailing moral shibboleths, he always assumes that the social whole, the universal, is merely an aggregate of self-actualizing individuals. "True spirit" or genuine ethical life differs from all these reasonable forms of consciousness because in it the individuals are implicitly aware that the universal is their "substance," the ground upon which they stand and the whole content of their actions.

Participation in common projects and the performance of family duties illustrate, respectively, the difference in this context between reason and spirit. In a cooperative endeavor, a shared goal holds men together and directs their efforts. They intuit in each other a commitment to a common end. Yet the bond between them is ephemeral. I can equally well choose not to participate, and I regard our efforts as temporary, limited by the purpose we share. Moreover, such cooperative activities are accidental to my self-identity, predicates which can be changed.

By contrast, our responsibilities to family members have a more profoundly obligatory character. The family is an end-in-itself, apart from any utilitarian goals that it pursues. Further, membership in a family is not contingent. The family bond permeates all the individuals who comprise it, determining their identity and giving significance to their lives. Finally, the actions of family members do not have the "accidental" character we encounter in mere cooperation: "In order for the familial relationship to be ethical, the nature of actions performed, in respect both to the person who acts and the person for whose benefit the act is undertaken, may not be contingent, as perhaps occurs in giving aid or rendering service."[8] Thus in the family and in ethical life as such one no longer regards the universal, the whole, or common ends as a predicate of independent subjects (really substances); instead, the universal is itself now a subject acting through the individuals. As in the *Logic*, the reciprocity of independent substances yields to a new, speculative relationship (the concept) in which the moments, formerly separate substances, now become differentiae of the same self-dirempting "one" that is wholly present in each. Furthermore, ethical actions concern the whole person, not the person as fragmented into different roles or quasi-independent social relationships: "The content of ethical action must be substantial or whole and universal: it can therefore be directed only toward the *whole* individual or toward him as universal and general."[9]

If Hegel's account of ethical life were merely a residual category to which almost every form of merely customary, traditional social organization could be consigned, one would see in him little more than a precursor of modern sociology. But for Hegel, ethical life does not exist in its perfected form until it has been purged of the arbitrary, patriarchal domination characteristic, for example, of ancient China or Egypt. It requires mutual recognition in which I intuit in my fellow citizens the same "self" which I am. This is not possible until a certain degree of political equality has been achieved, or until the *citizen* emerges from the world of primitive, patriarchal social existence: "[T]he *concept* which has arisen before our eyes [is]. . . self-consciousness as recognized, possessing the certainty of itself in the other free self-consciousness . . . In this concept is revealed the *realm* of *ethical life*. For this is nothing but the absolute spiritual *unity* of the individuals' essential being within their independent *actuality*: an implicitly universal self-consciousness."[10] Or, in plainer language, "I am only free, insofar as I posit the freedom of others and am recognized as free by others. Real freedom presupposes many free men."[11]

In its perfected form as mutual recognition, ethical life is *freedom*: "ethical life is the *idea of freedom* . . . the *concept of freedom which has become the world at hand and the nature of self-consciousness*."[12]

Where the individual described in the earlier section on reason regarded laws, institutions, and mores as external to his own will and projects, the "ethical" citizen sees such environing laws and folkways as integral to his very identity. Hegel stresses that the life of an ethical community provides us with an approximation of the concept, as instantiated in human affairs. The concept, we recall, is the paradigm of an entity whose existence involves self-differentiation, and yet the identifying of the moments that are thus separated from one another. A classical republic, in its ethical phase at least, was something like this. Its laws were not like an external bond, holding together an aggregate of independent individuals. Rather, the individuals derived their whole being from the laws. Taking the model of the "I" to describe this relation, we would say that laws and mores are like a pure in-itself which only *is* as differentiated into subject and object, here the citizens who all know their duty and carry it out. They see in one another only that identity (the laws as in-itself) which each, qua citizen, himself is: "The laws express what each individual *is* and *does*; the individual recognizes them . . . as particularized [*vereinzelt*] in himself and in each of his fellow citizens."[13] The concept is present here as freedom because each citizen is not a limit, a pure "other" to his fellow citizens (as is the case, for instance, in Hobbes' state of nature). The identity of each citizen is constituted through the movement of mutual recognition in which each citizen only *is* a citizen because he is acknowledged as such by all others, who are thus identical to him within the encompassing unity of the laws or ethical life. Recalling Hegel's discussion of the concept as freedom in the *Logic*, we can see that in ethical life each does indeed have his freedom in the others, not outside them.

Hegel's account of the demise of ancient ethical life will now be summarized. In the transition from reason to spirit, the universal—the social, religious, and cultural milieu of the individual—has become a subject rather than a predicate of independent individuals. Yet it is a subject, spirit, which still has the predominant form of *substance*. That is, the Greek citizen had not yet begun to reflect on the laws and thereby introreflect the ethical world into himself as the "point" in which all judgments arise. But we already know that the "I" or the concept is negative activity in which I exclude everything that is not-"I" from myself to become for-myself. To know itself as this sort of negative unity, spirit has to destroy the positive unity of citizen and law in Greek ethical life. Philosophically this "breach with the actual world" came about with the advent of the sophists and then even more clearly with Socrates. Thus, Hegel dates the emergence of modernity as far back as the Peloponnesian War.[14]

The emergence of subjectivity or reflective thinking shattered the fragile legitimacy of the laws because the citizen now asked the reasons for the laws' validity. At the moment we ask why we ought to obey, or what rational grounds can be adduced for performing our duties, we demand of customary law what it cannot provide. We alienate ourselves from the laws so that they suddenly appear to be a congeries of irrational commands and taboos in which we can discern no hint of rationality, no hint of our own self-consciousness and will.[15]

In the *Phenomenology*, the triumph of subjectivity or rational self-consciousness first takes the form of the victory of the polis over the family, as exemplified by Antigone's death in Sophocles' tragedy. For Hegel, this is essentially a triumph of human law over divine law, of universal, abstract justice over particularistic and customary obligations. The polis, albeit an "ethical" institution in its classical period, had set in motion a fatelike process in which it, too, would be obliterated by an even more rigidly universalistic entity, the Roman empire.

The universal citizenship and abstract legal system of imperial Rome already marked the inception of the self-alienated spirit we encounter in the modern Enlightenment. The Roman citizen is a *person*, an expression which, in its original significance, means "mask." The mask of personhood, the universality of abstract right conferred upon the Roman citizen by the emperor, bestows a superficial sameness upon the individuals of the imperial age. But their identity or mutual recognition is a mere surface phenomenon when compared to the profound ethical unity of ancient Greece. Behind the mask of personhood is simply the natural individual ("nature" in this context denoting the ensemble of one's spontaneous feelings and desires unorganized by reason and self-discipline). In the language of modern political science, the Romans were failures at "nation-building" because they could not foster a political culture in which the citizens felt any affinity toward one another as concrete human beings. Roman law and administration did not aim at "acculturating" the whole individual, but only at outfitting him with certain minimal rights and duties. From Hegel's viewpoint, the universal (here citizenship, personhood, mutual recognition, societal obligations) is merely grafted onto the particular. The two do not interpenetrate. The result is the alienation of the person from himself:

> [T]he personal independence of *legal right* [*Recht*] [is] . . . general confusion and mutual disintegration. For what is now considered as the absolutely essential being is self-conscious as the pure, *empty unit* of the person. In contrast to this empty universality, substance has the form of fulfillment and content. But now the content is left to its own devices and disordered; for the spirit is no longer present which had subdued it and held it together in its unity.—This empty unit of the person is thus a contingent existence in its *reality*, an inessential movement and activity which does not reach any sort of stability. . . . The consciousness of legal right therefore experiences, precisely in pressing its claims to personal worth, the loss of its reality and its complete inessentiality. To call an individual a person is the expression of scorn.[16]

Hegel here is discussing the ambiguity of the status of "personhood" or of "human rights" in general. Universal citizenship, succeeding the diverse and particular "ethical" citizenship of ancient Greece, appears in one sense to be a discovery or reappropriation of the "I" by itself. The notion of cosmopolitanism follows almost inevitably upon the insight that I am not necessarily a Greek, a Roman, a Carthaginian; rather nationality, mores, particularistic laws are inessential and contingent by contrast to my unassailable self-identity, which excludes everything specific. Yet by discovering my self as the absolute judge over all determinate existence, I seem to relinquish my actuality, to become nothing at all, a mere "unit" in Hegel's sense.

For Hegel, the development away from the concrete ethical life of a nation toward the abstraction of sheer humanity had a paradoxical and ominous character. When we no longer live in a genuinely political community where spirit is present as ethical unity or the recognition by each citizen of himself within the other, then our abstract rights (be these the rights of "personhood" or human rights as such) will be worth little. The more abstract the rights, the more natural differences will stand out, since these constitute the concrete *differentia specifica* of human beings in lieu of any bonds among them other than such merely formal rights. Moreover, if no one is willing to fight to guarantee my personal or human rights, if no one feels injured in his personhood when my rights are abridged, then their protection devolves upon a central power which constitutes, as Hegel says, the only continuity among the discrete personal atoms.[17] One of the hallmarks of the modern world, as Hegel interprets it, is the necessity for a centralized state power to overcome the "centrifugal" tendencies of atomized individuality. The story of the Enlightenment is in large measure the story of how centralized authority is gradually "rationalized" from feudal monarchy to the "concept" of the state in the *Philosophy of Right.*

But the inchoate self-alienation imbedded in the distinction between the legal person and natural individual does not yet give us a complete background for "comprehending" the Enlightenment as self-alienated spirit. Even in his earliest writings,[18] Hegel was profoundly interested in discovering the relationship between the disintegration of Greek ethical life and its civic religion, the establishment of Roman abstract right, and the spread of Christianity. In the *Positivity of Christian Religion,* Hegel interpreted Christianity's appeal as the inevitable outcome of the loss of civic freedom. Christianity's "objective," alien God found resonance in the world precisely to the extent that ethical life or Sittlichkeit, the subjective God, lost its power:

> Thus the despotism of the Roman princes exiled the spirit of man from the earth. The rape of liberty had compelled him to take flight toward the deity to preserve what was eternal, his absolute. The misery which that despotism had disseminated forced him to seek and await happiness in heaven. The objectivity of the deity kept pace with the corruption and enslavement of men; actually, that objectivity is only a manifestation or appearance of this spirit of the times. . . . Man himself became a not-"I" and his deity another not-"I."[19]

Despite the evident Fichtean influence in this early piece, Hegel never entirely abandoned this perspective. His treatment of the "unhappy consciousness" of early Christianity retains this image of God as an alien object, a not-"I," and man himself as a thing without an autonomous will. The simultaneous appearance of abstract personality and Christian otherworldliness delimits the pervasive dualism of human life within which the conflicts of modern politics and culture are played out. Indeed, the schism between human subjectivity, typified by the legal person, and an otherworldly God is for Hegel the most disastrous aspect of Cartesian dualism. The reconciliation of being and thinking postulated by Hegel's speculation cannot possibly occur in actuality unless the antagonism between faith and Enlightenment is put to rest.

The Modern State and the "Denaturing" of Man

Just as Sittlichkeit defined the essence of "true" or "immediate" spirit in antiquity, the word "Bildung" captures for Hegel the special features of the self-alienated spirit of modernity. Bildung may be translated as "education" in a number of contexts. But Hegel uses it in a much broader sense suggesting general culture or refinement. In many cases he employs it to convey a forming and shaping, the importation of system and order into an amorphous matter: "Form is an essential component of culture [Bildung]. Culture is the activation of the form of the universal which is thinking as such."[20] Similarly, Hegel notes that culture and upbringing (*Erziehung*) are meant to elicit the universal spirit in singular subjects.[21]

To form something (bilden) means to impart a form or *eidos* to it, to make it be something definite and universal. In culture, one universalizes the raw nature of singular individuals. Socialization or acculturation would not be bad equivalents for Bildung because these terms both suggest the process by which generally accepted norms and modes of thought are passed down from one generation to the next. Indeed, Hegel sometimes treats culture as an entire worldview, the paradigm or "horizon" of an age.[22]

However, in the *Phenomenology* Hegel treats culture as the special feature of modern self-alienated spirit. It will be recalled that the Roman Empire failed in its attempt to create an enduring body politic because it left the natural individual untouched. In the early modern period of transition from feudalism to centralized monarchical authority, Hegel discerns a second and more promising attempt to create a genuine state. The guiding principle in this nation- or state-building is that citizens must be made. Mutual recognition is still the basis for a body politic, but now it is not the abstract recognition of each as a bundle of rights and duties. Rather, to be recognized in the world of culture (Bildung), one must shape or form oneself (bilden), alienate one's own natural being and inclinations, and conform to universal norms of conduct. Thus, Bildung is a form of conscious self-alienation, the conscious renunciation of one's own particularity in favor of a "second nature" which is essentially universal or social.[23]

Hegel's interpretation of the modern period as an age of culture suggests that he has taken Rousseau as a model. In the *Emile*, Rousseau writes: "The best political institutions are those which are most calculated to divest men of their natural being, to substitute a relative for an absolute existence, and to swallow up the individual in the social unity."[24] The same principle applies across the board in Rousseau's *Social Contract*, where the natural and private will of the bourgeois must be alienated to the commonwealth as a whole to be replaced by the general will of the *citoyen*.

Hegel takes Rousseau's categories of alienation and "denaturing" as characteristic of the Bildung of the entire modern age. He seems to be arguing that these categories were always operative in the gradual evolution of modern states and in the nascent consciousness of freedom which accompanied them.[25] Rousseau merely gave conscious expression to a long development in which alienation and "denaturing" were already practically faits accomplis. In other words, Bildung in the sense of the conscious alienation of one's natural existence had, by Rousseau's time, become part of the universal Bildung—the cultural horizon—of the age.

Hegel's portrait of the artifical, self-alienated Bildung of early modern Europe seems at first rather one-sided. After all, this is also the age when natural right doctrines were being revived and given a new foundation by Hobbes and Locke. What is the relationship between the natural man of the English philosophers and Hegel's evocation of the cultured individual who "makes himself what he is"? The answer must be sought in the ambiguity of the concept of nature itself. When early liberal writers sought to express the idea that political authority is, or should be, constituted by an agreement made among atomic individuals endowed with certain prepolitical rights, they termed such individuals and rights "natural." While Hegel agrees that man as man possesses fundamental rights, he consistently rejects the view that such rights accrue to man by nature. It is rather the *concept* of man which compels us to acknowledge such rights. A long process of *denaturing* must occur which liberates man from the myriad corporative, religious, and family allegiances which hitherto defined his social existence. Only then can he begin to perceive himself *as* an individual who owes allegiance to a single sovereign authority and receives from it the guarantees of his fundamental rights.

The actuality of such rights depends on the recognition of each individual as a person and moral agent by every other individual. Hence "natural man" owes his entire existence to mediation. His identity as man and citizen is bestowed on him by society as a whole. In this sense it is a completely "artificial" identity, one constituted by the alienation of natural desires and inclinations. The artificiality and pretense of the ancien régime is thus not an antipode of the social contract state conceived by Rousseau. Both are necessary moments of a single Bildung in which men acquired an identity at once individual and completely mediated.

At the same time, the notions of alienation and denaturing take on a far more global logical significance in Hegel than in Rousseau. The Enlightenment is only part of a vaster enterprise: the reconciliation of being and thinking, truth and certainty, God and man. Within this more grandiose development, alienation fulfills a twofold function. First, it helps purge human spirit of its naturalness, raising it toward universality, toward the notion of the "I" as the absolute paradigm of whatever is. Second, this alienation goes far toward transforming substance into subject, or making divine spirit immanent in the world. The basic teaching of Christianity was that divine and human spirit were one; the divine spirit must alienate itself or become other (in the figure of Christ) in order to be what it implicitly (an sich) is: the concept, self-consciousness, a self-differentiating or absolutely negative activity. And the process of Bildung or alienation has, according to Hegel, exactly this significance for substance: "Culture . . . viewed from the standpoint of the individual, consists in the latter acquiring what is present at hand, consuming his inorganic nature and taking possession of it. But in respect of universal spirit as substance, this same process means that substance gives to itself its own self-consciousness or produces its own becoming and introreflection."[26]

Because we are now within the realm of spirit, culture or self-cultivation cannot have the meaning it did for "reasonable" consciousness, the resolve to "be oneself" or retain one's personal integrity as a predominately *individual* project. Both the self-alienated man of modern culture and the institutional milieu which is his "object" or "substance" are products of spirit. Therefore, the man of culture assumes that to claim personal worth and actuality, he must cultivate himself in accordance with the standards embedded in the institutions of his society, the preexisting Bildung of his culture. His idiosyncratic natural self will be subordinated to the essential, universal self he wishes to cultivate. The stubborn, individualistic romanticism which would be exemplified by Cervantes' Don Quixote and Schiller's Karl Moor is not really a spiritual viewpoint as far as Hegel is concerned, since it fails to recognize the objective, actual human world as genuinely rational.

But the sociocultural milieu of self-alienated spirit also differs in important ways from the Greek "true spirit" and its world. In the latter, according to Hegel, human and divine law, the polis and the domestic hearth were the competing institutions to which men were assigned with fatelike necessity. As Hegel interprets *Antigone*, the characters never have a real choice about the course of their actions. Human and divine law were all-powerful "substances" of which Creon and Antigone were only accidents lacking any depth of reflection or subjectivity. But in the modern world we have the competing institutions of political power and civil society or wealth. These are then the existing universals to which the individual must conform to acquire, as Hegel says, actuality and personal worth. The individual himself has at his disposal only the simple epithets "good" and "bad" to characterize these universals and his own conformity to them.

It is not entirely clear why Hegel regards "good" and "bad" as typical judgments of the early modern age. At first sight, they would seem more characteristic of ancient Greece. The only reason that seems at all convincing would be that Hegel wishes to illuminate the relatively inflexible code of behavior of the late middle ages which corresponded to the rigidity of estates and social ranks. It would appear that Hegel regarded this age as one in which the "either-or" predominated: an individual is either good or bad, either a nobleman or a merchant, etc. Neither fluidity of judgment nor social mobility had yet made themselves felt. Both judgments and social hierarchies were "self-alienated" in the sense that quality and personal status were thought to be rigidly self-identical and exclusive of all admixture of otherness: "each moment is specified as having an insuperable intrinsic worth and a stable reality vis-à-vis the other. Thinking pins down this difference in the most general way by absolutely opposing *good* to *bad* so that these fly apart and can never be the same."[27]

The rigid separation of good and bad in the world of culture corresponds to that stubborn adherence to the category of identity which typified the empirical understanding in its attempts to master nature. The separation of the object or substance (here, political power and wealth) from the judgments made about it also suggests that the early world of culture still works within "substance-thinking"; it assumes stable, self-identical entities to which predicates can be attached or withdrawn. Even so, the cultivated individual is not absolutely committed to either institution as Creon and Antigone were to theirs. The incipient conflict between the demands of state and of civil society did indeed reveal how internally "alienated" the modern world was from its very beginning. Yet the internal split within the modern world could be introreflected into the individual. He could become aware of his *freedom* precisely because he was not completely absorbed by any of the great institutions of modern society.

One notable feature of cultured and urbane people is their capacity to invert and confuse traditional judgments. What the sophists practiced on the simple ethical standards of fifth-century Greece, the early Enlightenment (Hegel will call it "pure insight") did to the standards of late medieval Christianity. But this inversion of values signifies, for Hegel, the necessity that mind should become aware of its own role in shaping social standards and relationships. In a sense, "good" and "bad" really are subjective judgments that can be applied in different ways by different individuals and classes. Any stable and definite value judgment such as "good" or "bad" has "as its very soul the immediate transition into its opposite; existence is rather the inversion [Verkehrung] of each determinate entity into its opposite, and this alienation alone is the essence and preservation of the whole."[28]

Because he takes universality to be the goal of his self-alienation, the man of culture first thinks of the good as "the self-identical, immediate, and unchanging essence of all consciousness."[29] Being-for-itself, the awareness of oneself as exclusively individual or particular (a "private" person) seems at first a mere adjunct to the universal self which the man of culture wishes to foster. Indeed, he regards as bad what only has being-for-another (that which seems to lack genuine universality of purpose) and thus gives him a sense of himself as a for-itself.

The man of culture at first simply assumes that the power of the state is good and wealth bad. The state seems to pursue universal ends and thus to demand that the individual cultivate in himself those very universal traits like self-sacrifice and loyalty which, as a man of culture, he regards as the core of his identity. And since "as much culture or self-cultivation as the individual has, so much actuality and power does he have,"[30] he naturally identifies himself with the state's power (*die Staatsmacht*) as the permanent, self-identical good. "State power, as well as being the simple *substance*, is also the universal work [*Werk*]—the absolute *matter-at-hand* itself [Sache selbst] in which the individuals find their *essence* expressed and in which their singularity is only consciousness of their *universality* and nothing else."[31]

But by a malicious dialectical reversal, the state, which is now *being*, something which *is*, must for that very reason be for-another, i.e., it must be wealth, the opposite of itself. The point of this baffling dialectic is that the state is no mere "ideal," the ineffable common good which each individual pursues. It is a real, existing institution which must have financial support to operate. Therefore it is thrown back upon the wealth of civil society, mocking the naïve supposition that universal ends could be so neatly separated from the more limited, private goals of the individuals who support and operate the state. At the same time, the cultured individual discovers the old saw of Mandeville that private vices are public virtues. Wealth cannot so easily be dismissed as "bad" simply because the individual is for-himself as an economic actor, consciously pursuing private ends. The economy also embodies the labor and activity of everyone, even though its end result is private consumption or enjoyment (*Genuss*):

> In consumption, the individual may indeed be *for-himself* or *singular*, but this consumption is itself the result of universal activity. Moreover, it gives occasion for universal labor and consumption by everyone. Each individual indeed *intends* to act selfishly within this moment [of consuming; L. H.], for it is in this moment that he comes to the consciousness that he is for-himself. Consequently, he does not take it as anything spiritual. But even when one considers the matter in an external fashion, it becomes evident that each person cannot help but provide for the consumption of all in his own consumption. And when he labors, he labors for all others as much as for himself, and they for him. Thus his *being-for-itself* is implicitly [an sich] *universal* and his selfishness only intended.[32]

Already, the internal fragmentation of the modern individual is adumbrated. He is both bourgeois (as economic actor) and citoyen (insofar as he internalizes the universal ends of the state's power); or, as Hegel says, he "intuits his dual essence [*Doppelwesen*]"[33] in these spiritual powers. But Hegel provides this fairly commonplace distinction with a logical significance when he sees in the citizen role the individual's being-in-itself, his universal identity, and in the bourgeois role the individual's being-for-itself, his identity as this specific person excluding other-being. This logical distinction is equivalent also to the differentiation of the individual into pure and empirical consciousness. The logical or speculative aspect of Hegel's discussion here links the opposition of faith and enlightenment to that between actual, empirical existence and pure or universal self-identity. Being-in-itself is an identity which can exist or have determinate being only insofar as it manifests itself in difference. To be manifest is to be dirempted. Thus the citizen has his specific, empirical being as bourgeois, just as the man of faith must live in this world, the world of the understanding.

According to Hegel, the competition between state and civil society drives the individual back upon himself, making him aware that his own pure consciousness is not indissolubly tied to either. He can choose between them. Consequently he comes to realize that he himself is their essence, that civil society and the state can only be actualized if concrete "selves" identify themselves with the respective ends of state and society: "[D]omination and wealth are thus present as objects for the individual, i.e., he knows that he is free of them and can choose between them or even refrain from choosing at all. The individual, now a free and *pure* consciousness, stands opposed to his essential reality as something that only exists *for him*. Thus he has the essence as *essence* within himself."[34] So good and bad become free-floating predicates, not tied by nature to either the state's power or wealth. The cultured individual realizes that these are "thoughts," not predicates inherent in the objects. As a result he believes he can make judgments about his objects. When Hegel speaks of judgments in this context, he has two meanings in mind. First, a judgment (Urteil) is simply the relating of the sentence subject to the predicates which define it. But also it is an original division or self-dirempting (*Ur-teilen*) of the self in which it simultaneously gives itself empirical existence as finite subject and actualizes the "substantial" ends of state power and wealth. This is why Hegel asserts that the individual "is the actual spirit of these objective entities and judgment is the demonstration of his power over them, a power which *makes* them be what they are only implicitly [an sich]."[35]

As judging power, the individual insists that the institution which he finds to be identical to him (gleich) will now be good, while the nonidentical institution will be bad. But the individual is both being-in-itself (pure consciousness, universal self) and being-for-itself (empirical consciousness, specific individual). Therefore the institutions to be judged do not give an unequivocal answer to the question "which one is identical to me and which is nonidentical?" As being-for-itself, the individual does not find his individuality confirmed in the state; rather, "he finds that, in the state, action as individual action is repudiated and subjected to the requirements of obedience."[36]

Wealth, on the other hand, seems to be good since it confirms the individual self-consciousness of each person without demanding self-sacrifice. It seems to be the "provider with a thousand hands,"[37] realizing the general welfare without resort to coercion. However, the individual is also being-in-itself. As such he finds the state's power identical to him since it expresses his permanent, enduring ends and gives him the sense of himself as a universal. Wealth, on the contrary, only satisfies his ephemeral consciousness of himself as a singular.[38]

The difficulties occasioned by the cultured individual's attempt to give an unequivocal meaning to good and bad induce him to adopt a new strategy. In a way somewhat reminiscent of Nietzsche's affirmation of life, the man of culture now asserts that the character of the judging person itself is the source of value. Whoever finds the institutions to be identical to him is noble (*edelmütig*), whoever finds them nonidentical is base (*niederträchtig*). This explicit shift from objective valuation to the character of the valuer sets the stage for a phenomenology of revolution. The noble consciousness adopts a naïve attitude of "inner respect" and "obedience" toward state power and of gratitude toward wealth.[39] He therefore appears at first to be an unequivocal supporter of the established order. The base consciousness, on the other hand,

> insists upon his disparity or nonidentity with these two essential institutions. He thus sees in the power of the ruler a fetter suppressing his being-for-itself and therefore he hates the ruler, obeys only with secret malice, and is always on the verge of insurrection. In wealth, which provides him the opportunity to enjoy his being-for-himself, he likewise sees only disparity with his permanent *essence*. Wealth gives him only the consciousness of his singularity and of ephemeral enjoyment, so he loves it while despising it. As soon as wealth vanishes—as it must, since it is the very nature of wealth to be evanescent—he regards his relationship to the wealthy patron as having disappeared as well.[40]

It is the noble consciousness which first claims our attention. Hegel intends to present a new version of the modern state (specifically the French state of Louis XIV) showing both the more profound internal unity of monarchy (as opposed to the Roman *imperium*) and some of the reasons for its impending collapse. The noble consciousness now appears more concretely as an estate of noblemen whose code of behavior demands fealty and self-sacrifice. The telos of this development will be the transformation of the medieval state (still only a mere ideal or substance, since it lacks self-consciousness) into a centralized monarchy.

> The noble consciousness thus finds in its judgment that the state's power, its object, is indeed not yet a self but still only the universal substance. Nevertheless, the noble consciousness is aware of that substance as its *essence*, purpose, and absolute content. Having thus established a positive relation to the state's power, it behaves in a negative way toward its own ends, its particular content and existence, permitting them to recede. The noble consciousness is the heroism of *service*,—the *virtue* which brings the universal into existence by sacrificing to it its own singular being.[41]

We thus have the double movement typical of the *Phenomenology* in which the state becomes real because certain individuals (the noblemen) adopt its purposes as their own. Meanwhile, the noblemen acquire self-respect and the respect of their peers by relinquishing their private existence, i.e., in their Bildung or self-cultivation.[42] But the noblemen identify themselves with the state only insofar as their *essential* being, their being-in-itself, is concerned. Their code of fealty demands only that they place themselves and their retinues in the service of the state when called upon to do so. Otherwise, they retain their honor and individuality or being-for-itself unimpaired.

The cultured individual portrayed here is the "proud vassal"[43] of late medieval Europe. His ambiguous position in respect to the state's power finds expression in his language. Because the state is not yet a permanently functioning government with clearly delimited sovereignty over all the individuals in the realm, it lacks the authority to make binding decisions. Consequently, when the nobleman speaks, his language takes the form of *counsel*, which has the ambivalent status of mere opinion. The nobleman may claim or even believe that his advice is meant to realize the common good, but it might contain only what is best for his estate:

> *Being-for-itself*, the *will* which has not yet been sacrificed as will, is the inner, still detached spirit of estates. This spirit yet retains the notion of its particular good despite all its talk of the *universal* good and tends to make this chatter about the universal good into a surrogate for action.[44]

Hegel here asserts that death is not really the ultimate self-sacrifice. The nobles are indeed willing to die for the realm, but as much for the sake of their own estate honor as for the state's power. So long as the noblemen treat the king merely as *primus inter pares* and are willing to tender counsel but not really to submit to sovereign state authority, willing to die for the abstraction of the state but not acquiesce to it as a concretely existing government, the state cannot truly be actual. It cannot be "self-consciousness," the expression of a single will or *volonté générale*. Thus the noble consciousness, in a new dialectical reversal, becomes base consciousness, always on the verge of insurrection. Only a more profound self-sacrifice or Bildung can make the state actual and turn the nobleman into a citizen:

> This contradiction which must be annulled by the noble consciousness has two related forms. First, there is a disparity [Ungleichheit] between the *being-for-itself* of this consciousness and the universality of the state's power. But also its alienation [*Entäusserung*] of existence, by fulfilling itself in death, remains in the form of being, rather than containing a return of consciousness into itself. . . . The true sacrifice of being-for-itself is therefore solely that in which consciousness abandons itself as completely as in death, but still preserves itself in this alienation. Only when the detached inner spirit, the self as such, emerges and alienates itself, can the state's power be raised to the status of a self.[45]

According to Hegel, only language can convey the complete sacrifice of self (or "denaturing" of man), "for it is the empirical *existence* of the pure self as self; in language the *singularity* of self-consciousness which is *for-itself* comes into being as such, so that it is *for* others."[46] In other words, actions, gestures, facial expressions, and the like remain an ambiguous "exterior" only partially evoking the real individual who is their "interior." Hegel considers language the most purely spiritual and hence the fullest expression of self-consciousness, for two reasons. First, since language is universal, it expresses the very nature of spirit, that human self-consciousness is completely singular and universal at the same time. Moreover, language has lost all traces of "thinghood"; it is a perfect *relation* between the speakers, a nexus which binds them together and yet separates and individualizes them. The nonactual medieval kingdom can thus only become a modern monarchy, and the medieval vassal a modern citizen, if language can be found which signifies a complete alienation of private will. According to Hegel, this language is flattery, and the noble consciousness renounces the "silent heroism of service" for the "heroism of flattery."[47]

As Hyppolite has pointed out, Hegel's description of the heroism of flattery amounts to a commentary upon Louis XIV's saying, "*l'état, c'est moi*."[48] On one hand, the vassal has undergone a loss of self more profound than death, giving up his honor and personal independence to become an "ornament" to the throne.[49] At the same time, the vague universal of the "common good," the substance of state power, becomes introreflected into self-conscious subjectivity: "[As a result of this alienation on the part of the noble consciousness], the spirit of the state's power becomes an unlimited monarch;—*unlimited*, the language of flattery elevates power to a purified universality."[50] The monarch is the last refuge of nature in a denatured world because his power depends not on Bildung, but on the natural succession within the royal house. He is obeyed because he is *this* specific individual and no other, an attribute of royal authority which finds expression in his name: "[Language] elevates singularity, which is otherwise only *intended*, toward pure existence by giving the monarch a proper *name*; for the name alone indicates that the distinction between this singular individual and all others is not *intended*, but made actual by all . . . by virtue of his name, the monarch is absolutely cut off and excluded from all others and alone."[51] For Hegel, the saying "I am the state" has its true significance only when transposed so as to read, "The state is an 'I,' a single will."

It is instructive to consider the differences between Hegel's phenomenology of absolute monarchy and earlier accounts of the same principle by Filmer and Hobbes. Like Filmer, Hegel insists that monarchical authority rests on a "natural" determination, devolving upon a specific individual because of his lineage. But like Hobbes, Hegel insists that royal authority derives from a form of alienation contained in language. Both Hobbes and Hegel realize that obedience creates power, or that sovereignty is only actual when it is recognized as such. But there is a tremendous difference between the language of contracts and that of flattery. In a contractual construction of sovereignty, I indeed relinquish my natural rights to everything (a principle consistent with the "denaturing" character of modern culture). But I retain my private existence, my being-for-itself, unimpaired; to put it bluntly, I agree to obey this particular sovereign as a matter of self-interest, and will continue to obey only so long as my private existence finds adequate protection. The Hobbesian language of contracts depicts a "bourgeois" form of self-alienation, convincing perhaps for certain strata of the populace, but not for haughty dukes and barons whose code of honor had taught them to despise the desire for self-preservation as a "base" form of consciousness. Because Hobbes has already abstracted so much from the historical circumstances of modern kingship in his "state of nature" construct, he posits as a reality or fait accompli the atomization and relative equality of all citizens. As

Hegel might say, Hobbes anticipates in thought social conditions which would not become actual at least until the French Revolution. Thus, Hobbes' contractual framework would obscure the very question of utmost importance: how such abstract, ahistorical principles of justice came to be predominant or "actual" in the modern world.

Although the language of flattery imbues the abstract substance of state power with individuality and self-consciousness, it does so only by undermining the foundations of the state on a deeper level. The self-sacrifice contained in flattery was not undertaken for nothing. The nobles received in return the wealth which stood at the monarch's disposal, so that their apparent suppression of their particular existence in fact only confirms and actualizes the latter. Hegel is probably alluding to the growing power of the *noblesse de robe*, who were drawn into the orbit of the monarch because of the official positions he could offer them. He notes that "the power of the state has devolved upon [the noble consciousness]. The state's power is only truly activated by [the nobility]."[52] The state might indeed now be a "self," but it is a pure self which cannot function without a bureaucratic apparatus composed primarily of office holders more interested in their own enrichment, at this stage, than in the "substantial" ends of the state. Thus, the very distinction between noble and base consciousness becomes untenable, since the basis for the distinction, sameness or disparity vis-à-vis the universal in-itself, state power, can no longer be upheld:

> If the noble consciousness thus specified itself as being related identically [*auf gleiche Weise*] to the universal power, its truth is rather to retain its own being-for-itself in its service and to be the actual abolition and fragmenting of the universal substance in the very renunciation of its own personality. Its spirit is a relationship of complete disparity. On the one hand, it retains its own will in its honor. On the other, however, by relinquishing its will, it in part alienates its own inner being, and becomes utterly nonidentical even with itself, and in part it subjects the universal substance to itself and makes this completely nonidentical to itself.[53]

The Fragmentation of the Self: "Rameau's Nephew"

Hegel finds in the relationship between the monarch as patron and the nobles as clients a microcosm of the entire society of prerevolutionary France. Although the impersonal market mechanism may have been operative, it was not immediately visible to most individuals. What they could see was wealth in the guise of wealthy men upon whom they had to depend. Where the classical master held his servant in bondage by force or the threat of force, the cultured person of this age wove his web of dependence by dispensing his largesse in measured amounts. The courtier finds his being-for-itself, his specific personal existence, alienated from him since it now depends on the power of another:

> [I]t is *being-for-itself* which is now something alien for [noble consciousness]; it encounters [*vorfindet*] its very self as alienated, as an objective, stable being-for-itself. Its object is being-for-itself, hence its *own*; but because the latter is an object, it is, at the same time, a reality that is immediately alien and has being-for-itself and will in its own right. That is, [consciousness] sees itself in the power of an alien will, and it depends upon this will, whether consciousness will be granted its selfhood or not.[54]

The situation of the courtier, the formerly noble consciousness, exactly parallels that of base consciousness as exemplified in Diderot's "Rameau's Nephew." Hegel regards the nephew as a prototype of the witty, unstable, cynical revolutionary man, and the Enlightenment itself only systematizes and disseminates the profound personal fragmentation of which the nephew could be considered a pure type. He merely expresses the fate of practically everyone in the "cultured" world of prerevolutionary France; he must sell himself or his wit and culture in exchange for his means of subsistence. What Marx later criticized as the alienation of the worker, his need to sell his labor power, is manifested in the *Phenomenology* as a cultural alienation. Since the individual is only what he has made of himself (his Bildung), he alienates the deepest layer of his personal identity when he must use his culture to make a dull-witted merchant laugh and thereby wangle a meal from him. And he stands in constant danger of being evicted if his buffoonery happens to touch a raw nerve in his patron (as befell the nephew in the dialogue). Consequently, says Hegel, "The spirit of his gratitude is . . . the feeling both of the most profound depravity and the most profound outrage . . . the pure 'I' itself is absolutely shattered."[55]

A few passages from the dialogue will illustrate Hegel's point. The nephew freely acknowledges that he is a plaything for the rich, that he has sold everything he has and is for their favor: "I was their dear

Rameau, pretty Rameau, *their* Rameau—the jester, the buffoon, the lazy dog, the saucy rogue, the great greedy boob. Not one of these epithets went without a smile, a chuck under the chin, a pat on the back, a cuff, a kick. At table it was a choice morsel tossed to me. . . . Anybody can do what he pleases with me, about me, in front of me. I never get on my high horse."[56] But at the same time, he rationalizes his humiliation by convincing himself that anyone would be a fool who did not try to obtain for himself a share of the wealth by whatever means he could. He fantasizes about the day when he himself might be wealthy enough to reduce his former benefactors to his own low station: "I would act like all beggars on horseback. I'd be the most insolent ruffian ever seen. I'd remember every last thing they made me go through and pay them back with slings and arrows. I love bossing people and I will boss them. I love being praised and they will praise me."[57] Moreover, the nephew declares (and Hegel agrees with him) that nearly everyone in this "world of culture" is like himself: "You don't seem to know that at this very moment I represent the most important part of Town and Court. The well-to-do of every description have either said or not said to themselves the words I've just confided to you; the fact remains that the life I would lead in their position is precisely theirs."[58]

Hegel goes on to point out that the wealthy patron, representing the status quo of prerevolutionary France, does not have the slightest idea how much his clients hate him, and certainly does not realize that he is creating implacable enemies of the Old Regime. It is not so much poverty that creates the potential for revolution, because poverty can result from the niggardliness of nature itself. Rather, revolutionary sentiments are fostered when poverty is connected to an arbitrary caprice that can alleviate or worsen it at will:

> What [the wealthy man] imparts, what he gives to others, is *being-for-itself*. But he does not give of himself like a selfless nature . . . [He is] power over the self and knows himself to be *independent* and *arbitrary* . . . Thus the wealthy man partakes of the same depravity as the client. For he knows, like the client, that in one respect *being-for-itself* is a contingent thing; but he himself is this contingency with power over personhood. In this arrogance—obtaining an alien self by means of a meal and supposing he has thereby purchased the subjection of that self's innermost essence—he overlooks the inner outrage of the other. He fails to see that the latter has thrown off all fetters and is totally frag-

> mented [*zerrissen*], and that, because [the client's] being-for-itself has become nonidentical, for him everything self-identical and permanent is fragmented.[59]

The completely fragmented "I" of the dialogue finds its most concrete expression in what Hegel calls "the language of fragmentation . . . [which is] the perfected language and the true, existing spirit of this whole world of culture."[60] This is first of all a language of flattery, but it differs from the courtiers' flattery since it tells the rich man not what he *is* (e.g., the state) but rather what he *has*, namely money, a mere thing. But on another level, the language of the fragmented self gives expression to a new, artificial, and implicitly revolutionary self-consciousness, an identity which Hegel calls "this innermost abyss, this bottomless depth, in which all stable orientation and substance has vanished."[61] In the language of culture, the individual (as subject) cultivates *images* of himself (predicates), a series of "made" selves that he can manipulate. The nephew, a pure example of the cultured man, sells these cultivated images of himself but still stands above them, knowing that they are his creations and despising the wealthy patron for accepting them as the "true" Rameau. It is, Hegel believes, the hallmark of the modern age of reflection that an individual can alienate himself so completely and still retain his self-identity. Diderot, through the nephew, has unwittingly discovered the *concept*, absolute identity within complete otherness:

> This self-consciousness, which incorporates the outrage which reviles [*verwerfen*] its own depravity [*Verworfenheit*], is immediately absolute self-identity in the midst of absolute fragmentation, the pure mediation of pure self-consciousness with itself. It is the sameness of the judgment of identity in which one and the same person is both subject and predicate . . . *Being-for-itself* has its own *being-for-itself* as object, as something utterly *other* and at the same time just as immediately as itself. . . . There is thus present here the *spirit* of this real world of culture which is conscious of its truth and of its *concept*.[62]

As we know from earlier encounters with the categories of reflection, the discovery that the difference of "I" and other is no difference points toward the same discovery for all reflective terms. The nephew's own alienated self-consciousness finds in noble and base, good and bad, and all the reflective terms of the world of culture the same sort of "inverted" [*verkehrt*] identity that he is. As the nephew tells his interlocuter, whom Hegel dubs the "honest consciousness":

> [R]emember that in a subject as variable as manners and morals nothing is absolutely, essentially, universally true or false—unless it be that one must be whatever self-interest requires, good or bad, wise or foolish, decent or ridiculous, honest or vicious . . . though when I say vicious I am merely using your language. For if we really thrashed things out, we might find ourselves calling virtue what others call vice and t'other way around.[63]

At the same time, it is for Hegel universal speech and especially that "judging which tears everything asunder" [*zerreissende Urteilen*] that reveals the concept at work and shows that the "I" in its negative activity lies at the core of all such seemingly stable valuations. The instability and inversion of all values (their "introreflectedness") reveals the infinitely protean "I" which can "be" good or bad, honest or vicious, and knows that it is *not* any of these terms, that it is the source of them and remains beyond good and evil in its negativity. The Enlightenment has become irresistible because it has discovered the power of *negativity*, namely, that whatever is, is the concept or the "I." For Hegel, this discovery is the decisive characteristic of all French philosophy during the Enlightenment, the one insight for which French "positive" philosophy (empiricism in all its forms) merely furnished convenient weapons: "This judging and speaking is thus what is true and unconquerable, while it overwhelms everything. It is the matter which, in this real world, is of *sole* and *true* concern."[64] Likewise, in the *History of Philosophy*: "[French philosophy] is the absolute concept turned against the whole realm of existing notions and fixed thoughts, destroying everything stable and giving itself the consciousness of pure freedom."[65] "Its character is especially remarkable, the character of the most profound outrage toward whatever had a claim to authority, whatever might be alien to self-consciousness and exist without it, against everything in which self-consciousness did not find itself."[66]

The "honest consciousness," or Diderot in his persona as naïve moralist, attempts to salvage the exclusive self-identity of good and bad, noble and base. But to do so he must speak and thereby open himself up to the witty repartee of the nephew. If he tries to escape the inversion of all moral values by citing examples of real or imagined virtue, he has succeeded only in showing that virtue could at most be an isolated case amidst the general depravity. Then the moral man could as easily be considered a fool as a paragon of virtue. In Hegel's words, "to portray the existence of the good and the noble in an isolated anecdote, whether it be imaginary or true, is the most bitter thing one could say about it."[67] He argues that the inverted world of the ancien régime cannot be set on its feet by an appeal to individual virtue or responsibility since part of the problem lies in the fact that each individual has made his specific, private existence into the ultimate criterion for all valuation. Still less can an appeal for a return to the innocence of nature have the desired effect when addressed to individuals whose self-cultivation has already turned them into artificial beings. Instead, Hegel follows Socrates in urging that only more profound and complete self-knowledge can prevail against the corrosive effects of critical thinking. In other words, nihilism is not so much the result of thinking per se, but of incomplete thinking: "The demand [that the world of culture should be liquidated; L. H.] can be directed only to the *spirit* of that culture itself, requiring that it should return as *spirit* into itself from its confused state and acquire a still higher consciousness."[68]

Thus far, the ongoing transformation of Western civilization described by Hegel appears to have borne bitter fruit. Although Louis XIV succeeded in creating a centralized state subordinate to his will, the price was exceedingly high. He helped produce a system of patron-client relationships extending from the highest court circles to the lowest strata of society, a system that alienated one man from another and generated profound feelings of envy and hatred on the part of its dependent elements. The state corrupted the economy by replacing the essentially impersonal mechanisms of the market by the measured largesse of wealthy patrons (replacing abstract wealth by concrete wealthy men). And the economy corrupted the state as soon as the state became dependent on men who bought and sold political offices with an eye to the profit that could be exacted from them.

The second great accomplishment of prerevolutionary Europe—the liberation of individual self-consciousness—appears to have had equally unfortunate results. The modern age rediscovered an inestimably important principle in its assumption that citizens are not created simply by the bestowal of abstract rights. They must be acculturated, formed, and educated (*gebildet*). As merely natural human beings, they will lack the more profound self-identification with the common good that an ethical state requires; hence they must alienate their natural existence in Bildung.

But the inner fragmentation of modern societies produces unwonted results when the individual submits to this sort of self-cultivation. He learns that nothing is what it seems. When he purports to act for the state, he ends up enriching himself. When he yields to his acquisitive impulses, he contributes to the enrichment of others by the mediation of the market, and thus he indirectly strengthens the state. The introreflection of all activities and institutions into their putative opposites culminates in a reversal of all judgments. The apparent independence of the patron proves to be a total dependence on his clients, whether of the king on the noblesse de robe or the wealthy merchant on his paid wit. The man who profits most in such a world is the one who best understands how to manipulate its vanities to his own ends. Thus the liberation of the "I" proclaimed in theory by Descartes becomes in practice the cultivation and manipulation of "images." Only the man who has no stable self-identity can adopt and discard any identity as circumstances dictate.

Like Plato in the *Republic*, Hegel wishes to show how the degeneration of the state both mirrors and fosters the declining moral standards of its typical citizens. But the fragmentation of individual self-consciousness and political authority provides some insight into the underlying weakness of the ancien régime. As long as political institutions depend upon the will and caprice of a single person, the state cannot be put on a firmer foundation than that typified by the web of dependencies spun by Louis throughout his kingdom. The state must be made to incorporate the rational will itself as a universal and not simply the will of one man. Likewise the nephew proves that the rigid and self-identical categories of finite thinking can always be confounded by dialectic. The "I" as negative activity is always more and other than any of its specific roles or moral precepts. Thus, morality from an individual perspective must yield to an ethical life that fully incorporates all aspects of the moral will. Accordingly the Enlightenment and French Revolution, despite their shortcomings, will begin from the principle that man as such, and not isolated, idiosyncratic individuals, is the proper subject of thought and action.

ENLIGHTENMENT, FAITH, AND REVOLUTION

5

So far we have examined Hegel's obscure but evocative portrait of wealth, power, and self-cultivation in early modern Europe. The central theme of his arguments has been the inability of the individual completely to identify himself with the world of culture he inhabits. In the Enlightenment and Revolution, the breach between the self and world becomes an explicitly social problem that threatens to destroy the entire society. The individual no longer speaks merely for himself but on behalf of the whole country or even of all mankind. And in this sense, spirit has approached more closely to self-knowledge within human thought, since one of its essential moments, universality, has been given its due. Yet the Enlightenment and its persistent shadow—religious faith—are still plagued by the old nemesis of abstract, incomplete thinking. Its program is premised on the negativity of the concept or the "I." But it still operates within the framework of the understanding and its reductionistic empiricism. Hegel must now demonstrate how the experiences of the world of culture will cause spirit to "return into itself" and define itself in increasingly adequate terms until the pure "I" or concept becomes its explicit object.

The return-into-self of spirit has a twofold significance for the world of culture. First, a self-consciousness that finds nothing but contradiction in the actual world may attempt to preserve its self-identity by a flight into the "beyond," in which case it appears as Christian faith. In this sense faith, the in-itself aspect of human consciousness, is a successor of the noble consciousness, the honest consciousness, and their self-identification with substantial or universal ends. But it is far more self-alienated than these, because their objects were at least *in* the world, though remaining unactualized thoughts. The fragmentation of the actual world has driven this universal side of consciousness to the conviction that only a God who is not part of the world can be spared its fragmentation.

On the other hand, the cultured individual typified by Rameau's nephew will come to understand that even the ends he still holds worthy of pursuit—money and power—are as vain as the "higher" purposes he scorns. He realizes that even these ends appear significant only because they are recognized as worthwhile by some or many other selves. Thus, the very wit and cultured speech of the prerevolutionary bohemian spirit suggest that whatever has any value enjoys this status only because *I* acknowledge it to be so.

Hegel is, I think, trying to explain in philosophical terms the distinction between a cultured cynic and a political radical. The former attacks and undermines many of the same dominant values and pretenses as the latter. Yet he does so out of the conviction that people are only concealing their (inevitably) base and self-interested motives behind pious rhetoric. The cynic would presumably feel more at home in a society where everyone pursued his selfish goals without any shame or hypocrisy. He does not want or expect anyone to alter his or her values; he just wants people to stop trying to deceive themselves and others with high-sounding cant.

A political radical, by way of contrast, has a somewhat greater appreciation for the power of values and ideas to shape human society and individual conduct. While lashing out at hypocrisy, a true radical wishes to convince his fellow citizens to reexamine their lives and the interpretations which they customarily place on their own and others' behavior. He expects that his rhetoric might actually change the way others think and act and eventually, perhaps, even lead to a complete revolution in government and society.

In Hegel's sense, then, the radical has a deeper insight into the power of the self over reality than the cynic does. The latter would admit (as Rameau does) that human beings do not have the potential to become much different than what they are now. Their lives are controlled by passions and desires that they can only mask or adorn, not change. Indeed, the barely concealed self-hatred of Rameau's nephew reflects his realization that his life and values are as empty and vain as the lives and values of the pompous courtiers and bourgeois whom he mocks. To overcome such cynicism, Hegel thinks, the erstwhile cynic must reflect on the totality of his own existence and see, as clearly as he can, that the pursuit of such things as wealth and power is not the only way to live. One can choose a way of life; it is not foreordained by any biological or cultural necessity. From this angle, the cynicism or nihilism of the nephew appears to be itself an act of "bad faith," as a modern existentialist might say. What is truly significant is not the pursuit of desires per se, but the power of the self to shape its own self-presentation so as to obtain the objects of desire. To focus on the latter means to see the remarkable power of thought over material reality. As Hegel says:

> [P]ower and wealth are the supreme goals of the efforts of this consciousness. It knows it can obtain possession of these things by subjecting itself to the renunciation and sacrifice needed to become truly cultured and thereby to attain a generally acknowledged status. These goals are really recognized powers. But the personal worth which is thus obtained is itself vain; and just by demonstrating its power to gain possession of these goods, this consciousness knows that they are not ends in themselves: rather it now knows itself as the power that dominates them and that they are something vain.[1]

In philosophic terms, the "I" has now made itself into an object of reflection. Cultured cynicism proves to be a phase of spirit's self-development and not a final stopping point beyond which there can be no appeal. From now on cultural protest will take on an explicitly political coloration.

The Enlightenment and Faith

We have reached the point at which Hegel introduces the Enlightenment in its specific form as an opponent of faith or superstition. It is the same fragmented consciousness of the nephew except that now it is called "pure insight" and is purged of its still "natural" affinities for wealth and power. Its object is the "pure 'I,'" and it lacks any definite content since it is "negative being-for-itself."[2] Hegel thinks of the Enlightenment as a completion of the denaturing process of culture both because it helps create the abstract citizen of the French Revolution and because it accepts as valid only what accords with reason, not what is merely natural or ancestral.[3] His contention will be that the Enlightenment and faith are really just two moments of the same spirit, implicitly identical in their phenomenal difference.

In his lectures on the history of philosophy, Hegel energetically defends the French Enlightenment against its recent detractors by pointing out that the philosophes "carried out the Lutheran Reformation in a different form."[4] The guiding principle of the Reformation was contained in the demand that the laity should be abolished.[5] On one level, the argument simply is that the philosophes and Luther both attacked the supposition that an exclusive caste (whether of lawyers, hereditary estates, or priests) should be in a position to lay down authoritative rules and precepts for the rest of mankind. But in a broader sense, Hegel interprets the Reformation and the Enlightenment as distinctive contributions to the same ultimate end of the actualizing of human freedom:

> What Luther had initiated in the heart [Gemüt], for the emotions, was the freedom of spirit. But this freedom, still unaware of its simple root, had not yet grasped itself as it really is—as the universal itself. In thinking, all content vanishes and the thought is fulfilled by its own activity—the French established general determinations and thoughts and adhered to them; general principles for which individual conviction was essential. Freedom now becomes a general condition of the world and forges a link to world history, indeed becomes an epoch of world history.[6]

The French philosophes, however, tended to interpret religion in terms of the language and psychological principles they were most familiar with: self-interest. Being in many cases deists or atheists, they lacked any real experience of or sympathy for the outlook of religious believers. Consequently, they simply tried to draw attention to those aspects of religion where, it seemed, Church authorities were duping an untutored people for their own gain. They hoped, in effect, to emancipate their fellow citizens from religious thralldom by appealing to their enlightened self-interest. However valid their criticisms were (and are), Hegel thought that they were misinterpreting and distorting the very nature of religious faith. They should have realized, he suggests, that the essential character of faith, stripped of its supernatural trappings, coincided with their own demands for freedom. Still, faith cannot be entirely exempted from blame since from its beginnings in Roman times, it always carried the stamp of otherness, worship of an alien being outside the world.

The *Phenomenology* assigns to the Enlightenment two important tasks. First, it will have to "purify" religious faith by purging the latter of its remaining secular character. In plain terms, this means attacking the Catholic Church on its most vulnerable flanks: its political and social power and its tendency to stress the dogmatic and ritualistic, rather than the inward, aspects of religion. The "result" will be a new conception of faith that places it in the heart of the individual, as the Reformation had done in Germany centuries before. Second, the Enlightenment will have to demonstrate by its practical deeds (the French Revolution and Terror) that political freedom cannot be realized without a revolution in the human heart, one characteristic of religious faith. In Hegel's picturesque expression, the French Revolution will pave the way for a reconciliation between the "Sunday and workaday of life."[7]

The task Hegel sets for himself—and for the Enlightenment—proves to be one of the most intriguing and important in the entire *Phenomenology*. Indeed, it goes to the very center of his critique of the Enlightenment. He is not satisfied simply to show that faith and enlightenment share some points in common. More ambitiously, he wishes to argue that they are two aspects of a self-same, transindividual spirit, different yet also identical. If he is right, then he can draw a very strong conclusion: any individual mind or spirit that sets out on a quest of self-knowledge and self-completion cannot succeed in this without actually seeing and experiencing both the rational and "negative" power of Enlightenment and the inner tranquility and depth of religion. Hegel makes his argument by renewing an already familiar distinction: faith is now assigned to the sphere of "being-in-itself," while pure insight is given the title of "being-for-itself." Faith is, in effect, an immediate or positive identity of itself with itself, while insight is the same identity constituted *via negationis*:

> [D]riven back upon itself from a world in the midst of disintegration and devoid of essence, spirit is in its truth and in inseparable unity both the *absolute moment* and *negativity* of its appearing, as well as the essence of this negativity which is inwardly *satisfied*, its positive tranquility. But since both moments are determined as such by their *alienation* they split apart into a double consciousness. The former is *pure insight*, the spiritual *process* that is epitomized in *self*-consciousness . . . . the simple con-

> sciousness of the positive or tranquil self-identity has . . . the inner *essence* as essence for its object.[8]

This passage evokes Hegel's earlier description of the concept as "pulsating within itself, without moving, trembling within itself without losing its tranquility."[9] The concept is as unthinkable apart from its self-differentiating activity as these differentiated moments would be apart from the identity of which they are the differentiae.

Hegel also distinguishes faith from pure insight by calling the former *thinking* while identifying the latter with the concept. He admits that the ordinary consciousness of faith tends to treat God as a Vorstellung or presentation, a definite being residing somewhere beyond the world. However, he insists that God is really a thought, "pure consciousness of the *essence*, i.e., of the simple interior of things . . . —the principal moment of faith which is usually overlooked."[10] It is actually mythology rather than religion per se that treats the object of faith in a representational fashion.[11] Since Hegel defines thought as the universal-in-action, the universalizing activity which is the very core of human consciousness, he has made a good point, at least in respect to the great monotheistic religions. These do indeed wish to see every event and every sort of relationship as the work of a single spirit that could certainly be understood as the "essence" or "interior" of things. The reason we tend to interpret faith as a matter of the heart is that we take thinking to refer exclusively to explicit or *reflective* thoughts.[12]

The identification of religious faith with thought, even if only implicit thought, plays an important role in Hegel's critique of the Enlightenment. If faith were only a matter of the heart, then it would remain beyond the pale both of Enlightenment and speculative philosophy, an irreconcilable "other." Modern man would then live in two separate worlds without being whole in either. Moreover, religious faith would then be immune to rational criticism, a breeding ground for whatever barbaric superstitions might strike a responsive chord in the individual. Nevertheless, merely because faith has a thought content does not mean that it can be properly assessed by *finite* thinking, the categories of the understanding employed by the Enlightenment. In fact, the "natural" religion of the eighteenth century distorts the real significance of faith as much as its reduction to a wholly irrational feeling does.

Although Hegel attempts to be evenhanded in his treatment of faith and enlightenment, acknowledging each as a necessary but incomplete expression of spirit, it is here above all that he reveals himself to be a stepson of the Enlightenment. The key to Hegel's philosophical enterprise is the assertion that mind can have knowledge of itself not as a natural "thing," but as the proximate instance of the concept. It is surely true that what Hegel means by mind is not the unique mind of a particular person; still, absolute mind or spirit (*der absolute Geist*) only thinks and knows within finite minds. Therefore, to say that religious faith is thinking, the universal-in-action, means that it is an aspect of mind's self-knowledge even if the mind doing the knowing is conceived as the divine mind in man. If, as Hegel says, the real purpose of the Enlightenment is to achieve pure *immanence*, to eliminate any sort of beyond or "outside" that could be the source of knowledge and meaning for man, then Hegel himself outdoes even the philosophes in this enterprise, since they leave either a shadowy *être suprême* or matter as a sort of absolute object.

Pure insight is thus one result of the self-alienated world of culture,[13] since it merely universalizes the fragmented speech of Rameau's nephew: "It is . . . pure *being-for-itself*, but not as this *singular individual*; rather as the self that is inwardly *universal*, the agitated movement that penetrates and attacks the *tranquil* essence of things."[14] Having taken on this universal form, pure insight is now enlightenment. Unlike the nephew, the man of the Enlightenment expects and demands that everyone should share his insight: "This pure insight is thus the spirit that calls out to *every* consciousness: *be for yourselves*, what you all are potentially [an sich]—rational."[15]

In order to make everyone rational and fulfill its claim to possess a pure and true insight into the irrationality of the status quo, the Enlightenment cannot rest content with the witty talk and desultory judging of the bohemian nephew. It must synthesize and collate such insight into a compendium: the *Encyclopedia*. Here we can see what Hegel meant when he noted that an appeal for a transformation of the actual world could not so much be directed toward individual virtue but toward the culture of the age. If everyone could be convinced that what is true must stand the scrutiny of one's own insight, then the ancien régime would lose all legitimacy.[16]

The Enlightenment, with its conviction that everyone is potentially rational, attributes the influence of what it considers superstition to a conspiracy of priests and despots. These latter may see through the superstitions they foist on a passive populace, but even if they did, they would not jeopardize their privileges by admitting it. So the Enlightenment directs its attention to the simple, untutored people. It spreads, as Hegel says, like an aroma through the atmosphere or a communicable disease whose symptoms are so mild that they are at first barely noticed. By the time a counterattack is launched, the Enlightenment has gone too far to be stopped.

The question which first concerns Hegel is how the Enlightenment was able to win such an easy victory over faith, especially since faith represents a fundamental aspect of all self-consciousness. Furthermore, if enlightenment and faith are indeed implicitly identical, then this identity must be experienced, since Hegel does not accept as real what lies entirely beyond experience (a thing-in-itself). As we observe the arguments the Enlightenment marshals against faith, we should also be able to see its intentions become inverted. It should become plain *for us*, and gradually for the man of the Enlightenment, that his accusations against faith might equally well be turned against his own philosophical views. Hegel here makes the puzzling argument that, since the Enlightenment presumes that whatever is, is the concept or the "I," then it cannot accuse religion of lies and distortions without accusing itself of these. Perhaps he means by this that all institutions (including religion and monarchy) must be in some way rational if their creators, human beings, are themselves rational as the Enlightenment claims they are. Hence, if the Enlightenment attacks such institutions, it undermines the model of human rationality that it uses to interpret its own activities, and therefore undermines itself. Though this argument appears specious, it is almost certainly what Hegel is driving at, as a lecture remark suggests: "It is absurd to think that priests invented religion to defraud the people for their own selfish ends. It is as shallow as it is perverse to regard religion as a matter of caprice or deception. . . . [in the notion of an absolute Being] there is not just rationality per se, but universal, infinite rationality."[17]

The Enlightenment's troubles begin as soon as it declares God to be a creation of the human mind. When d'Holbach or any other philosophe argues in favor of atheism, he is inclined to classify God as a fictitious being, like a unicorn or a centaur. But Hegel seizes on the ambiguity of this creation of God and insists that it is quite true, but in a different sense than the Enlightenment intended. In Hegel's comprehended version of Christianity, religious faith has as its object the "essence of its own consciousness."[18] In other words, God is in a way produced by human consciousness, but by the *pure* self, not by man as a contingent empirical being. In his conception of an absolute, man is giving speculative expression to his own self-knowledge. One could conclude from this that God does not really "exist," but Hegel would simply reply that real existence does not signify finite empirical being.

The latter is an imperfect low-level mode of existence and hence less real than the speculative relationship which is the nature of spirit. The conclusion that spirit is *not*, does not have being in the sense of thinghood, has in fact already emerged in the section of the *Phenomenology* devoted to "observing reason." But because the Enlightenment employs arguments derived from the empiricism discussed in that section, we might say that it has not yet "learned its lesson."

Thus faith, in its "comprehended" form, would not deny that God is produced by human consciousness; the man of faith would only aver that such production should be understood in a speculative and not empirical way. Furthermore, says Hegel, the faithful experience the unity of self and object (man and God) in their religious services. When they assemble in church they invoke or produce God for themselves, transforming him from an abstract other into a present spirit.[19] At the same time, the invocation of God as the spirit of the congregation is a self-invocation by divine spirit. Only in this way can substance become subject or God become self-conscious as and in human consciousness.[20] Thus, when it is comprehended, faith perfectly fulfills the criterion of the Enlightenment that we should only acknowledge as true that in which we find ourselves or our self-consciousness.

But the proponents of the Enlightenment did not only claim that religion is a creation of the human mind, that God is just an anthropomorphic fantasy. They also pointed out that the whole idea of a God judging and condemning humanity through his intermediaries, the priests, was an outrage. As noted, the philosophes would characteristically say that this God was dreamed up by the clergy to defraud their parishioners and keep them under control.[21] Hegel finds these charges contradictory, I think, for the following reason. The first charge implies that the conception of a deity is an inevitable and natural one for human beings. It stresses the continuity between man's mind and the mind of the deity he constructs. The second charge suggests, however, that people would not believe in a deity were it not for the cunning machinations of a priestly class who foist the idea on an ignorant populace. The second charge stresses the incompatibility or difference between the human mind and the divine, at least as far as "natural reason" is concerned. In evaluating the Enlightenment's indictment of religion, Hegel focuses especially on its cynical and iconoclastic side. He finds that the high-mindedness of the Enlightenment is betrayed and sold out in its biased, almost libelous attacks on the attitude of faith. The supposedly pure intentions (*reine Absichten*) of pure insight (*reine Einsicht*) are compromised when it tries to "demonstrate to faith . . . that it is a conscious lie."[22]

Hegel does not mean that the Enlightenment is playing a devious game with religion, that it intentionally and maliciously picks on religion's weakest and most ambiguous doctrines for its own nefarious ends. Rather, he is convinced that philosophes like Voltaire were honestly describing organized religion as they saw it—a confused muddle of superstition and fraud. The truly intriguing question for Hegel, then, must be formulated on a different level: What does it tell us about the Enlightenment and the modern mind in general that the philosophes should have displayed such a complete lack of comprehension for religious experience? It appears to have been Hegel's view that the Enlightement was actually feeling its way toward the position taken ultimately by Fichte, that the "I" or self achieves its identity only in struggle against and conquest of the sphere of the not-"I" (everything outside of the self understood generally as "mere nature" or "inclination"). In his perversions of religious experience and doctrine, the man of the Enlightenment was simply manifesting his failure to grasp the symbolic or spiritual oneness and harmony that the man of faith feels toward his objects of veneration. To sum up Hegel's point, then, the Enlightenment has indeed achieved an insight into the "negative" power of the "I," which plays so striking a role in Fichte's philosophy. But its empiricist predispositions and political concerns prevent it from articulating this experience in a rigorous, metaphysical manner (as we shall see shortly when we review its "positive" program).

The most egregious examples of the Enlightenment's denigration of spiritual and symbolic truth involve the rituals of Catholicism. The Enlightenment seizes upon the outward symbols of faith (statuary, communion wafers, etc.) and in accordance with its own empiricist views, transforms these in the image of its own unacknowledged metaphysics. A believing Catholic would of course see in these rituals and objects a fusion of sacred and profane, eternal and ephemeral. But the philosophes, reasoning according to the principle that all ideas ultimately must have come from sense experience, dismiss the "sacred" aspect of Catholic symbolism as sheer illusion, and thus "see" only the profane and nonspiritual side of things.

Likewise, the Enlightenment accuses faith of basing its religious beliefs upon contingent historical events and even more contingent preservation and transmission of those events by scores of anonymous scribes in times past. Here Hegel insists that the Bible, as a record of specific events, is not really the source of faith: "In fact, it does not occur to faith to attach its certainty to such testimonies and contingent events; faith is rather, in its immediate certainty, a naïve and unreserved [*unbefangen*] relationship to its absolute object, a pure knowledge of it which does not permit letters, paper and scribes to become mixed up in its consciousness of the absolute being."[23] Of course, it does occur to faith in its "uncomprehended" form (i.e., the form in which nearly every religious person thinks and feels) to base its certainty on the contingent events of the Bible. Hegel solves this problem by asserting that faith "has already let itself be seduced by the Enlightenment"[24] to the extent that it attempts to ground its convictions on historical facts or sense data. From one angle, Hegel has made a poor argument because it is easy to show that, even prior to the Enlightenment, faith meant belief in specific facts about Jesus' life, the miracles he performed, his sermons, and so on. That faith had always had this "contingent" character could not have been lost on Hegel, especially since he makes much of the medieval penchant for venerating sensuous things like relics. I believe his real intention is not so much to give us an unbiased account of religious faith, as to reinterpret it speculatively in order to immunize it against the Enlightenment's attacks. Faith had never been shaken quite so much as it was by the Enlightenment simply because the empiricist belief in the absoluteness of sense data had never before enjoyed such widespread acceptance. In trying to justify itself, faith adopts willy-nilly the standpoint of the understanding, the home ground of the Enlightenment. Consequently, its apology appears confused and contradictory, eventually even to the man of faith himself, so that faith degenerates into silent brooding, irrational superstition, or some variety of historicism or Unitarianism. Such, at least, is the fate Hegel envisioned for faith if it were not rejuvenated by speculative philosophy.[25]

For Hegel, the impending loss of faith has potential consequences which go far deeper than what immediately meets the eye. Religious faith is not for Hegel a social role, an attitude, or a contingent set of beliefs that man can discard at will and still retain his essential self intact. It is rather an indispensable dimension (the in-itself) of all consciousness, the one "actual" case in which even nonphilosophical individuals have an intuition of themselves as *spirit,* as universal in their specific existence, or as something more than a refined form of res extensa. If even religious faith is "finitized," shorn of its speculative content, then man will have relinquished a crucial aspect of his self-knowledge, namely the relation of human self-consciousness to the absolute. The Enlightenment, if entirely successful, will thus signify a loss of self-consciousness, perhaps even a regression to something like a highly sophisticated animal existence.

Hegel discerns in the Enlightenment's condemnation of fasting and donations to the church a token of its real intentions. He thinks such small sacrifices on the part of faith bespeak an attempt to transcend one's private, solipsistic "being-for-oneself" and achieve a sense of oneself as universal.[26] But the Enlightenment considers such practices both impractical (*unzweckmässig*) and unjust. It assumes that a person's real ends concern the satisfaction of his physical needs and wants, despite high-sounding phrases about benevolence and virtue. The Enlightenment harks back to the base consciousness that made wealth its object and took the model of *homo œconomicus*, the bourgeois of the market economy, to be the sort of person one should "identify" oneself with. Thus, the "enlightened" philosophes "find it foolish that the individual, who is only a determinate, absolutely specific person by excluding all others and possessing property, should absolve himself of his determinate existence by relinquishing his property itself."[27] Indeed, it seems to such champions of a market economy unjust that someone should act in ways not consistent with the principles of enlightened self-interest, since such behavior undermines the whole system of exchange of equivalent values: "[The Enlightenment] also finds it *unjust* to deny oneself a meal and to give away butter and eggs without receiving money in exchange or to give away money without getting butter and eggs back, simply giving these things away without getting back anything at all for them; [the Enlightenment] declares a meal, or the possession of such things, to be an end in itself."[28]

Of course, Hegel realizes that the attitude of faith is still incomplete because it too is self-alienated, lacking as it does the philosophical *knowledge* of its object. But the Enlightenment attacks faith from the wrong perspective (the perspective of finitude) and therefore can only substitute for it a smug mediocrity: "The fundamental character of eudaemonism and the Enlightenment [has been] to transform the beautiful subjectivity of Protestantism into an empirical subjectivity, to transform the poetry of pain, which scorns any reconciliation with empirical existence, into the prose of satisfaction with finitude and a good conscience about it."[29]

The devastation of faith by Enlightenment has, in the *Phenomenology*, a twofold consequence. First, faith is purged of its last tenuous connections with the world of finite reality. The strategy of Enlightenment has been to seize upon finite aspects of human consciousness, which faith cannot gainsay precisely because it *is* in part finite, and to extend these to encompass even the sacred sphere of religious belief. This appears to spell the doom of religion. The latter has no content at all left, it lacks any definite, stable object to believe in, because such an object would, as a self-identical "this," be finite and open to the attacks of the Enlightenment. But Hegel discerns in the dilemma of faith a "cunning of reason" at work, because faith is introreflected from its double world, the sacred and profane, into a pure consciousness of itself as the focal point of each, the absolute activity which posits the two spheres to begin with.

> The behavior of [the Enlightenment] toward faith appears to rip asunder the latter's *beautiful* unity of *trust* and of immediate *certainty*, to pollute its *spiritual* consciousness by low thoughts of sensuous *reality*. . . . But in fact the Enlightenment initiates the abolition [*Aufhebung*] of a *separation* which has not been *thought* through or rather not *comprehended*. The consciousness of faith had always applied a dual criterion to its experience, it had two different sets of eyes, ears, tongues, and speech, it had always seen every notion in duplicate without drawing together the dual significance of its experience in a comparison. Faith lives in two separate modes of perception: one, the perception of *sleeping* consciousness, pure and abiding in uncomprehended thoughts; the other, of *waking* consciousness, living purely within sensuous reality, each keeping its own house. The Enlightenment illuminates that heavenly world by means of notions from the earthly world, and demonstrates this finitude to the former, a finitude faith cannot deny, because faith is self-consciousness and hence the unity to which both modes of presentation [Vorstellung] belong, and in which they do not diverge; for they belong to the same, inseparable *simple* self into which faith has now passed over.[30]

The "Positive Program" of the Enlightenment

Having lost all objectivity, faith is driven back into itself, and it collapses into "pure longing," the form it will take in the German Enlightenment.[31] But this is not the only result of the work of the Enlightenment. The latter has erected its "edifice of finitude" everywhere and must work out some positive program to replace religious faith. It is in this feeble attempt that Hegel discerns the real "poverty of the Enlightenment," and the impending loss of self-consciousness that a consistent empiricism would entail if it could vanquish faith once and for all: "When all prejudice and superstition has been banished, the question arises: *now what? What is the truth which the Enlightenment has disseminated in place of these prejudices and superstitions?*"[32]

The "positive" side of the Enlightenment has in fact already emerged in its critique of faith, and, of course, in the empiricist worldview. The Enlightenment now has a twofold attitude toward its object which we can roughly classify as the aspects of identity and difference. Having stripped the divine being of all predicates, Enlightenment only retains, as Hegel says, a "pure vacuum" or pure abstract identity as its absolute. At the same time, its strict adherence to the principles of the understanding seems to open up a vast field of singular entities in this world, each self-identical and different both from the others and the empty absolute. In fact, as Hegel remarks, the Enlightenment has returned to the consciousness of sense certainty: "Consciousness, which in its very first actualization is *sense-certainty* and *opinion* [*Meinung*], here returns to that first position from the long road of its experience, and is again knowledge of what is purely the *negative of itself* or of *sensuous things* that *exist* and are indifferently opposed to the *being-for-itself* of consciousness. But now it is not *immediate* natural consciousness, but rather it has *become* such under its own eyes [sich]."[33]

Hegel's final caveat is important, because it reminds us that the empiricism of the modern age is no longer the naïve confidence in the world of sense which characterized prephilosophical consciousness. It is an artificial sense-certainty adopted in an age of culture to combat corrupt and authoritarian religious institutions as well as the political despotism that profited from such corruption. Therefore, one cannot justifiably greet the demise of the *Hinterwelt*, or the "other" world beyond experience, with such high expectations as did Nietzsche. In effect, the Enlightenment's commitment to this world is always plagued by the shadow of the other world that has now lost all content. The experience we have of sense-certainty in its post-Christian phase would then be the presence of an absence, a nagging feeling that the secular sphere has been defined or determined by a now absent "beyond." It is the classic Hegelian negation of the negation, an affirmation including the prior negations and therefore not really tantamount to the status quo ante or original affirmation (i.e., the sort of "yea-saying" that Nietzsche and Hegel both found in Greek ethical life and the Greek acceptance of fate and tragedy).

Moreover, for Hegel there can never be *pure* immanence outside of speculative philosophy. Although we may suppose (*meinen*) that we have abolished the supersensuous, the dialectic of consciousness, culminating in the understanding, has demonstrated that we always require a universal ("this," the thing, force, law) to give an account of our purportedly immanent experience. Thus, even the most tough-minded man of the Enlightenment is driven to some form of unacknowledged dualism precisely because dualism is inherent in the fundamental cognitive principles of the understanding: the rigid separation of exclusive self-identity and exclusive difference or negation.

In the "positive" program of the Enlightenment, the universal (now devoid of content) actually takes on two forms to which correspond two "parties" of philosophes. The first party, deism, defines God as a supreme being of which nothing further can be known than his bare existence. The second party dispenses with God altogether and acknowledges matter as its absolute principle. As far as Hegel is concerned, the dispute between materialism and deism is empty talk, because these two principles are in fact the same, namely, "pure thought itself."[34] This is not hard to see in respect to deism, but it is somewhat puzzling in the case of materialism, because we normally think of matter as a richly diverse and concrete totality of all that we know through our senses. But Hegel has already tried to show, in the first chapter of the *Phenomenology*, that notions such as "the certainty of sense," "this," and "pure being" are emptier than we might suspect. Something similar appears to be the case with materialism. What we actually perceive are definite, distinct objects like trees or houses—or better, the sensory properties of such things. It requires an act of abstraction to disregard this sensory diversity and to propose that "behind" it, all of these objects are really the same basic stuff. For Hegel, the category "matter" looks beyond experience and posits a supersensible interior of things which is, however, entirely abstract and empty. And this supersensible interior is most emphatically a creation of thought rather than a direct experience of the world.

Hegel's critique of these two "parties" of the Enlightenment reveals a good deal about his critique of that entire movement. He interprets both materialism and deism as propositions advanced about the nature of the absolute since the latter is nothing other than an unconditioned principle or the "ground of experience" (Fichte). But as we know, his absolute is nothing outside of what it knows itself to be, a knowledge that is actual only in human self-consciousness. And since both parties of the Enlightenment define the absolute as an abstract principle lacking any necessary relation to its differentiae, they have in fact retrogressed to a conception of the absolute as unself-conscious substance, the level of "Oriental" religions which "cling to a still abstract concept of God and of spirit, something the Enlightenment also does when it wishes only to know God the Father; for God the Father, for Himself, is still sealed off from the world, abstract and therefore not yet the spiritual, true God."[35] In the *History of Philosophy* Hegel even calls the abstract religion of the Enlightenment a regression to "Mohammedanism."[36] But most often he characterizes the materialism and deism of the French philosophes as Spinozism, since Spinoza's substantially conceived God could be described as *deus sive natura*, as though there were no essential difference between God and matter or nature: "[T]his philosophy has advanced toward atheism, and has determined matter, nature, etc. as the ultimate, active, efficient principle; one can say that it is on the whole Spinozism, where the one of substance has been advanced as the ultimate principle."[37]

In both cases, there is no attempt made to explain how identity and difference are related. In materialism, we have identity posited as pure matter. But matter is nothing at all unless it is formed, differentiated into specific "somethings" which can be thought. Deism posits God as a pure thought or form without matter, entirely unconnected to the manifold of experience. Thus the deist is as hard put as the materialist to explain why there is something to be experienced and not nothing at all. Moreover, because the philosophes regard materialism and deism as exclusive principles, they have in fact fallen back behind Cartesianism, for Descartes at least had the notion of God as a third thing outside being and thinking who guaranteed that our thoughts would correspond to the order of nature.[38]

For Hegel it is the Enlightenment's concept of *utility* which binds together these moments of identity and difference into a unity, permitting pure insight to intuit its own concept. In both deism and materialism we have a pure abstraction or a being-in-itself "behind" the world of experience which is for-us. Yet no attempt has been made to think through the connection between these two moments. Now in utility, I acknowledge that the world as a whole is for-me, or that its value is determined in relation to the uses to which it can be put. But at the same time, it can be useful or valuable only by virtue of what it is in-itself. Yet its identity takes on a definite form only in respect to its possible utility or its being-for-another. To take an example, if I define something as a means, as having utility for some end, it clearly becomes a means (i.e., becomes what it is) only insofar as it is for-another (here the end to which it is the means). But we would not say that just anything would do as a means; some things possess intrinsic qualities that make them better suited to be means to certain specific ends than other things. However, those intrinsic qualities are irrelevant to the thing's being a means (which is its peculiar mode of being in a system of universal utility) until the end is posited for which those qualities of the thing can serve as means. Thus, as in the dialectic of thing and perception, we have an oscillation between being-in-itself and being-for-another that reveals the instability of identity and difference when these are taken as stable, discrete forms.

Hegel, following his own *Logic*, takes being-for-itself (the concept) as the higher principle expressing the identity-in-difference of the moments of utility. Specifically, this is the being-for-itself of human self-consciousness in a system of exchange or market economy:

> [E]verything is thus just as much *in-itself* as it is *for-another*, or everything is *useful*. . . . For man, as the thing which is *conscious* of this relationship, his essence and relative position result from the dialectic of utility. . . . Just as everything is useful for man, he too is useful, and his vocation [Bestimmung] is to make himself into a generally useful member of his band [*des Trupps*]. As much as he takes care of himself, just so much does he have to contribute to the others; and to the extent that he contributes, he also takes care of himself.[39]

In utility, the dialectic of wealth is repeated where the individual finds that he can confirm his own freedom and independence (being-for-itself) in private consumption while at the same time contributing to the general good (utility) by providing jobs for those who produce what he consumes. And likewise his contribution (i.e., his labor) is in proportion to what he receives in return from the other members of civil society. Here and in the *Philosophy of Right*, Hegel adopts an ambivalent attitude toward the "invisible hand" of the market economy that seems to produce the general utility without any conscious effort or self-sacrifice on the part of individuals. Civil society does indeed help to provide the confirmation of individual judgment and self-consciousness which only the modern state has been able to institutionalize. But Hegel discerns in it a certain insipidity, even a loss of self-consciousness, which is exemplified in the Enlightenment's confidence that man is by nature good (as a coparticipant in the system of universal utility): "[Man] is *good* just as he is immediately, as a *natural consciousness* in-himself [an sich], and he is *absolute* as a singular being while other-being is *for him*; in fact, . . . for him as the animal who is conscious of himself, *everything* is there for his pleasure and delight, and he walks around in the world as though it were a garden planted just for him and as though everything in it had come right from God's hand."[40] The only evil he admits might possibly consist in eating or drinking too much. And even religion is drawn into the system of utility, because it is "pure usefulness itself."[41] Hegel is probably thinking of the philosophes and French revolutionaries who frankly admitted that religion was necessary to uphold the system of private property and exchange that they wished to establish.

Hegel finds in this naïve affirmation of man's natural goodness a complete misunderstanding of the nature of evil and, for this very reason, a loss of self-consciousness by man of his essential nature as spirit. The language Hegel uses in describing civil society—man as a "self-conscious animal"; his contribution to the "band" or primitive social grouping; and the "spiritual animal kingdom" (*das geistige Tierreich*)—suggests that it can never be more than a highly sophisticated survival mechanism. It seems to confirm to the individual that he and his own material ends are the center of the universe and that his fellow men (as well as nature) exist to provide for those ends. Like Tocqueville, Hegel thinks that the institutions of civil society work to prevent the individual from "getting outside himself," breaking through the confines of his solipsistic Cartesian self and establishing nonutilitarian ties to other people:

> To the profound doctrine of original sin taught by the church, there stands opposed the doctrine of the modern Enlightenment, that man is good by nature and should therefore remain true to nature. . . . To the extent that man . . . only knows and wills himself in his particularity, excluding the universal, he *is* evil and this evil is his subjectivity. Man, insofar as he is spirit, is not a natural being; insofar as he behaves like one and pursues the ends of his desire, then he *wills* his natural being. Thus the natural evil of man is not like the natural being of animals. Naturalness in man has more precisely the sense that natural man is a

singular being as such, for nature lies *eo ipso* enchained in singularity. Thus, insofar as man wills his naturalness, he wills his singularity.[42]

The emergence (or reemergence) of natural man in the *Phenomenology* bespeaks the ambiguity that has beset the Enlightenment from the beginning. On the one hand, the world of culture has gradually shredded the web of encompassing circumstances and concrete ties that prevented man from intuiting himself as a human being as such. The result was a new self-consciousness (the Enlightenment) that would acknowledge nothing as true or real in which man, as a rational being *tout court*, could not discover himself. The cogito of Descartes, once only a metaphysical theory, becomes a reality in France on the eve of the Revolution. If Tocqueville could say of Americans that they were Cartesians who had never read Descartes, Hegel would advance this claim even more forcefully of prerevolutionary France. But if man was no longer willing to tolerate institutions in which he could not discover himself, the urgent question arises: what—or who—is man? The metaphysics of utility suggest that he is a natural being, a bourgeois, an isolated, singular individual. As such, he would discover himself only in institutions like the market economy that seem designed to satisfy his material wants more or less automatically.

Thus in one sense, Bildung has laid bare "natural" man insofar as we understand by human nature man in his singularity, the homo œconomicus of civil society and the calculus of utility. On the other hand, Bildung and Enlightenment have "denatured" man by severing the temporal bonds of religion and philosophy that provided meaning and continuity to history. Just as empiricism tears asunder the sensuous concrete into simple abstract determinations without trying to reconstruct the whole in thought, so too culture and Enlightenment rip man out of the matrix of tradition in order to pose him as an abstract human being as such. Thus, if we think of nature as the ensemble of pregiven social, religious, and familial ties that make up the warp and woof of a person's concrete existence, then culture and Enlightenment have indeed "denatured" man or made him *artificial* by inducing him to regard the "sacred chain"[43] of tradition in a negative way, as an alien power circumscribing his freedom.

It is in this latter sense that Hegel regards the culture of utility as the precursor of absolute freedom. From a logical point of view, utility simply states that nothing has value in-itself, but only for-another. And this logical formula, in turn, contains the same idea we found in

Bildung, that a person makes himself into what he is by suppressing his pregiven, merely natural existence for the sake of universal ends. These ends have the significance of being-for-another because they are actual only in the context of a universal recognition of them. An individual's status as economic actor or citizen, for example, expresses a role he has assumed, which contains an explicit relation to all other citizens who acknowledge the role of citizenship or to all other participants in the economy who buy the commodities he produces and furnish the commodities he consumes. Or, to return to Rousseau's language, each person alienates his whole natural existence (being-in-itself) and receives in return the status of citizen, a mode of being which is only actual for-others (the other citizens as a whole). Finally, utility expresses the notion that social and political institutions have no claim to legitimacy in-themselves, but only for-another, i.e., for man conceived as the abstract, rational being that the Enlightenment exhorts him to be. So, in all its permutations, the principle of utility tells man that there is no genuine objectivity, nothing "out there" or even in himself that is not suffused with the power of the self as negative activity. When consciousness comprehends the true significance of utility, and "takes back" the last vestiges of objectivity (the in-itself) into itself, it becomes absolute freedom.[44]

The French Revolution

Superficially, Hegel's critique of the French Revolution bears some resemblance to that of Edmund Burke. Both writers indict Rousseau (probably unjustly) for having instilled in the French the dream of putting into practice abstract rights and liberties. For Hegel and Burke, the French Revolution seemed to reveal the impossibility of erecting any stable, legitimate political order upon the foundation of an atomized "mass" society. That is, so long as individuals insisted upon participating in government and demanding rights as abstract individuals rather than through intermediary, corporate bodies and institutions to which they belong, the state would continue to oscillate between anarchy and dictatorship. However, a closer examination of Hegel's arguments will indicate just how widely he and Burke diverged in interpreting the historical significance of the Revolution.

For Hegel, the French Revolution was above all a philosophical event, for two related yet distinct reasons. First, the philosophes seemed to Hegel in a large measure responsible for discrediting the ancien régime. Thus, in the sense that their vaguely philosophical ideas contributed to the Revolution, it could be said to have its origin in philosophy. However, Hegel only grudgingly concedes to the abstract empiricism of the Enlightenment the title "philosophy." So his endorsement of the Revolution as philosophical merely because the views of the various Encyclopedists influenced it is only half-hearted, at best.[45]

Yet the Revolution was also a philosophical event in a more profound sense. According to Hegel, the men of the Revolution were the first to try to rearrange actuality according to thought. By so doing, they demonstrated that thinking lies at the heart of actuality, the fundamental principle of Hegel's speculative idealism: "As long as the sun was in the firmament and the planets revolved around it, no one had ever seen man stand on his head, i.e. upon thought, and construct reality in accordance with it. Anaxagoras was the first to say that *nous* rules the world; but now man had come to recognize that thinking should govern spiritual actuality. This was therefore a splendid dawn."[46]

Because thinking is the "universal in action" itself, the Revolution signified both that human self-consciousness had become universal and that actuality should be governed by universal principles. This is the meaning of the oft-quoted Hegelian assertion that recent history is less a battle of passions than of ideas:

> If history has hitherto seemed to present itself as a conflict of passions, in our time, while passions are not lacking, it exhibits a different character. In part, it is predominantly a conflict among thoughts which attempt to justify themselves, and in part a conflict of passions and subjective interests, but essentially only under the rubric of such higher justifications.[47]

> What makes men morally dissatisfied . . . is that they find the present incommensurate with the purposes they consider to be right and good (these days especially ideals of political institutions). They oppose to what exists their *ought*, their notion of how matters should rightly be. Here it is not particular interest or passion which demands satisfaction, but rather reason, the right, and freedom.[48]

The universality of consciousness and of the principles of political legitimacy are inseparable from the "absolute freedom" that the French Revolution attempted to actualize. Since freedom has already been defined as being-with-oneself, not having an absolute other outside oneself, universality is its prerequisite; only the universalizing activity (or thought) can absorb other-being into the self: "[T]he *universality* of consciousness constitutes freedom. When I know myself as a universal being, I know myself as free. . . . The will as free is this: that its content be universal; in this universal I have my essence, my essential being; I am then identical to myself. And as a corollary, the others too are identical to me, for they are the same universal as I am."[49] Here we can see clearly the influence of Rousseau's *Contrat Social* (not to mention Kant's moral theory) on Hegel's interpretation of the Revolution. In the *Phenomenology*, he identifies absolute freedom with Rousseau's volonté générale:

> [T]he world is [for consciousness] utterly its own will, and this is general [or universal] will. And this is not at all the empty thought of the will, posited in tacit or represented consent; rather it is the real general will, the will of all *singular* individuals as such. For the will is implicitly the consciousness of personality or of each person, and it is supposed to exist as this true, actual will, as the *self*-conscious essence of all and of each personality, so that each person indivisibly does everything and so that what emerges as the deed of the whole is the immediate and conscious deed of each.[50]

To this we may compare Rousseau's account of the social contract:

> *Each of us puts his person and all his power in common under the supreme direction of the general will; and in a body we receive each member as an indivisible part of the whole.*[51]

What appeared in utility as a loss of self-consciousness, a return to naïve naturalism and hedonism, here displays its reverse side. Of course, each person is a bourgeois, a specific being-for-itself interested in private consumption; but just as wealth had its alienated opposite in state power, the singular bourgeois has his alter ego as the revolutionary citoyen. The paradoxes of the Enlightenment are now laid bare within one and the same individual. When the Enlightenment in its various guises has completed the process of stripping away from each individual every contingent aspect of his being, has severed every historical tie among individuals and broken the "sacred chain" of tradition, the Janus-faced atomic individual stands revealed. If he looks within himself he can see that he is a specific, singular person. But he is not a natural man in the sense that a savage would be, like

Rousseau's *homme naturel* in *The Second Discourse*. He is also a pure self, a human being as such, or what Hegel calls pure self-certainty, the cogito of Descartes. And as pure self-identity, the "I" = "I," he is identical to everyone else. In other words, religious affiliations, estate and family ties, regional loyalties—the ensemble of circumstances that hitherto constituted a person's station in life—have become in principle contingent and irrelevant to his essential identity as homme or citoyen. The citizen sees that the identities of other citizens as well as his own were posed in a common act of self-alienation in which they traded in their natural existence for their new artificial status as citizens.

Hegel considers the Rousseauian general will a dramatic advance in political philosophy and in spirit's self-consciousness as such. The notion of a general will comes close to Hegel's own conception of *one* spirit differentiating itself within finite human consciousness. This is the case because the general will is not an aggregate of singular wills (a *volonté de tous*), but a single will activated within each individual. Consequently, a state founded on the general will exhibits a far more profound principle of unity than what we encountered in either the Roman empire or the ancien régime. In these latter, unity is either a "mask" of legal personality or a sort of fraud in which estate privileges are retained intact despite the personal abasement of flattery. Legal rights touch only the surface existence of the individual, flattery claims his honor, but the general will absorbs the whole person into a political unit. Hegel makes this point explicitly in comparing the Roman and modern worlds.[52]

Moreover, the Rousseauian general will constitutes a great advance over the contingent natural right theories of early liberalism, for example those of Hobbes, Locke, or Hutcheson. Such "empirical" theories of natural law abstract from a great number of historical circumstances to arrive at their natural man, but they do not reach the *concept* of man, which is freedom: "What concerns us is this, that [Rousseau's political philosophy; L. H.] made consciousness aware of the content, that man has freedom in his spirit as something utterly absolute, that free will is the concept of man."[53] Hegel therefore believes that the French Revolutionary state, insofar as it embodies Rousseau's political philosophy, is founded on an absolute principle—the certainty of self—rather than on opinion [Meinung]. It is the discovery of this principle in its application to practical affairs that really makes the French Revolution a philosophical event and a moment of speculative reconciliation.[54]

By interpreting the French Revolution in Rousseauian terms, Hegel can also make the transition from the French to the German Enlightenment more plausible. It is not a long step from Rousseau's general will theory to Kant's categorical imperative. And this is precisely the step that Hegel wants consciousness to make in the *Phenomenology*. There and in the *History of Philosophy* he remarks that the general will is a "transition to Kantian philosophy."[55] The common feature is the principle of "certainty," which Hegel has already identified as the underlying notion of the Revolutionary state and will now show to be the same notion as Kant's transcendental "I." We know from earlier discussions that the "I" as Kant understood it is pure self-identity, "pure" in the sense that it makes experience of objects possible but is not itself an object of experience. It is an identity that lacks self-differentiation or negativity, i.e., it is not yet the Hegelian concept that exists only insofar as it dirempts itself into empirical subjects and objects. Or, to use Hegel's language, the transcendental "I" or pure certainty lacks *truth*, a diverse content through which identity is constituted mediately or by introreflection. In historical terms, only the Greek polises were founded on truth, because in them the citizen unself-consciously did his duty, obeying the concrete laws (the content) in which he found the confirmation of his own identity. The deficiency of the French Revolution as well as its world-historical significance will be attributed to the one-sidedness of the principle of certainty, empty identity without internal differentiation.

The principle of certainty, Hegel thinks, conceals a tension between two distinct aspects of the "I" to which we have already alluded. I am, on the one hand, a unique individual with a consciousness and personality all my own. I think, feel, and perceive things from my own peculiar angle of vision and act on the basis of needs and interests that I regard as paramount. I am, in other words, the experiential referent of Descartes' cogito that knows its own thinking (self-certainty), but doubts all else.

At the same time, "I" designates a transcendental consciousness which is not identical to the empirical self that I know myself to be. As a unique individual I am an object of experience. But the transcendental "I" makes experience possible (in Kant's description of it) and so stands outside experience. But since all transcendental egos synthesize experience in the same way (see chapter 1), all are implicitly identical.

Hegel's point is that these two aspects of the "I" are indissolubly linked; indeed, he would call them identical-in-difference. There can be no consciousness of one's own individual personality without the transcendental function of the "I"; yet the transcendental "I" or spirit, as Hegel has argued so often, always exists in determinate subject-object relationships in which I perceive myself to be a unique individual, interchangeable with no one else.

The epistemological ambiguity in the "I" has, of course, a moral dimension as well. In German idealism, the transcendental "I" or spirit figures as the source of personhood and hence as the referent of moral obligation. I must treat the other as a moral being because he is like me (a self) and not because he is utterly unlike me in being a unique individual. The empirical "I," the "I" of individual personal identity, appears by contrast as the focus of private, selfish, particularistic aims. This is why, in the French Revolution, the decisions of individual citizens or leaders evoked suspicion. They reflected—or seemed to—only the will of the particular person and not the general will. Where this opposition hitherto took the form of a schism between noble and base, faith and enlightenment, or good and bad, it is now concentrated in the consciousness of every individual who is just as much a pure self as he is an individual actor: "[T]he opposition thus consists solely in the distinction between singular and universal consciousness; but the singular consciousness itself is, in its own estimation, only what *seemed* to be opposed to the universal; it is universal consciousness and will."[56]

In the French Revolution, the dialectic of singular and universal consciousness takes the following form: the citizen is no longer content with playing a mediate role in the state; instead, he wishes to participate as a whole person in political affairs. In terms of Hegel's *Logic*, he is renouncing his empirical or singular existence (say, as a nobleman, artisan, merchant, or peasant) in favor of a universal consciousness or general will. Consequently the network of *corps intermédiaires* which made up pre-revolutionary France collapses because these bodies limit and circumscribe the incipient universality of consciousness.[57] When each citizen confronts the state directly, rather than as a member of an estate, guild, or any other subordinate and partial social grouping,

> each individual consciousness emerges from its assigned sphere, no longer finding its own essence and work [Werk] in this particular corporate organization. Instead each conceives its own self as the *concept* of the will and conceives that will to be the essence of all such corporate organizations. Thus it can only be actu-

> alized in a labor [*Arbeit*] which is whole and entire. In this absolute freedom, all estates are thus eradicated, for these were the spiritual powers in which the whole had been articulated. Individual consciousness, which had belonged to an estate and confined its will and accomplishments to the latter, has now abolished [aufgehoben] this barrier; its purpose is the universal purpose, its language the universal law, and its work [Werk] the universal work.[58]

Once the self as universal or as general will has emerged from the debris of the ancien régime, the problem arises of how anything so abstract as the general will can be implemented and actualized. Or as Hegel says: "The next question, however, is: how can the will be determined? For by willing itself, it is only an identical relation to itself. . . . A content, determinate being is required for the will; the pure will is its own object and content, a content which is none at all."[59] We should not think of Hegel's question primarily as a matter of practicability—for example, of how the citizens could be brought together in one place. Rather, it concerns the very grounds for the legitimate exercise of political authority. Rousseau had argued that only the general will, not an aggregate of individual wills, however numerous, can provide legitimacy to the laws. For if a given law were enacted merely because one faction happened to be stronger than another, then all grounds for obedience on the part of the weaker faction would dissolve. Right would in effect become might, and the rule of the strong over the weak would replace legitimate political authority. Rousseau consistently denied that superior force entails any obligation to obey on the part of those who are oppressed by it; therefore, the state would cease to exist as a true state if it could not legitimately place obligations on its citizens. That Hegel accepted Rousseau's argument appears to be substantiated by his comment on the nature of the general will: "The general will must not be regarded as composed of expressly particular wills, or in such a way that these particular wills would remain absolute. Where the minority must obey the majority, there is no freedom."[60]

Thus for Hegel the problem of how the general will can take on a determinate form is tantamount to asking whether legitimate authority can be exercised at all. How can the general will direct the actions of the state if it is always real, flesh-and-blood individuals who must act and decide matters of common interest? His conclusion is that the general will cannot act, at least not in the positive sense of enacting specific, binding legislation or making decisions concerning the state as a whole. The consciousness of the French Revolution "cannot accomplish any positive work [Werk], neither the general works of language nor those of actuality. It cannot enact the laws and establish the institutions of *conscious* freedom, nor can it perform the deeds and works of the freedom *of will*."[61] So the Rousseauian or revolutionary republic cannot be a genuine state either in the legal-philosophical sense of exercising legitimate (universally recognized and morally binding) authority or in the practical sense of establishing more or less permanent and stable sovereign power.

The Revolution therefore culminates in dictatorship and anarchy, which flow from the same deficiency in the doctrine of the general will. If laws are to be passed and decisions made, some specific individual or group must be put in a position of authority: "If the universal is to accomplish any deed, it must be concentrated in the unit of individuality and a singular self-consciousness must be put at its apex, for the general will is only *actual* will in a self which is a unit."[62] But the will is no longer general if it is exercised or proclaimed by a specific, singular person or group, since all other individuals (as singular) are then excluded from active participation: "[If a singular self-consciousness is put at the head of the republic], however, *all others* are excluded from the *whole* of this deed and only have a limited share in it, so that the deed would then not be the deed of *actual universal* self-consciousness."[63]

Politically, the dialectic of universal and singular wills leads to a deadly factionalism in which one faction loses its claim to articulate the universal will as soon as it gains any real power:

> The government is itself nothing but the point or individual expression of the universal will, but now as the establishment. As willing and execution that emanate from a single point, it simultaneously wills and executes a specific ordinance and action. It thereby excludes the rest of the individuals from its deed, and furthermore constitutes itself as having a specific, determinate will opposed to the universal. Therefore, the government can simply not present itself as anything else but a *faction*; only the *victorious* faction is called the government. And precisely because it is a faction it is necessarily doomed; as a government it is a faction and hence guilty.[64]

The paroxysms of factional politics display the anarchic side of the revolution, but dictatorship is equally implicit in the principle of the general will, because the latter can be turned against *any* citizen. To the extent that the general will is distinct from the specific acts of empirical individuals, one can always apply the interior-exterior category and impute selfish intentions to a person no matter what his specific deeds may indicate. Thus we see the (logical) potential for the French Revolution's law of suspects, especially in light of Robespierre's campaign for civic virtue: "*Being suspected* . . . takes the place of or has the meaning and effect of *being guilty*."[65]

Throughout Hegel's long discussion of Enlightenment, he has consistently emphasized its negative character. The "positive" philosophy of empiricism and the natural right theories derived from it functioned primarily as intellectual weapons against the Old Regime. In the Revolution, this negativity of Enlightenment turns upon itself once the old beliefs and institutions have been demolished. As we have observed in the cases of dictatorship and anarchy, the Revolution has stripped consciousness down to its essential, bare components of singularity and universality: "[Absolute freedom], on account of its own abstractness, divides into equally abstract extremes: simple, unrelenting, cold universality on one hand and on the other the discrete, absolute, hard rigidity of actual self-consciousness, a stubborn 'point.'"[66] Now with nothing left to demolish, the abstract universality of the understanding turns against the only thing remaining which is not universal, namely, the discrete physical existence of the individual self. As Hegel says, it becomes a "fury of disappearance,"[67] the terror which can strike at anyone, citizen or dictator, because all, qua empirical individuals, are suspect.

When Hegel speaks of the "fury" of absolute freedom, we should take him quite literally. The furies of ancient mythology and tragedy pursued those like Orestes who were guilty not so much because they chose to do evil, but because they became ensnared in the web of fate or incomprehensible necessity. In the French Revolution's "negative work" of death-dealing, the universal pursues everyone like a fury because everyone *is* guilty simply by virtue of being a particular self. The natural innocence of the individual in utility proves with equal justification to be natural guilt. But death in the ancient world at least had some meaning, because the tragic figure upheld an essential principle (human or divine law). In the aftermath of the Enlightenment, death has no meaning at all since the individual has, in effect, been reduced to a "this" of sense certainty: "The sole work and deed of universal freedom is . . . *death*, and more exactly a *death* without any inner scope or fulfillment, for what is negated is the unfulfilled point of the absolutely free self. This is the coldest, most insipid death, without any more significance than chopping through a head of cabbage or taking a drink of water."[68]

In Hegel's *Phenomenology*, as well as in the actual course of events, the Terror spells the end of the French Revolution. The revolutionary citizens, sensing "fear of their absolute master—death—are again ready to put up with negation and differences. They subordinate themselves to corporate organizations, and return to a partial and limited work, but, for that very reason, to their substantial activity."[69] In the *Philosophy of Right*, Hegel broadens this experience of the Terror into a metaphysics of the state: the will as such is not an abstraction but a self-differentiating concretum modeled after the concept. Hence the state too must be self-differentiating or organic if it is to embody the general will. "Abstract" rights such as those enunciated in the "Declaration of the Rights of Man and Citizen" cannot be sustained unless they rest on secure foundations of morality and ethical life.

The problems inherent in actualizing absolute freedom also condition Hegel's attitude toward Napoleon. Although he ranked the latter alongside Caesar and Alexander as a world historical individual, Hegel also realized that Napoleon's grand design for Europe had failed. While he esteems the Corsican's military genius and stern measures against those he sarcastically labels "advocates, ideologues, and men of principle," Hegel remarks that "the impotence of victory has never appeared in a harsher light" than it did at the time of Napoleon's conquests.[70] His abstract brand of liberalism took root only in France and a few Rhenish states. Elsewhere, most notably in Spain, abstract right demonstrated its inability to displace national tradition and religious conviction. On the whole, Hegel asserts, liberalism "went bankrupt" in almost every country of Europe.[71]

The failure of both the Revolution and Napoleonic liberalism to provide a solid foundation for liberal institutions is one of Hegel's foremost political concerns. If formal equality and civil liberty were the only goals of historical development, then the Revolution and Code Napoléon would have completed history's task. Freedom would be actual and man reconciled to his world. But this is not the case. Abstract right and absolute freedom must always be understood against the background of Greek Sittlichkeit, where man was truly at home with himself in his political surroundings. The French brand of liberalism, far from recreating a modern form of ethical life, fosters a mass society of atomized individuals held together either by terror or (under Napoleon) a machine-like bureaucracy. It is still symptomatic of the world of "self-alienated spirit" even while presaging a higher principle.

Hegel is quite consistent, throughout his writings, in locating the deficiencies of the Revolution. He asserts that no revolution can succeed if the ethos or inner life of the citizens has not prepared them to accept the freedom of abstract legal rights, an ethos provided only by Protestantism:

> It must be deemed an act of foolishness of modern times . . . to have made a revolution without a reformation.[72]

> [I]t is a false principle that the fetters upon legal right and freedom can be cast aside without the liberation of conscience, that a revolution can exist without a reformation.[73]

In this context it is significant that Hegel refers to revolutionary citizens as geometric "points" without any dimensions. He means that the Enlightenment has stripped them of any positive, concrete self-identity so that all that remains of them is a hollow core. In Hegel's view, this is the particular fate of Catholic countries where religious faith was still commingled with "superstitious" attachment to external things and hierarchical authority. When the Enlightenment drove faith underground or banished it into the vacuous être suprême of Robespierre's cult, it left the French no alternatives but a thinly disguised atheism or nihilism, or else the crypto-Catholicism that many returned to under the guidance of the so-called recalcitrant clergy.

In the *Phenomenology*, this "historical" explanation of the Revolution's failure appears as a failure of the general will doctrine. Rousseau, like the liberals, began by postulating a state of nature in which singular, atomized individuals would give their express consent, as individuals, to the social contract. From this angle of vision, the individuals appear to be the "absolute" basis of the universal or the general will, even though Rousseau insists always that the latter is not a mere aggregate or volonté de tous. What must be reconciled then are the absolutely atomized individuals on the one side and the "cold, unrelenting" general will on the other. This is equivalent to asking how it is possible for discrete, atomic individuals ever to acquire the notion of universal good that may differ from or even impair their interests as private persons.

The solution is to "internalize" the general will as the very essence of human self-consciousness. In Kant's moral theory, I am only free when I obey a law I have given myself. If I follow the inclinations I have as a natural, empirical being, my will is no longer autonomous, but subject to the heteronomy of impulses which do not have their source in my self-conscious "I." And because the only law that satisfies those conditions is the doing of one's duty for duty's sake rather than for the advantages it might bring, then freedom, morality, and self-identity all coincide in Kant's ethics. The self, as pictured in the social contract doctrine, is an empirical being which must try to discover the general will. In Kant's moral theory, the self *is* the general will. Hegel expresses this transition by saying that consciousness now loses its "abstract *being* or the immediacy of being a point without substance." In its new, "internalized" form, "it knows the [pure will] as itself and itself as essence, but not as the essence *immediately in being* [*seiend*]. Pure will is neither the revolutionary government, nor anarchy endeavoring to constitute itself as anarchy, nor is it the center of this faction or its opponent; rather, the *general will* is the *pure knowledge and willing* of consciousness."[74] The universal will, in this new form, became *conscience*, and specifically the conscience of Protestantism. Thus, the Revolution demonstrates that it requires a reformation to succeed, that freedom cannot be made actual in a "mass society," but rather only where the citizens have an inner life and inner resources commensurate with freedom.

The explanation of why the Revolution failed gives us the key to showing what it accomplished and why it was necessary from the standpoint of the *Phenomenology* and of Hegel's project of speculative reconciliation. We recall that there is a double path to the reconciliation of Cartesian dualism, one starting from experience of the natural and human world and leading to the thought or concept of that experience, and the other beginning with man's inner life (religious faith) and giving it a rational form. The loss of Greek ethical freedom tore the world apart into abstract personhood (certainty) and otherworldly Christianity (truth). These self-alienated fragments of lost integrity cannot be reconciled and reconstructed until they can be experienced as identical-in-difference. And this experience is provided in the Revolution:

> Luther had gained possession of spiritual freedom and concrete reconciliation. He triumphantly established that man must work out and discover for himself what his eternal vocation [Bestimmung] is. But the *content* of what takes place in man's inner life and of what truth must animate him, this Luther assumed to be

> a given, something revealed by religion. Now [in the Enlightenment and Revolution; L. H.] the principle has been set down that this content must be present, that I must be able to convince myself of it inwardly and that everything must be derived from it as the inner ground of truth.[75]

Hegel, unlike Burke, does not condemn the Revolution simply for demolishing historically legitimized rights and privileges in favor of thought principles. Rather, he discerns its failure in the abstractness of its thought, its inability to account, theoretically and practically, for the truth contained in Christianity. Hegel accepts the validity of Rousseau's attempt to construct a political philosophy on the basis of free will. What doomed Rousseau's *Social Contract* and (as far as Hegel is concerned) its stepchild, the Revolution, was Rousseau's failure to comprehend the *concept* of the will. If the will is understood speculatively, as identity-in-difference or self-differentiating unity, then it can generate its own content and hence get beyond the merely "negative" work of the Revolution. For ancestral institutions and historical entitlements, however, Hegel has little sympathy, as his remarks about England reveal. He notes that the particularistic prerogatives and principles in England display "the most extreme inconsistency and the most extreme injustice [*Unrecht*]. In England of all places one is least likely to find institutions of real freedom. In private law and in freedom of property they are incredibly backward."[76]

Hegel's speculative philosophy thus locates him in a unique position between the autonomous, abstract self of all enlightenment and the unself-conscious ethical life which the former undermines. Like Socrates, he is convinced that the only solution to the problems raised by the negative labor of abstract thought and the collapse of traditional morality and institutions lies in a deepening of our self-knowledge. The pure "I," the self as detached from an erstwhile ethical whole, is a fact of European civilization, just as it had become (on a different level) in the Athens of Socrates. It is neither possible nor desirable to restore the discredited ideologies and political forms of the ancien régime, because these were conceived in a time of "gloom and selflessness of consciousness"[77] when freedom was not yet explicitly recognized as the concept of man. But the pure self, in its uncomprehended form, threatens to destroy everything of value in European civilization. As finite, "natural" self, man can become at best the insipid hedonist that utilitarianism imagines; and as the abstract citoyen, he can accomplish only the negative work of the Terror. So it becomes urgently necessary to think through the nature of the pure self and thereby deepen its self-consciousness so as to include the moments of civilization—religion, metaphysics, concrete ethical life—that the self qua enlightened had negated. In short, it is necessary to write a phenomenology of appearing consciousness that will be nothing less than an account of the "I" in its quest for self-knowledge. The problems raised by the Enlightenment and French Revolution bring us full circle to the speculative core of Hegel's philosophy.

But the speculative reconciliation sought by Hegel is by no means complete. We have witnessed the bankruptcy of absolute freedom and its underlying principle, the enlightened, abstract "I." It remains to be seen how abstract freedom and abstract selfhood can be made concrete and brought into accord with religious faith. In other words, the principle of *certainty* or the abstract "I" must be reconciled with the *truth* of religion if wholeness in thought is to be recaptured. This will be the task of the German Enlightenment.

THE GERMAN ENLIGHTENMENT: FROM ABSOLUTE FREEDOM TO PURE SUBJECTIVITY

6

In his article "Was ist Aufklärung?" Kant defined enlightenment as "*the emergence of man from the immaturity for which he himself is responsible. Immaturity* is the incapacity to make use of one's intellect without the guidance of another."[1] From this it would seem that Kant has wholeheartedly embraced what Hegel called the slogan of the French philosophes: "Become for yourselves what you are potentially—rational!" Kant was unquestionably a man of the Enlightenment in his emphasis on reason and autonomous thinking as the defining characteristics of man. But in fact his place in the Enlightenment is quite ambiguous. And if one hesitates to classify him as a philosopher of the Enlightenment, one's reservations must be all the greater in respect to Fichte and Jacobi, who also figure in the period of "critical" philosophy in Germany.

We saw in chapter 1 how Kant and Fichte outlined a theory of the self profoundly at odds with notions current in empiricism, offering a radically new conception of the "I." But as Fichte observes, these theoretical conclusions do not make complete sense apart from their implications for practical activity: "[R]eason cannot even be theoretical, if it is not practical; . . . there can be no intelligence in man, if he does not possess a practical capacity."[2] In fact, in the German Enlightenment, self-identity becomes a moral and practical rather than an empirical or material issue. Consequently it is in the moral theories of Kant, Fichte, and Jacobi, as much as in their metaphysical principles, that we can appreciate how they both expanded and transformed the fundamental outlook of the Enlightenment.

As Hegel interprets them, these German thinkers returned to the dualism that had been so prominent in Descartes' philosophy. But they refined and developed it by analyzing much more precisely the nature of the "I" and its contribution to experience. Indeed, Hegel reads their works as the logical culmination and explicit working out of the great themes of the Enlightenment—the harsh antagonism and irreconcilability of thinking and being, morality and nature, "I" and not-"I." Moreover, he sees in the German Aufklärung at once a deeper appreciation of faith and a failure adequately to express or comprehend the truth of religious experience. Unlike the French, the thinkers of the German Enlightenment all try to assign an important role to theology in their systems.[3] Yet in Hegel's view their misunderstanding of religion threatens the latter far more significantly than the cynical incomprehension of the French philosophes ever could. For all their pious rhetoric, he thought, the German Aufklärer put the seal of inevitability on the alienation of human and divine. A passage from *Glauben und Wissen* expresses Hegel's judgment on critical philosophy: "There is thus nothing to be seen in these philosophies but the elevation of the culture of reflection to a system. . . . the torture of a better nature under this limitation of absolute opposition expresses itself in longing and striving . . . but in perennial incapacity . . . to raise itself above limitation into the self-transparent sphere of reason in which all longing ceases."[4] Or, more simply, the German Enlightenment is a "speculative Good Friday," an "absolute suffering" in which "God Himself is dead," but which contains within itself the potential for resurrection or speculative reconciliation.[5]

The Moral Worldview in Kant

Kant's moral philosophy actually begins in the *Critique of Pure Reason*, in which he tries to demonstrate the limits of pure reason in order to make room for faith. His refutations of the traditional proofs of freedom, the soul's immortality, and God's existence are not intended to culminate in skepticism or nihilism but to confirm that we can (and must) believe in these metaphysical principles as a precondition for the use of practical reason.[6] As in the deduction of the categories, transcendental apperception or the pure "I" is the linchpin of Kant's practical philosophy. Since it is not a part of experience or given in the phenomenal world, it can, as noumenon, be taken as a possible source of free acts. To see what Kant means by this claim, we must understand his notion of freedom: "I understand by freedom . . . the capacity to initiate a state of affairs of one's own accord [*von Selbst*] such that the causality of that state of affairs would not in turn be subject to another cause that would determine it temporally and in accordance with the law of nature. Freedom in this sense is a pure transcendental idea that . . . contains nothing that has been borrowed from experience."[7]

The question that immediately arises once freedom has been defined as extranatural causality is how we would ever gain an idea of it at all. If all we experience are phenomena subject to causality (an a priori category), what would lead us to suppose ourselves to be exempt from natural laws in any respect? Says Kant: "In inanimate nature, or in nature consisting only of animal life, we find no ground for thinking of any faculty as conditioned otherwise than merely by the senses. But man, who otherwise comes to know all of nature solely through his senses, also knows himself by means of pure apperception and, more specifically, in actions and inner determinations that he cannot at all account as sense impressions."[8] Of course, the "faculties" which we find not conditioned by the senses are the a priori faculties of reason and the understanding. Both are aspects of our very self-identity ("I" = "I") which is the precondition for any experience at all. Since the understanding can apply categories only to what is given in experience, reason—more specifically, practical reason—would seem to be the logical candidate to sustain the faculty of freedom.

In his writings on morality, Kant goes into the matter more deeply. He first defines the will as the author of causality, insofar as such causality emanates from practical reason. The question then becomes: how must an imperative be constituted so as to allow us to assert that the will which obeys it is free? Kant answers that "freedom would be that attribute of causality in which it could have effects independent of any alien causes *determining* it."[9] Furthermore, since the notion of causality implies lawlike necessity, the notion that a given cause will necessarily produce a certain effect, we must imagine that the causality of a free will would act according to a special kind of law. This law would be of the sort that, by obeying it, the will would determine itself and not be determined by any alien cause. That is, the will would be autonomous, obeying a law it had given itself. To the extent that I obey a law dictated by my physical, natural existence (e.g., pursue pleasure at all times), my will is not truly autonomous. This is because my physical existence (what Kant calls sensuousness) is distinct from my pure self-identity, my transcendental "I." In pursuing such an "empirical" imperative I am in effect merely obeying the law of nature, allowing my will to be determined by an "alien" object. Hence, autonomy and freedom of will must reside in obedience to a law which my pure self would will, a law devoid of any admixture of empirical, sensuous motivation.

The only law that fulfills the conditions for autonomy is the categorical imperative in any of its several formulations:

> Act only according to that maxim which you could simultaneously will to be a universal law.[10]

> [Act] only in such a way that the will could regard itself simultaneously as universally legislating through its maxim.[11]

In the categorical imperative there is no reference to any object (like pleasure or happiness) of the will. It is a purely formal or procedural principle that instructs us to universalize our maxims and ask ourselves whether we would be willing to obey them if they were valid for any and every will.

It is important to emphasize the assumptions underlying Kant's theory of freedom. First, it assumes that the pure, noumenal, or transcendental "I" is the true self, what I really mean when I say "I." Only by making this assumption can Kant distinguish so neatly between an individual as part of the natural, sensuous order and the individual as free agent, or practical reason. Indeed, reason *is* this capacity to split ourselves apart into noumenal and phenomenal existence, a remarkable capacity that Kant believes is essentially incomprehensible: "Now man finds actual within himself a faculty by means of which he distinguishes himself from all other things, indeed even from himself insofar as he is affected by objects, and that is *reason* [which is] . . . pure self-activity . . . pure spontaneity."[12] In other words, autonomy is indeed a justified demand, the very essence of enlightenment, but it is inconceivable so long as man is understood empirically in terms of utility, pleasure and pain, eudaemonism and the other naturalistic, materialistic categories of eighteenth-century liberal philosophy. Under these assumptions man would be only a modification of res extensa and thus unfree.

Second, the true self, as noumenal, is also universal. Once empirical, sensuous attributes of the self have been thought away, there is no way to assert that one "I" is different from another. This is indeed the condition for the possibility of a categorical imperative. When I universalize my maxims, I am trying to determine what a rational being as such would will, quite apart from his contingent circumstances and specific personal identity. Kant himself puts considerable emphasis on the universality of the pure self. He asserts that the dignity of a human being, his claim to be treated as an end rather than a means, rests on his capacity to act according to the categorical imperative, conceiving of himself as a universal self.[13] And the notion of the community of rational, free beings (as opposed to empirical beings), Kant calls the "realm of ends" (*Reich der Zwecke*), the ideal of practical reason.

Finally, Kant's practical philosophy implies that freedom and morality are identical. The categorical imperative is both a moral law and a law of the free causality of the will. Kant's view certainly has considerable support in common sense. We hesitate to call an action good, virtuous, or moral unless the agent acted voluntarily. And on the other hand, the actions we are most likely to regard as free are those that are undertaken contrary to impulse and inclination. Nevertheless, we normally assume that freedom means the capacity to choose whether we will act morally or immorally. For Kant, only the moral choice is a free choice. If we act immorally we have acted according to inclination. Inclination, in turn, comes from our empirical, sensuous existence, which is to say that our will has been determined by an alien object and is not autonomous.

Kant's position may seem radical, but it follows from the metaphysics of freedom. The moral quality of an act, he argued, cannot be said to reside in its consequences (the worst intentions may sometimes result in good consequences). Hence morality must be sought in the agent's motive or "principle of volition." But if every act is motivated by empirical sentiments like pleasure and pain, then there could be no moral acts at all since all acts would have the same fundamental motivation. Therefore, if moral acts are to be distinguished from nonmoral ones, we must postulate a separate source of motivation for each: namely, pure practical reason and sensuousness, respectively.

Kant's moral philosophy resurrects, on a new basis, the profound dualism of being and thinking characteristic of Cartesian metaphysics. Whereas for Descartes the cogito was an empty principle of self-certainty, for Kant it becomes the focal point for an entire system of practical reason that is located outside experience in a noumenal world. Descartes only posited a fundamental difference between res cogitans and res extensa as two separate substances. But Kant, and still more Fichte, insist upon a continual struggle between morality and nature, pure and empirical wills. In Fichte, the more radical and perhaps more consistent thinker, the entire world is defined merely negatively as not-"I." And since "I" and not-"I" are located on a quantitative continuum, the task of the "I" is to abolish the not-"I" or to act in such a way that moral law replaces natural law. In effect, the absolute "I" only posits the not-"I" so it will have a resistance to strive against, and hence make itself conscious of its true nature as nonempirical. Fichte expresses this in his characteristic, uncompromising fashion:

> This demand, that everything should conform to the self, that all reality should be posited absolutely through the self, is the demand of . . . practical reason.[14]

> What is required is the conformity of the object with the self; and it is the absolute self which demands this, precisely in the name of its absolute being.[15]

For Hegel, the problem is to demonstrate by means of an immanent criticism why the dualisms of practical reason lead to insoluble contradictions. The point of the section of the *Phenomenology* devoted to "spirit certain of itself" is to reintegrate the pure, noumenal "I" of abstract morality with empirical existence. This dialectic leads us away from abstract morality, by way of Fichtean conscience, to pietistic Protestantism. Hegel considers Kantian morality a bowdlerized, truncated Protestantism that must be made to see its essentially religious core.

In the *Phenomenology*, the moral theories of Kant and Fichte appear under the rubric of "the moral worldview" and "displacement" (*Verstellung*).[16] The expression "displacement" indicates that this sort of abstract morality avoids contradiction only by displacing it into a nonexperienceable future or postulated God. Hegel discovers the weak point of Kantian morality in the radical disjunction between morality and nature, or "I" and not-"I." As Kant envisages their relation, these spheres are so completely separated that an act that is part of the causal nexus as a phenomenon would be a free act, when taken as a noumenon. In this respect Kantian ethics is an extreme example of the philosophy of reflection and of the "inverted world" it generates. The world is seen as so internally shattered and polarized that an event in one sphere can have a diametrically opposite character in its inverted counterpart, something like the negative of a photograph.

The tension between morality and nature leads the "moral world-view" to propose three postulates which it believes will reintegrate these rigidly separate spheres. The first of these is the supposition of a highest good as the final purpose of all moral actions. Kant, in the *Critique of Practical Reason*, insists that the highest good is not a determining ground of the will (only the moral law can determine the will if it is to be free and moral), but is nevertheless its ultimate object.[17] As Hegel reads Kant, the latter introduces the postulate of the highest good to resolve a nagging problem in his moral theory, the problem "that nature is unconcerned about providing moral consciousness with the awareness of the unity of its actuality with that of nature. And thus nature will *perhaps* allow moral consciousness to be happy and *perhaps not*."[18] In other words, the highest good is supposed to encompass both morality and individual happiness in one ideal notion.

It would at first appear that Hegel is demanding something Kantian morality cannot provide (and which is indeed irrelevant to it) when he writes: "Moral consciousness cannot dispense with happiness and omit this moment from its absolute purpose."[19] But Kant himself says essentially the same thing: "To be happy is necessarily the demand of every rational but finite being, and thus an unavoidable determining ground of his appetitive faculty."[20] And he criticizes the Stoics precisely because, in his view, they did not take into consideration every human being's desire for happiness. Kant's concern is certainly justified. If morality does not ultimately bring happiness, then to will that the moral law be universally obeyed would mean willing that men should be unhappy, which makes a mockery out of morality. Hegel interprets the postulate of the highest good as a roundabout way of admitting that the noumenal (transcendental) and phenomenal (empirical) selves are really *one* self, and that man cannot consistently be regarded as a dual being.

The second postulate (actually the first in Kant's *Critique*) likewise concerns the opposition of morality and nature. Nature is not merely "indifferent" external nature, but also my own nature insofar as I am a sensuous being. As we know, the essence of moral action consists in suppressing one's inner nature so that the sole determining ground of the will is the pure self or moral law. But this gives rise to a new difficulty and a new postulate which Kant describes: "The complete congruence of the will to the moral law is holiness, a perfection of which no rational being is capable at any point of his existence. But since this is nevertheless postulated as practically necessary, it can only be encountered in an infinite progress toward complete congruence. And it is necessary, according to the principles of pure practical reason, to assume such a practical advance as the real object of our will."[21] This "infinite progress" toward holiness requires an infinite time in which to complete itself, so we must postulate the immortality of the soul, as a condition for conceiving of morality at all.

Hegel again interprets Kant's argument essentially as a logical puzzle. The self has differentiated itself into "I" and not-"I," here moral self and inner nature. This is only an embellished account of *what* consciousness is, i.e., of the fact that it is always intentional. If there is no object, there is no subject and vice versa. In moral terms, this means that if there is no nature to overcome, there is no morality. If I did what I ought to do because I always wanted to do it, there would be, strictly speaking, no moral action, just as without an object for consciousness, there would be no consciousness. Kant avoids confronting this difficulty by banishing it into an infinite future. It is, as Hegel says, "an absolute task" and must remain one.[22]

The first two postulates can be summarized, according to Hegel, as the harmony of morality and objective nature (the final purpose of the world) and the harmony of morality and sensuous will (the final purpose of self-consciousness). The third postulate, in Hegel's account (which differs substantially from Kant's), is supposed to unite these elements in a notion of moral action. Since the moral law is pure and formal, it is not immediately obvious which specific duties should be subsumed under it. So Hegel's version of moral consciousness postulates another consciousness in which the specific duties are sanctioned. He regards this relating of specific, multiple duties to the *one* law as the same relationship that we found in the postulated harmony of morality and happiness. That is, we have the concept, or the unity of universal and particular, ethics and nature, which is "a lord and ruler of the world who effects the harmony of morality and happiness and simultaneously sanctions duties as *multiple*."[23]

The same postulate (God's existence) follows when we take seriously Kant's warning that no action is ever entirely moral. In this case (the secular equivalent of original sin) we feel unworthy of happiness and conclude that it can only be a gift of grace from another consciousness. Both forms of the postulate, as Hegel describes them, deviate from Kant's account. The latter makes the straightforward argument that the highest good, in order to be a credible object of moral willing, must somehow include the congruence of morality and happiness. This is only possible if we postulate the existence of God as a cause of both nature and morality who has provided that these moments will eventually coincide.[24] Hegel eschews the notion of cause as inadequate to explain the relationship between morality and nature (subject and object). He takes God to signify the *concept* of the unity of these moments, the activity by which they are posited as different and yet held to be (ultimately) identical.

However, only we phenomenological observers, guided by Hegel, can grasp the direction and meaning of these criticisms. The "moral consciousness," Hegel's personification of Kant's ethic, clings to the traditional idea of a transcendent God distinct from human consciousness. Accordingly, Hegel makes the moral consciousness resort to "displacements" to avoid the conclusion he himself will draw—that the dualisms of morality and nature, man and God, cannot be sustained:

> For moral consciousness itself, however, its moral worldview does not have this significance, that it is developing its own concept and making it into an object to itself. . . . For it only knows the pure essence [*Wesen*] or the object as pure knowledge or as itself insofar as the latter is *duty* or *abstract* object of its pure consciousness. It thus acts only as thinking, not as comprehending. Therefore, the object of its *actual* consciousness is still not transparent to it; it is not the absolute concept, which is alone able to conceive *other-being* as such, or its absolute opposite as itself.[25]

In the first postulate, which hypothesized a highest good as the ultimate object of a moral will, we already find a displacement. It was assumed that there could be no harmony in the present between morality and the actual world. Happiness appears to be entirely contingent and unrelated to morality. But, insists Hegel, the congruence of happiness and morality is in fact present in every moral act. Kant did not realize this because he had such a crude notion of happiness: "Happiness is the condition of a rational being in the world, when, in the totality of his existence, everything occurs as he would wish and will it to."[26] In other words, Kant's "highest good" would see to it that the moral man won all the lotteries and trips to Hawaii, while the immoralist would stub his toe at every crack in the sidewalk. Hegel, however, thinks of happiness as tantamount to satisfaction or being "at home with oneself" (bei sich) in other-being. I am happy or satisfied when, as in a moral act, I can intuit the actualization of my essential being: "[B]ecause in the accomplished act consciousness actualizes itself as this singular individual, or intuits empirical existence as having returned into it [i.e., the consciousness; L. H.], this being the meaning of enjoyment, there is therefore contained in the actuality of moral purpose that form which is designated enjoyment and happiness."[27] In short, Kantian morality displaces into the beyond what is implicitly present here and now: "Thus action immediately accomplishes in fact what was not supposed to happen and was supposed only to be a postulate, a beyond."[28]

What is more, Hegel accuses the Kantians of not taking even moral action seriously. First of all, the postulate of a highest good, a perfect congruence of morality and happiness, seems to be so hopelessly unachievable that it renders individual moral actions absurdly insignificant. It becomes virtually impossible to see the connection between some nebulous highest good and my own puny actions. So, as Hegel remarks: "Because what is generally best is supposed to be effected, nothing good is done."[29] One could, I think, justifiably defend Kant against Hegel's criticism on this score. But there is more to his argument. Kant defines moral action by way of its opposition to the causal nexus of natural events. But the highest good postulates that this opposition will somehow be effaced. Hence, argues Hegel, to will the highest good means that one wills the elimination of morality.

This same displacement becomes even more obvious in the second postulate which foresees an infinite progress toward holiness in which sensuousness and morality will entirely coincide. It is easy to see that if they ever did coincide, there would, by Kant's definition, be no morality at all, and indeed no consciousness. What Hegel objects to in both versions of the postulated harmony of morality and nature is the assumed quantitative relation between them. It appears as though an increase in morality signifies a decrease in sensuousness or even in natural causality, an absurd suggestion in Hegel's view: "Progress as such as well as *diminution* would assume differences of magnitude in morality; but there can be no talk of such quantitative relations in morality. In it, as the consciousness for which *pure* duty is the ethical purpose, one cannot think in terms of any difference at all, let alone such a superficial one as magnitude; there is only One virtue, only One pure duty, only One morality."[30]

The contradictions within these two postulates impel moral consciousness to reveal its true colors. Since morality is not present *now* (but only in an infinitely removed future), consciousness cannot be serious about postulating an equivalence between morality and happiness. There is no morality; hence no one can claim happiness (in

Kant's sense) as a just recompense for his own merit. A person can only petition for it as a gift of free grace. That is, he admits he is not moral, but wants to win the lottery anyway, so he shows the world that he is really more interested in happiness than in morality: "Non-morality here expresses what it is,—that it is concerned not about morality but about happiness pure and simple, with no relation to morality."[31]

In both of the displacements discussed above, the conflict between morality and nature is the key issue. And in each case, the moral consciousness admits that the conflict will—and must—somehow be resolved. Otherwise, morality would be an absurd or unfulfillable requirement for man. But it postpones the final harmonizing of morality and nature into a distant future. To Hegel, this really is a dishonest move, because the time element (future vs. present) should not have any relevance to the question at hand. If morality and nature can be harmonized in the future, why not now? If the Kantian moral consciousness had confronted the problems raised by the reconciling of its antagonistic terms in the here and now, it would, Hegel believes, have to abandon its original dualistic premises. One way of doing this (the way Hegel chooses) is simply to point out that man never really confronts nature in quite the unmediated and antagonistic manner described by Kant and Fichte. Both our inner nature and the physical world have long since been humanized and overlaid with a "second nature" of socially determined laws, customs and values. Our feelings, our thoughts, our apparently spontaneous responses are already shaped by the "spiritual" forms of life into which we are socialized. Moreover, a purely moral will is an abstraction. The content of our moral will is also socially mediated, as we have seen. Thus, the really crucial question is not so much how pure morality can ever be made congruent with our natural inclinations (e.g., the wish to be happy). Rather, we must ask what kind of society would satisfy the highest moral standards while also permitting the individual to actualize himself (his will) to the fullest, i.e., to be happy in Hegel's sense. In the last two chapters, we shall explore the characteristics of such a society as Hegel outlines it. But meanwhile Hegel must confront the final issue of Kantian ethics: theology.

It is the third postulate, the existence of God, that represents for Hegel the most untenable displacement of all. To reduce his argument to the simplest terms, he objects to the separation of human and divine spirit in such a way that the latter remains a shadowy "beyond" for finite self-consciousness. If the reflective categories of Kantian morality cannot stand scrutiny in the here and now, it avails nought to dispel them into a remote beyond, for as soon as one focuses on the foggy regions of an infinite future, the contradictions return in full force. If human self-consciousness (as morality) is self-contradictory, then divine consciousness is too. Like the attitude of perception, analyzed by Hegel toward the beginning of the *Phenomenology*, Kantian morality seeks to ground the unity (or sanctification) of diverse duties in a pure, untainted consciousness beyond diversity, or, alternatively, it proclaims itself as the pure unity of the one moral law and wishes to have a divine legislator sanction multiple specific duties. In either case, moral consciousness is unwilling to confront contradiction, which means it is unwilling to abandon the rigid exclusivity of identity and difference as fundamental categories of the understanding. And because it refuses to think through the relationship between identity and difference, it cannot comprehend human or divine consciousness, nor see how they can be identical in their differentiation.

The point of Hegel's analysis of Kantian theology comes most clearly into view in some of his other writings, notably the inaugural address he delivered upon assuming his duties at the University of Berlin. On one side, he appreciates the effort that "critical philosophy" has made to show why God is a necessary idea of reason and why human freedom and morality would not be entirely meaningful without divine sanction. To this extent, the German Enlightenment seems to him much superior to the French. But both Kant and Fichte retract what they have granted by insisting that reason cannot really obtain any concrete knowledge about religious matters. Hegel believes that Kant and Fichte, much like Descartes, introduce a divine being only to paper over the displacements and contradictions in their systems. "[God] is assumed [to exist] by consciousness for the purposes of harmony, just as children make a scarecrow and then agree among themselves that they will let themselves be scared by this mannequin."[32]

By so restricting the meaning and range of religious faith, the critical philosophers had harmed more than religion itself. They had also called into question the traditional mission of philosophy to pose and answer mankind's most important questions. If, as Hegel thought, the religious impulse was something inevitable—because spiritual—in man, then philosophy's self-declared agnosticism would only open the floodgates for the ever-present tendencies toward charlatanry in religion. He notes caustically that critical philosophy was well on the way to reducing philosophy to a triviality.[33]

It is interesting to examine Hegel's early theological writings, for these show us quite clearly why he broke with critical philosophy. In 1795–96, he composed an article on the "Positivity of Christian Religion" in which he asserted that "the essence of all true religion and also of our religion is the morality of man, and . . . the more specific teachings of the religion of Christianity [are] all means to disseminate morality."[34] Here he is an orthodox man of the Enlightenment applying the categories of natural and positive (borrowed from jurisprudence) to religious faith. There is only *one* human nature, obedience to the moral law, and therefore whatever in religion does not promote or concern morality is positive and contingent.

By 1800, however, Hegel had come to question the very rationale of this venerable distinction and says as much in a revised version of the same article: "General concepts of human nature are too empty to provide a criterion for [judging] the particular and necessarily more diverse needs of religiosity."[35] He goes on to argue that "human nature" cannot be comprehended at all if we ignore its historical dimension. Spirit only is what it knows itself to be, and its quest for self-knowledge takes place in time. Hence religion, as one form of spirit, will inevitably have a historical aspect that cannot be "thought away" without impoverishing our understanding of human nature and religion.

But Hegel's early criticism of Kantian moral theology transcends conventional historicism. The counterpart of man as moral agent is nature as mere res extensa, a spiritless mechanistic flatland devoid of significance. In a world so conceived, the moral self has no meaningful field for its self-realization: "Because the pure 'I' has defined itself rigidly in its abstraction and lack of content, it has all of existence, the fullness of the natural and spiritual universe, opposed to it as a beyond."[36] But for Hegel the core of religious faith is the intuition of the sacred in the world of experience, the sentiment that the things and events of ordinary life are infused with an eternal truth and hence point beyond their mundane existence toward the divine. Thus, in proposing to defend religion, critical philosophy unintentionally emasculates it by "demystifying" the world and parching the wellsprings of religious experience:

> In a religion, actions, persons and memories can be considered sacred. Reason demonstrates their contingency; it demands that what is sacred should be eternal and unchanging. But it has not thereby demonstrated the positivity of those religious things, for men can and must attach immutability and sacredness to what is

> contingent. In his thinking of the eternal, he attaches the eternal to some contingency of his thinking.[37]

Thus Kant proves himself to be a man of the Enlightenment rather than a theologian in the final analysis. His attempt to reconcile reason and religion amounts to a reduction of religious man to "natural" man (albeit the "nature" of man is no longer empirical, but consists in the pure "I" of transcendental intuition). Consequently, Kantian practical philosophy shares the same defect as the outlook of the entire Enlightenment. It is a "Trojan horse" within the ramparts of religious faith because it banishes religion entirely from the world of experience and equates it with the noumenal realm of morality, thereby effacing the very aspect of faith which distinguishes it from Enlightenment.

Kantian practical philosophy, as one German version of Enlightenment, has attempted to "combine" reason and faith instead of treating them as irreconcilable enemies. But the result of this synthesis is entirely unsatisfactory. Reason cannot know anything important, and faith cannot venture into the world for fear its objects will be transformed into dead things before its very eyes. Hegel sums up his suspicions about the German Enlightenment in a striking passage from "Glauben und Wissen":

> The question is, whether the winner, reason, has not suffered the same fate which usually befalls the victorious might of barbarian nations at the hands of the weak but cultured nations which have succumbed to them. They retain the upper hand as far as their external authority is concerned, but succumb spiritually to the vanquished. The glorious triumph which the Enlightenment has celebrated over its opposite, faith (or what it takes to be faith in the minimal extent of its religious comprehension), once it is seen in the light of day, turns out to be nothing but this: The positivity with which it took issue has not remained religion, nor has reason, which triumphed, remained reason. The progeny which hovers over these corpses as the child of peace, common to each and unifying them, has within it as little of reason as it does of genuine faith.[38]

Hegel's task in the *Phenomenology* is to disrupt the "unholy alliance" between Enlightenment and faith in the critical philosophy of Kant. He believes he has succeeded at least in demonstrating that the postulates of practical reason are untenable because they make distinctions that cannot be consistently maintained if morality is to be real. Above all, consciousness distinguishes between the finite moral self (which can never be entirely moral but must advance toward an infinitely receding horizon of holiness) and the divine self, which is entirely moral but in a way incomprehensible to us. Hegel's argument is simply that Kant has made a distinction that is none at all. The divine legislator is merely a thought construct (*Gedankending*) and hence not an "other" of moral consciousness.

Conscience

The need to postulate a divine will in the beyond arose because Kant distinguished so rigidly between morality and sensuousness. The idea of a divine will is in fact nothing other than the idea of a self that is a unity of the moral and empirical "I," a being who knows his concrete duty and can act morally in a specific situation. To advance beyond Kantian morality, a new consciousness must arise in which the moments of pure morality and empirical existence are united, just as they are in the idea of a divine will.[39]

The new shape of consciousness which Hegel introduces at this point is called simply "conscience." It scorns the abstractness of the moral worldview because "it is simple, self-certain spirit *within itself* [*in sich selbst*], which acts conscientiously in its immediacy, without the mediation of the notions of the moral worldview, and which has its truth in this immediacy."[40]

> [Conscience] knows that being as itself in whom the *actual* is simultaneously *pure knowledge* and *pure duty*. It retains, even to itself, its complete worth in its contingent being, and it knows its immediate singularity as pure essence and action, as true actuality and harmony.[41]

It might at first appear as though conscience were a retrogression from Kantian morality. After all, the entire course of the *Phenomenology*, beginning with ancient ethical life, has been designed to shatter the immediacy of self-knowledge and duty. That is, enlightenment in the broader sense was a necessary incursion into the immediate integrity of Greek life, the detaching of the "I" from all bonds of ethical existence so that it could come to know itself as universal. Here we seem to encounter a return to immediacy in the midst of the cultured, self-alienated world of modern Europe. On confronting this unexpected return to immediacy, we must wonder whether the odyssey of consciousness has ended and speculative reconciliation been accomplished. If so, we would have reason to complain that conscience hardly seems to be a satisfactory solution to the problem of lost ethical integrity.

To address these issues one at a time, we must first bear in mind that "conscience" is in fact an allusion to the philosophical position Fichte adopted in *The Vocation of Man*. Fichte undertook to explain the ground of all experience in his *Science of Knowledge* and concluded that it lay in the activity of the absolute "I" by virtue of which it posited itself as finite "I" and (in a separate act) posited a not-"I" which is simply the negative "other" of the self. But insofar as we merely contemplate the sphere of the not-"I" in theoretical activity, we are in fact determined by it; that is, the "I" is in a sense extinguished in theoretical activity. So the question becomes, how and why do we ever tear ourselves loose from the bonds of nature (the not-"I") and pose ourselves as subjects confronted by objects which we know to be different from ourselves? This is essentially the same as asking how self-consciousness is possible (and hence consciousness itself, since there can be no consciousness without self-consciousness, as Kant demonstrated in the *Critique of Pure Reason*). Fichte answers by saying that practical activity precedes theoretical knowledge.

> It is . . . the necessary faith in our own freedom and power, in our own real activity, and in the definite laws of human action, that lies at the root of all our consciousness of a reality external to ourselves. . . . We are compelled to believe that we act, and that we ought to act in a certain manner; we are compelled to assume a certain sphere for this action; this sphere is the real, actually present world, such as we find it. . . . From this necessity of action proceeds the consciousness of the actual world; and not the reverse way, from the consciousness of the world the necessity of action. . . . We do not act because we know, but we know because we are called upon to act:—the practical reason is the root of all reason.[42]

The moral law is merely the abstract, formalized version of pure certainty of self which is the root of all moral action and (hence) all self-consciousness. Fichte continues: "The laws of action for rational beings are *immediately certain*; their world is certain through that previous certainty. We cannot deny these laws without plunging the world, and ourselves with it, into complete annihilation."[43] What is immediately certain (*gewiss*) is nothing but the voice of conscience (*das Gewissen*). This is not a play on words on Fichte's part. He is merely capitalizing on a linguistic analogy to illuminate the relationship between self-consciousness and the moral activity that conscience bids us perform. By subordinating theoretical knowledge to the immediate intuition of ourselves as moral beings, Fichte circumvents the implicit skepticism of Kant's *Critiques* and places morality on what seems to him an unshakable foundation.

Conscience, because it is immediate and concrete certainty, seems to provide us with the immediate unity of pure self and empirical existence which was lacking in Kant's postulates of practical reason:

> That voice within my soul in which I believe, and on account of which I believe in every other thing to which I attach credence, does not command me merely to act *in general*. This is impossible; all these general principles are formed only through my own voluntary observation and reflection, applied to many individual facts, but never in themselves express any fact whatever. This voice of my conscience announces to me precisely what I ought to do, and what leave undone, in every particular situation of life. . . . It carries with it immediate conviction, and irresistibly compels my assent to its behests. . . . To listen to it, to obey it honestly and unreservedly, without fear or equivocation—this is my true vocation, the whole end and purpose of my existence.[44]

We seem to have found a tentative answer to our first question, namely, why conscience should be considered a higher form of consciousness than Kantian morality. In fact, it *is* Kantian morality but now with its underlying assumption laid bare: to be a self and to be moral or conscientious are one and the same. But our second question remains in doubt. Is the Fichtean doctrine of conscience a modern equivalent of Greek ethical life, an immediate concrete knowledge of one's duty purged of the reflection and skepticism of the Enlightenment? Hegel argues that conscience *is* an ultimate principle, at least to the extent that it includes Protestant religious faith within it. Conscientious performance of duty is the indispensable basis for the state in its specifically modern form. Yet on the other hand, conscience is still not equivalent to speculative knowledge. It is still a one-sided, subjective principle that has not overcome the deficiencies of Kantianism: "[Moral consciousness] by retreating back into itself cannot become essentially anything other than what it already is."[45] In its most extreme form, the "beautiful soul," conscience will have retreated so far into subjectivity that it eschews and even condemns all action. Here we will encounter the turning point of the entire *Phenomenology* and Hegel's speculative enterprise as a whole. Either the subjectivity of romantic protest and religious faith must be reconciled with the world-transforming but amoral actions of the Enlightenment, or the most extreme personal fragmentation is a permanent feature of our world, and modern life cannot be restored to anything like the immediate integrity that infused Greek Sittlichkeit.

The logical categories that conscience initially embodies are by now familiar: being-in-itself and being-for-itself. The in-itself is equivalent first to pure consciousness or the self qua universal, while the for-itself refers to the "I" as specific, personal, and empirical. We recall that the earlier selves of the world of spirit—the person of legal status and the self-alienated individual of modern culture—had not been able to integrate these moments. The universal was a "mask" of status in the Roman Empire and did not penetrate and inform one's specific individuality. In the world of culture, the universal self (the in-itself) of Rousseau's general will behaved as a Moloch devouring specific individuals and governments just because they were specific. It is also important to realize that the lack of unity between in-itself and for-itself signified that substance had not yet become subject. Insofar as substance is the universal or the in-itself, it must be animated and actualized by individual selves (i.e., consciousness as for-itself).

In Kantian morality, the in-itself (as moral law) is ostensibly identified with the specific individual, but this identity is "displaced" because as a specific person (for-itself) I can never be moral, but only approach morality asymptotically. Consequently the in-itself is detached from the for-itself and displaced into a beyond (the divine legislator). Another way to express the same point would be to say that the universal is empty of content (it is only the form of law); it does not give itself its own content. But the concept of the concept or of the subject (as opposed to substance) is that it should be a self-differentiating, self-particularizing universal. Hence Kantian morality has not overcome the self-alienation or the reflective culture characteristic of the Western world since the decline of the polis. But conscience, because it is immediately concrete, appears to reintegrate the moments of being-in-itself and being-for-itself.

As Hegel portrays the attitude of conscience, it is essentially an unreflective performance of duty that "knows and does what is concretely right."[46] In fact, he suggests that anyone who took Kant's morality too seriously could never act at all. The emptiness of the categorical imperative makes it possible to regard many different specific duties, even diametrically opposed ones, as equally valid moral possibilities. Thus in any specific case, the Kantian will not be able to act because he will not know how to reconcile the conflict of duties. Conscience, on the other hand, abjures any reflective casuistry and follows its convictions with the unerring certainty of their rectitude, simply because it does not acknowledge a conflict between its specific existence (being-for-itself) and the in-itself.[47]

Because conscience can and does act, it enters into a new relationship with other individuals. It performs an action that, according to its own judgment and conviction, is the right thing to do. But because it does act (and not merely reflect), its "interior" or self-certainty takes on an objective form which is there for others to see and judge. Hegel therefore reintroduces the category of being-for-another to illuminate the public, social character of conscientious action. The in-itself, which is the universal aspect of conscience, detaches itself from the individual and appears, qua being-for-another, as the social fabric that holds human beings together in a civilized community. Hegel notes of this newly introduced aspect of conscience: "*Being-for-another* is thus substance, being-*in-itself* that is distinct from the individual. Conscience has not abandoned pure duty or the abstract *in-itself*, rather the in-itself is the essential moment of behaving toward others as *universal*. It is the common element of self-consciousness, and this element is the substance in which the deed has *stable existence* and *actuality*. It is the moment of *being-recognized* by the others."[48]

In other words, morality, acting as a universal "I" toward other selves, can never be a solipsistic withdrawal into oneself. It does not consist in comparing concrete cases of moral actions with a formal law. Probably no really moral individual ever acted that way. Rather, morality designates our concrete and specific appreciation of others' rights and needs, an acute sense of the value, and also the frailty, of human community. Morality is thus not so much a relation between my specific situation and a universal law, but between me and you. It becomes a reality when we recognize each other as free individuals and are aware of that mutual recognition as the essence and source of our obligations. According to Hegel this is not really the case with Kantian practical reason: "The *in-itself* [of Kantian morality] is for it either the abstract, *unactual* essence, or being as an *actuality* that is not spiritual. But the *actuality* which *is* for conscience is of the sort which is *self*, i.e., existence conscious of itself, the spiritual element of being recognized."[49]

But the moment of being-for-another that conscientious action introduces also draws our attention to its ambiguity. When I act, I transform conscience from an inner conviction into an outward deed. My action enters the public realm and becomes actual. However, it is not mere being in the way a tree or rock is. It points beyond itself toward my convictions as a conscientious person.

On the other hand, my conscientiousness is never exhausted in any specific act. The act is separate from me because it is now a frozen "something" that does not express my inner convictions. If my conscience impels me, I will act differently, even in the opposite way, under identical circumstances. I may decide to donate all my money to a noble cause, or enlist in the army, put my life in danger, and intentionally take the lives of others. Conscience obeys no law and recognizes no need to be consistent because inner conviction and immediate knowledge are its essence.

At this point, the ambiguity of conscientious actions expresses itself in the disparity between the deed and its recognition by others:

> The consciousness for which the action is present [with its implied claim to be recognized as conscientious; L. H.] is completely uncertain about the acting, self-certain spirit. The latter acts and determines himself in the element of being; the others take this *being* as the truth of acting spirit and are thereby certain of him. He has expressed in his deed what he holds to be *duty*. Yet he is free from any *determinate* duty. Where the others think he is actual, he has already departed. . . . For his *actuality* is, as far as he is concerned, not the duty and determination which he has exhibited, but rather the duty and determination he possesses in the absolute certainty of himself.[50]

What is missing is a mediating term between my silent, ambiguous action and the in-itself, which has now become being-for-another or mutual recognition. My deed has to be infused with my own subjectivity for it to be recognized as conscientious. It must become a presentation of self and not, as Hegel says, "vulgar actuality."[51] The mediating element between self and accomplished deed cannot be a "third thing" for we would not have the concept of their unity in another entity existing outside them. Thus, says Hegel, it must again be language that transforms the mere being of the deed into an externalization of selfhood, and indeed of the universal selfhood of conscience:

> Here we again see *language* as the empirical existence of spirit. It is self-consciousness as *being-for-another* that is immediately *present as such* and as *this* universal. It is the self divorced from itself and become objective to itself as pure "I" = "I." It preserves itself as *this* self in its objectivity yet also converges with the others and is *their* self-consciousness. It thus apprehends [*vernimmt*] itself just as it is apprehended by the others, and this apprehension is precisely *empirical existence that has become self.*[52]

Only in language do I, as subject, become objective to myself at all, and at the same time the objectivity of my physical existence and actions acquires a subjective dimension (as the expression of a self) when I speak about them. As long as my actions are silent, says Hegel, the others "do not know whether this conscience is good or evil, or rather they not only cannot know this, they must take it to be evil."[53] Action unaccompanied by speech appears to be merely natural, the pursuit by consciousness of its own "pleasure and desire."[54]

Whatever the specific content of conscientious speech may be, it always says the same thing: "*The self . . . knows itself as the essence.*"[55] Or, more simply, it expresses my conviction that this action was my duty. Further, it acknowledges the moral bonds of society, the universality of conscience. When I explain or justify my act, I imply that only mutual recognition, the social milieu, can put the stamp of duty upon an ambiguous action. Just as flattery acknowledged and created the power of the state as a specific individual (Louis XIV), speech acknowledges and constantly recreates the human community.

The Beautiful Soul

Yet even language cannot completely eradicate the ambiguity of action because that ambiguity is rooted in the concept of action and, indeed, in the concept of self-consciousness as such. "I" refers both to the self as a specific, natural being and the self as the universal present in moral action and human community. I am both being-for-itself and being-in-itself, although the latter has now assumed the form of being-for-another, since morality is no abstract law but the fabric of human community as such. At this point Hegel introduces a new form of consciousness that acts out the dialectic of universality and specificity one last time. This is the "beautiful soul," the last finite form of consciousness in the *Phenomenology* and hence the prelude to absolute spirit in religion and philosophy. More specifically, the beautiful soul incorporates the aspect of judgment or recognition that the conscientious agent tries to gain for his deeds. Thus we will in fact deal with conscience divided into two distinct *personae*, the acting conscience that petitions for recognition and the judging conscience (the beautiful soul) that may accord or withdraw it.

As Goethe portrays her in his novel *Wilhelm Meisters Lehrjahre*, the beautiful soul is a pietistic Protestant who exhibits a degree of romantic, narcissistic self-preoccupation that increasingly alienates her from the social world, her friends, and relatives, and eventually even her fellow pietists. She confesses that she "would rather abandon my country, my parents, and my friends and earn my living abroad than act contrary to my own insight."[56] As she withdraws into the interior of her own heart, she feels so strongly the presence of God that even her own body begins to seem indifferent to her.[57]

The beautiful soul represents the most extreme form of conscience because she believes herself capable of that which Kant could ascribe only to divine will: always doing, out of inclination, what is right. She has no use for laws and proscriptions because the inner voice is far superior to any formal codex. Fichte's doctrine of conscience was only a pale, secularized version of this sort of incredible inner self-assurance:

> I always advance and never retreat. My actions are becoming more and more similar to the idea I have formed of perfection. Daily I feel it becoming easier to do what I think is right. . . . I scarcely recall a commandment; nothing appears to me in the form of a law. There is an instinct which guides me and always leads me to do what is right. I freely follow my inner dispositions [*Gesinnungen*] and know as little of restrictions as of repentance.[58]

When the beautiful soul does emerge from her self-preoccupation, it is mostly to hold meetings with other pietists. In these little congregations, spirit is indeed present, but, as Hegel suggests, "the spirit and the substance which binds the members together is thus the mutual assurances they make about their conscientiousness, and good intentions. They rejoice in their mutual purity and revel in the splendor of knowing, expressing, and cherishing such excellence."[59] Although this pietistic version of Protestantism may hold to the doctrine that

God is an "other," a being somewhere "out there" in a beyond, the real significance of the beautiful soul's conscientiousness is the immediate identity of human and divine spirit: "Consciousness . . . knows the immediacy of the presence of the essence [i.e., the divine being; L. H.] within it as the unity of the essence and itself. Thus it knows itself as the living in-itself and it knows this its knowledge as the religion which, as intuited or existing knowledge, is the speech of the congregation about its own spirit."[60]

But the immediacy of the unity between human and divine spirit is its Achilles' heel. Because it is only immediate unity it is not comprehended as speculative. Speculative unity (unity according to the concept) requires differentiation and mediation, since to be at all means to be something definite or enter into the realm of difference. The "I," as pure negativity, cannot acquire self-knowledge except through the mediation of its self-objectification in a finite relationship. And since divine spirit thinks only in and through human spirit, divine spirit cannot know itself or even be what it is outside the series of finite subject-object complexes within which it is manifest. Hence the beautiful soul, as pure inwardness and extreme subjectivity, impoverishes both human and divine spirit.

Since the beautiful soul is sheer inwardness, she cannot really participate in the human world, but only judge it. Her whole being is a permanent reproach to anyone who attempts to act in the imperfect world of human society. In Hegel's words,

> [This consciousness] lacks the power of externalization, the power to make itself into a thing and to endure being. It lives in fear of tarnishing the splendor of its inwardness. In order to preserve the purity of its heart it flees all contact with actuality and persists in the stubborn powerlessness to renounce its self, now driven to the apex of ultimate abstraction, and thereby give itself substantiality. It refuses to convert its thinking into being and entrust itself to absolute difference. . . . Its action is a longing that loses itself only in becoming an object with no essence. . . . This unhappy, so-called beautiful soul, in the transparent purity of its moments, glimmers away within itself like a dying ember and vanishes like a formless vapor that dissolves in air.[61]

For Hegel, the pitfalls of this form of consciousness are best exemplified in Jacobi's philosophy. (In fact, the entire section on self-certain spirit in the *Phenomenology* appears to be a concretization of Hegel's earlier article "Glauben und Wissen" which dealt with Kant,

Fichte, and Jacobi as advocates of the philosophy of reflection in its special form of subjectivity.)

Jacobi is of course a man of the Enlightenment insofar as he adopts the empiricism of Hume as his starting point. But he differs from nearly all empiricists and from the Enlightenment as a whole in his insistence that religious matters are exempt from scientific scrutiny. He wishes to save God and religion by posing an unbridgeable gulf between rational but limited scientific inquiry and nonrational faith that gains an intuition (albeit not a concept) of the absolute. Hegel cites with approval Jacobi's remark that "cognition which advances by means of *finite* mediations only takes cognizance of what is finite and contains no truth."[62]

However, Jacobi does not draw what, for Hegel, would be the appropriate conclusion from the deficiency of finite knowledge. Instead of forming a notion of infinite or absolute knowledge that would retain the rationality and stringency of science while yet encompassing religion, Jacobi turns against all speculative philosophy, criticizing it in the name of Humean empiricism. Jacobi in effect tries to preserve religious faith from the onslaught of enlightenment by embracing the narrowest possible version of rational thought (Humean skepticism). Using Hume's arguments, Jacobi attacks those such as Spinoza, Kant, and Fichte who try to ascertain rational grounds for religious beliefs, sensing that a rationalized deity, a mere postulate or deus sive natura, can never be a substitute for the intense conviction of private, personal faith.

Hegel, of course, agrees that absolute spirit must be conceived as subject and not as any abstract être suprême. However, he is equally convinced that Jacobi's form of subjective religious conviction not only does not preserve faith from the Enlightenment, but hands to the latter a total (and undeserved) victory. For if religious faith is detached from rational cognition, it can be the vehicle for the most irrational sentiments and superstitions. In some remarks from the preface to the *Phenomenology*, Hegel shows that he has clearly understood the powerful attraction of Jacobi's religiosity; yet he is also determined to prevent religion from lapsing into a shallow, arbitrary irrationalism:

> This prophetic talk indeed supposes that it has permanently seized hold of the center and depth of everything. It looks down with scorn upon determinacy (*horos*) and intentionally keeps its distance both from the concept and necessity and from reflec-

> tion, whose domain is the finite. But just as there is an empty breadth, so too there is an empty depth. Just as there is an extension of substance whose effusion into the infinite manifold is unchecked by any power which might hold it together, so too there is an intensity devoid of content, a pure force that refrains from any expansion, and this is the same as the merely superficial.[63]

Jacobi's philosophy and the beautiful soul that portrays it exemplify this empty intensity. Hegel points out that an immediate relation to God must necessarily contain only the conviction "that God is, not *what* God is; for the latter would be cognition and lead to mediated knowledge."[64] In other words, Jacobi's faith is only an emotional, irrational version of the Enlightenment's être suprême. Here again, we find confirmation of the charge Hegel levels against the entire German Enlightenment: that it has compromised both reason and faith. In Jacobi, reason cannot know anything important, while faith is arbitrary, immediate, and empty. Hegel even suggests that Jacobi's philosophy would have to ratify not only Christian faith, but also faith in God as the Dalai Lama, a bull, or an ape.[65] This is because he does not interpret faith as a conscious adherence to a specific doctrine, but rather as a matter of intense emotional commitment.

Jacobi's philosophy is in fact a philosophy of reflection in both senses of the word. Faith and reason, the ultimate irreconcilable dualism of his system, is a dualism of reflection in the special Hegelian sense. But faith itself, as Jacobi understands it, also contains the other element of reflection, conscious deliberation upon a matter (Nachdenken). Jacobi's form of subjectivity and faith is not the naïve adherence of an untutored person to ancestral beliefs. It is a self-conscious attempt to efface rational thought and return to the naïve faith of a prereflective culture. As far as Hegel is concerned, this is a hypocritical pose, an egotistical repudiation of egotism: "It may thus appear that Jacobi has retrieved Protestant subjectivity from its Kantian conceptual form and given it back its true shape as subjective beauty of sensation and the lyric of heavenly longing. But, on account of the essential ingredient of reflection and consciousness of subjective beauty, faith and individual beauty are in fact torn loose from the naïvety and directness in which alone they are able to be beautiful, pious, and religious."[66]

From Hegel's critique of Jacobi, it should be plain that the beautiful soul represents more than simply a passé version of Protestantism. In a way, she stands for every attempt to recapture the lost wholeness of our lives by taking refuge in attitudes, forms, and customs that enlightenment has made impossible for us. Where Burke sought a stable foundation for political authority in the wisdom of ancestors, the beautiful soul (following Jacobi) wishes to place religion on the seemingly unshakeable basis of immediate conviction. However, a conscious, reflective attempt to reconstitute unreflective, unconscious modes of life is self-defeating. If one consciously repudiates the Enlightenment, one is still determined by it. The "negations" performed by Burke and Jacobi are *concrete* negations of abstract rights and rationalized religion. Hence the restored immediacy that they both envisage is in fact no immediacy at all but a negation of negation, an immediacy conscious of itself as being immediate by contrast to the repudiated culture of the Enlightenment.

Nevertheless, the beautiful soul, in spite of its "untruth," succeeded in giving a new, more profound meaning to spirit's self-alienation. In self-certain spirit, the opposition between universal and singular has been *internalized* as a distinction between the in-itself (now defined as being-for-another or mutual recognition) and the for-itself (the "I" as specific individual). We now have a world of conscientious selves each certain that he knows and does what is right, and each prepared to judge the actions of all others. Hegel simplifies matters by reducing the complex world of conscience to the single case in which an acting conscience seeks recognition from a judging conscience (the beautiful soul). Since duty no longer has any reference to an abstract law (and still less to positive laws of a given state), the acting conscience finds himself in an ambiguous position:

> This universality and duty has the utterly opposite significance of being *singularity* which is determinate and represents an exception to the universal. For this *singularity*, pure duty is only universality which has become surface appearance and has been directed outward; i.e., duty only resides in words and only has the status of being-for-another. Conscience, now only *negatively* oriented toward duty which has been defined as *determinate* and *present*, knows that it is free from such duty. But because it concretizes empty duty with a *determinate* content drawn *from out of itself*, conscience has the positive consciousness that it provides content for itself as *this* self. Its pure self, as empty knowledge, is devoid of content and determination. The content which it provides is taken from its self *as this* determinate self or from itself as natural individuality.[67]

In other words, there can be no "pure" self as such. The pure "I" exists only within finite, empirical situations. We can indeed separate, in thought, the moments of self-consciousness, but as concrete selves our personal, individual identity is inseparable from our determination as pure "I." For this reason, all our supposedly conscientious acts can be taken as evil and our speech in defense of them as hypocrisy.[68] At this point, spirit has reached what Hegel calls its "deepest reflection into itself."[69] It has come to the realization of what theologians would call original sin and existentialists, guilt. This is recognition that the "I" is simultaneously both universal and singular, conscientious and evil. The same pure negativity that allows me to tear myself out of animal existence and enter into ethical and moral relationships with others, also cuts me off from them and seals me into the ineffable interiority of my own self. Socialization is at the same time individuation:

> This pure self-certainty, driven to its extreme, appears in the two forms of *conscience* and *evil*, which immediately merge into each other. The former is the will to *good*, which, however, in this pure subjectivity is something *non*objective, nonuniversal, and ineffable. The subject knows that it *itself* decides what conscience dictates in its *singularity*. But *evil* is this same knowledge that one decides as a singular individual, insofar as singularity does not remain abstract, but takes on the content of subjective interest opposed to the good.[70]

The confrontation between the acting conscience and the beautiful soul must somehow result in a reconciliation between good and evil. The individual, cut off from his social world precisely because he is a particular, specific self, must be reaccepted into it. At the same time, the beautiful soul must be driven to abandon her arrogant, deedless subjectivity. At first, the beautiful soul seizes upon the ambiguity of all action and seeks to explain a seemingly conscientious deed on the basis of an ignoble, self-serving motive. In this respect she adopts the strategy of empiricist historiography that applies the interior-exterior category in such a way that the virtuous exterior is introreflected into a putatively vicious interior. "There are no heroes for the valet, but not because the hero is not a hero, rather because the valet is a valet."[71] The acting conscience cannot deny the partial truth of these judgments because all action includes the aspect of particularity and natural individuality.

Hegel points out that this self-righteous attitude displays an appalling lack of honesty. The beautiful soul can retain her purity only by refraining from all action and merely judging. Yet judgment too is a form of action, and indeed a base action when he who judges sees only base motives in the deeds of others (*honi soit qui mal y pense*!). When the acting consciousness recognizes that the beautiful soul is as guilty as he, he is moved to confess his own guilt. But such a confession is not a humiliation or self-abasement; it is an attempt to reestablish continuity with the other, to mend the torn fabric of human community on the basis of a mutual insight into human weakness.

Here the beautiful soul of pietistic Protestantism demonstrates its true ugliness and reveals the limitations of religious faith in its irrational, unspeculative form. The beautiful soul refuses to accept this confession and repudiates all community with the acting consciousness. In so doing, she proves that she has no grasp of spirit and hence of Christianity. She does not realize that spirit can redeem the past and undo what has been done. She does not understand the power of speech over deeds.

The beautiful soul, as such, can never achieve the reconciliation of fragmented human existence except in death, where all humans are equal because they are mere being without spirit. The only true redemption of the past lies in forgiveness, in which the judging consciousness would abandon its arrogant posture and extend recognition to the acting consciousness of their common humanity. To Hegel, forgiveness is the presence of absolute spirit in human affairs: "The word of reconciliation is spirit *existing*, intuiting the pure knowledge of itself as a universal being in its very opposite, i.e., in the pure knowledge of itself as *singularity* that is absolutely self-enclosed. This is a mutual recognition that is absolute spirit."[72]

While forgiveness appears here in the context of religious faith, it extends into political life as well. Hegel holds that a legal system must apply strict, inflexible standards of justice, paying no heed to the character of a criminal or to the circumstances surrounding his deeds. Justice cannot dispense forgiveness because to do so would negate its essence *as* justice. But the executive power, because it embodies a higher and deeper mode of spirit than formal legality, can and should issue pardons when it is appropriate to do so. The right of pardon, as an attribute of sovereign authority, bears a strong resemblance to the power of forgiveness that Hegel so strongly emphasized in the *Phenomenology*. Both in effect affirm the fundamental continuity of human life present in mutual recognition. To forgive someone means that we acknowledge his deed and its bad consequences for ourselves or others, and yet we treat the deed as though it had never happened. We believe that the bonds that unite us are strong enough to withstand the divisive force of an evil act; so we refuse to demand or exact retribution for it. On the level of an entire state, the sovereign likewise affirms the affective unity of its citizens by granting pardons. In a properly organized state, one in which the citizens find a confirmation of their spiritual identity in the laws, there is no need to exact retribution for every single crime.

With the concept of forgiveness we have reached the turning point of the *Phenomenology* in which finite, human spirit becomes speculative knowledge. Thus far there has been a gulf between self-consciousness and consciousness or between res cogitans and res extensa. Hegel believes he has shown that the mind's knowledge of itself finally comes to include, as moments, all its objectifications, the whole series of subject-object relationships that the absolute gave itself as finite human existence. In forgiveness I acknowledge, in effect, that being is thinking. The past has been. It is frozen being because it is no longer present and subject to change. Yet forgiveness, the mutual recognition by the two selves that they are moments of a community or continuity, undoes what is done and redeems the past for the present. This signifies that the "I" has only itself as its object. You are absolutely other than I am as a specific person or for-itself. But because I comprehend the power you have to cast aside the rigidity of your being-for-itself, you and your past deed cease to be alien to me. Thus, I have the concept of spirit before me, an "I" that is we, and a we that is "I."

By the same dialectic, substance has become subject. Substance is subject when the absolute diremperts itself in human self-consciousness in such a way that its differentiae (within the nexus of mutual recognition) are immediately identical and known to be so. As Hegel says in one of his most poetic passages: "The *Yes* which reconciles, in which both 'I's' relinquish their opposed *empirical existence*, is the *empirical existence* of the 'I' extended to duality, which yet remains self-identical and retains its self-certainty in its complete externalization and opposite. It is God appearing among those who know themselves as pure knowledge."[73] God remained substance so long as he was determined as force, divine law or fate, the être suprême, or the divine legislator who coordinates morality and happiness. In all these cases, He appears as an *object* of man's consciousness. But the experience of reconciliation shows that the divine is an activity that dissolves the barriers between one self-consciousness and another.

Taken together, the German and French Enlightenments laid the foundation for Hegel's concept of the state. The French developed the idea of abstract political freedom based on the general will. But freedom as it was defined by the French Enlightenment was both too individualistic and too barren of content. Although Hegel rejects the German Enlightenment's dualistic premises, he welcomes its attempts to find a place for religious faith in the new world of rational thought. Religion allows us to see the communal or spiritual aspect of human consciousness and thus the limitations of the modern natural law tradition that so influenced the French revolutionaries. In developing his theory of the state, Hegel will draw on both Enlightenment traditions, or at least on his interpretations of each. The individual freedom and rational legal system of the modern state, argues Hegel, presupposes a deeper solidarity and sense of tradition that, at least in the West, cannot easily be separated from the Judeo-Christian legacy. In the following chapters, we shall see how the more spiritual bonds of the modern state gradually emerge as freedom becomes more concrete and developed.

THE TRANSCENDENCE OF LIBERALISM: SPECULATIVE FOUNDATIONS OF THE MODERN STATE

7

In both its moral and political dimensions, the Enlightenment has precipitated a crisis of identity for modern man. He is exhorted to define himself and make his decisions according to universalistic, rational norms or else to harken to the inner voice of conscience. In neither case can he wholeheartedly identify himself with traditional institutions, be these secular or ecclesiastical. From the viewpoint of abstract reason, utility, the moral law, or the inner light, such institutions are bound to appear as merely conventional and even arbitrary. But the personal autonomy conferred by enlightened self-reflection, aptly symbolized by Fichte's pure "I," remains what Hegel calls a mere "ought." The individual is driven into a state of permanent, irreconcilable tension between a tradition that has become meaningless and an empty self-identity incapable of actualization in the real world. This tension manifests itself in a variety of extreme and self-destructive modes of behavior: the nephew's iconoclasm, revolutionary terror, the impossible quest for moral perfection, and pietistic longing. Yet all these phenomena point back to the rigid dualism of being and thinking first formulated by Descartes. It is the ultimate barrier to the development of a stable identity on the part of the individual, an identity which would permit him to comprehend his social, political, and religious milieu as an extension of himself rather than as an indifferent or even hostile force.

The problems of identity that Hegel raised in the *Phenomenology* are taken up again fourteen years later in the *Philosophy of Right*. It is apparent from the outset that he is still seeking a solution to the legacy of the Enlightenment:

> Only by destroying something does this negative will acquire the sentiment of its own existence. It may indeed intend to will, let us say, some positive state of affairs, for example the state of universal equality or universal religious life. But in fact it does not will that such a state of affairs become actual. For in this case some sort of order would have to be created in which both institutions and individuals would become particularized. But it is only in the annihilation of particularity and objective determinations that the self-consciousness of this negative freedom emerges at all.[1]

And, referring specifically to the French Revolution, he points out to his students: "Fanaticism wills an abstraction rather than an articulation. So when differences emerge, fanaticism finds this repugnant to its indeterminacy and annuls them. For this reason, too, the people destroyed again the institutions they themselves had made in the Revolution, because any institution is repugnant to the abstract self-consciousness of equality."[2]

Besides laying bare a conspicuous thread of continuity in Hegel's thought between 1807 and 1821, these remarks also indicate the wider context within which the *Philosophy of Right* must be interpreted. The Cartesian dualism of being and thinking is reproduced, in the modern Enlightenment, as a rupture between subjective will and the specific structures and institutions that circumscribe it. The political crisis that the Revolution helped precipitate is, in fact, only one aspect of a more global problem extending from pure logic to the everyday lives of modern citizens. Thus we should not expect any radical disjunction between Hegel's *Logic* and *Philosophy of Right* since they share essentially the same "cognitive interest" in reconciling man with himself and his natural or spiritual world. Indeed, Hegel hints that the political and ethical problems bequeathed by "enlightened" inquiry first made it necessary to rethink the nature of logic: "The need to conceive of logic in a more profound sense than as a science of merely formal thought is occasioned by the interest of religion, the state, law, and the ethical life."[3] One might paraphrase Kant here and assert that logic without a concern for political and moral existence is empty, while a concern for political and moral existence is blind without logic, and specifically Hegel's logic of the concept. Yet in the *Philosophy of Right*, as elsewhere, Hegel assumes that the dilemmas engendered by the ratiocinations of Verstand can be laid to rest only by further, more speculative thought, not by a rejection of philosophy as such.

The Origin and Meaning of Right

THE PHILOSOPHY OF RIGHT AS A SCIENCE OF ACTUAL STATES. In order to preserve his *Philosophy of Right* from misinterpretations, Hegel finds it necessary, once again, to distinguish a science—and specifically a science of right—from other modes of cognition. The need for this explanation, which Hegel provides in the "Preface," has itself arisen because of the crisis of political authority brought on by the Enlightenment. The latter has unquestionably taught men to think for themselves and to demand that state and society be organized according to the principles of reason. But since there is no generally accepted criterion for what is rational, we find a wild proliferation of theories about the state, each claiming to have discovered its truly rational basis. All these competing theories have, in Hegel's view, succeeded only in discrediting philosophy altogether. And by so doing, they indirectly advance the cause of wholly irrational phenomena such as the romantic nationalism of Hegel's contemporary, Jacob Fries, and his allies in the *Burschenschaften*.

Hegel exempts his own work from this charge precisely because it is scientific. By this he means that it makes use of the speculative principles he developed in the *Science of Logic*. He assures us that "the whole [of the *Philosophy of Right*; L. H.] as well as the formation of its internal structure rests upon the logical spirit,"[4] and he recommends that his readers judge it in this light. We recall from our review of the *Logic* that reason, which is logic's special domain, must not be taken either simply as ontology (a logos of being) or as a canon of the rules of inference (logic in its usual subjective form). Rather, the absolute, as activity, expresses itself as subject and object and is hence present in both. In the context of the *Philosophy of Right* this implies that we must not construct theories about the state that would be merely subjective, that would ignore the presence of reason in actual states. If we grant that nature is a rational whole (rather than mere random chaos), then why should we refuse to acknowledge the rationality of our social and political institutions, whose laws (*Gesetze*) are posited (*gesetzt*) by spirit itself?[5]

Thus, for Hegel, a scientific treatise on right or law must attempt to fathom the rationality of what is actual:

> Philosophy, because it is the *investigation of the rational* and, precisely for this reason, the *apprehension of what is present and actual*, does not set up any *beyond*, supposed to exist God knows where.[6]
>
> Thus, this treatise, to the extent that it contains a science of the state, is not intended to be anything but the attempt to *comprehend* and *portray the state as immanently rational*.[7]

The rationality of actual states has long been a sticking point with critics of Hegel, although some of his more recent commentators have come to his defense on this issue.[8] The speculative significance of the term "actuality" has already been discussed in chapter 2, but a few additional remarks may clarify Hegel's meaning. First, it is quite consistent with his entire philosophical position that he should seek to uncover the rationality immanent in modern states. He always contends, even in the case of nature, that objectivity displays an immanent rationality. Indeed it could not be otherwise if the absolute only defines itself through its objectifications. Hence it should not surprise anyone that Hegel does not jettison his speculative position in the *Philosophy of Right*. The latter is simply an application of principles found throughout his philosophy.

Second, Hegel insists again, as he did in his critique of Lockean empiricism, upon the distinction between genesis and truth. We may be able to explain why certain institutions first came into being and even why they have continued down to the present. But this sort of explanation does not entitle us to infer that these institutions are right or rational: "A determination of right [*Rechtsbestimmung*] may prove to be quite well-founded and completely consistent in respect to *circumstances* and *existing* institutions of right and still be irrational and contrary to right in and for itself."[9] So while Hegel does reject abstract theories of natural right that measure existing states against a nonactual "beyond," he refuses to abandon the principle that right differs in its very essence from mere positive existence or historical longevity.

Obviously Hegel's unusual position raises serious difficulties. If we do not judge the rationality of existing institutions according to a transcendent, nonactual standard, how can we avoid identifying right with positive law and existing institutions? The only solution would be to demonstrate that historical development has finally led to the creation of actual states that incorporate the institutions and principles which the "idea of right" would require. Of course, it is Hegel's contention that this convergence of right and history has occurred, at least in its basic outlines. Both the *Philosophy of History* and the *Phenomenology* describe the process by which the consciousness of universal freedom (the freedom of man as man) penetrated and transformed European states. The *Philosophy of Right* will show this freedom to be the essence of the idea of right and the principle that governs the diverse institutional forms of the modern state.

However, matters are not quite so simple as Hegel sometimes makes them seem. Both the *Philosophy of History* and the section of the *Phenomenology* devoted to finite spirit end with a problem, not a solution. As we recall, the nature of modern subjective freedom dissolves the traditional bonds of political authority, and tries to replace them with what, to Hegel, seems an intrinsically unrealizable requirement. Authority should henceforth embody the abstract principle of popular sovereignty which is inherently empty since it demands that only the general will or the moral imperative should rule. As Hegel points out at the end of his lectures on the *Philosophy of History*:

> On account of this formal principle of freedom, this abstraction, they [the atomized individuals of a liberal state; L. H.] do not allow any stable sort of organization to arise. Freedom right away opposes itself to the specific decrees of the government, for this is a particular will and hence arbitrary. The will of the many brings down the ministry and a previous opposition now takes over. But the latter, insofar as it is now the government, has the many against it once more. In this way the movement and unrest continues. It is this collision, this knot, this problem which history confronts and which it must resolve in future times.[10]

While "future times" may provide some sort of solution, Hegel is not entirely willing to wait that long. He believes he can outline a state that will meet the highest standards of rational right and freedom, while simultaneously including stable political authority and a wealth of "articulations" or institutions. We would misjudge Hegel, then, if we assumed that he were merely putting the seal of philosophical legitimacy on existing states. Instead he wishes to resolve a problem whose origins can be traced via the Enlightenment to Cartesian dualism and even, in a way, to the breakdown of Greek Sittlichkeit. In effect, he has adopted the same strategy toward the state as he did toward religion. He maintains that his ambition is only to "reconcile" man to what is—Lutheranism, the modern German state—while in fact he gives to "what is" a completely new meaning by subjecting it to philosophical comprehension. Although one may discern in the *Philosophy of Right* some institutions with analogues in contemporary states, these are still only analogues. In most cases, Hegel's definition of such institutions diverges nearly as much from the self-understanding of those who operated them, as his "comprehended" Christian trinity differs from the trinity of ordinary, pious Lutherans.

THE ORIGIN OF RIGHT AND FREEDOM IN THE STRUGGLE FOR RECOGNITION. In the *Encyclopedia*, the contents of the *Philosophy of Right* are included under the heading of "objective spirit." Here individual self-consciousness is already aufgehoben, or absorbed into an ensemble of more or less permanent institutions and structures. If one assumes that an objective moral-political order already exists (even if only embryonically), then some very vexing philosophical issues have been sidestepped: Where does order come from? In what sense do individuals "fit into" the ongoing order? Are they ontologically prior to it, or vice versa? Are the members of society "natural" men in Hobbes' sense, or are they "denatured" men in Rousseau's sense?

For a political tradition such as classical liberalism, Hegel's concept of objective spirit would thus beg all the important questions since it would start out by assuming the presence of a political order whose genesis and legitimacy are precisely at issue. I would argue that Hegel's political philosophy is simply incomplete if one considers the *Philosophy of Right* exclusively. It is necessary to move back into the realm of "subjective spirit" in order to find any account of the origins of political order per se. Fortunately for his readers, Hegel is strikingly consistent on this point from the *Phenomenology* onward. Legal status, or a condition in which right prevails (*Rechtzustand*), must be preceded by a struggle for recognition in which individual self-consciousness sheds its merely subjective, natural character and eventually becomes universal self-consciousness or spirit. Accordingly, before investigating Hegel's *Philosophy of Right*, we shall try to reconstruct the relevant passages in his other works which illuminate the transition from a situation where there is no right or established order to one in which, *mutatis mutandis*, right is an accepted principle. This will be Hegel's equivalent to the liberals' state of nature.

In the *Phenomenology*, the dialectic of self-consciousness marks the beginning of genuinely social relationships among human beings. In the previous sections, consciousness had groped its way toward comprehension of the concept. At the conclusion of chapter 3 (on force and understanding), the "I" had finally attained a clear theoretical vision of its active structure, its character as an identity of identity and nonidentity. But once the "I" sees what it is, it must grasp, however dimly, that it cannot rest there. Its very identity calls for a new cycle of differences, a new series of subject-object complexes. Now it must become appetitive and practical. Like Fichte, Hegel believes that the self must become practical to get a clear sense of its power over nature (Fichte's not-"I"). The theoretical attitude, however sophisticated, lacks the dimension in which the self actually creates and posits its own reality, rearranging the world according to self-generated standards and goals. The most rudimentary level of practicality is consumption of physical objects because, in consuming, the "I" demonstrates that it is a negative power over its environment. It does not take things as they are; it changes them in accordance with its own needs: "[T]he simple 'I' is . . . the simple universal for which differences are none at all only by its being the *negative essence* of the formed, independent moments. And self-consciousness is thus certain of itself only by annulling [aufheben] this other which presents itself as independent life. It is *desire*."[11]

In other words, self-consciousness does not exist merely in the mode of thinghood. It must constantly produce itself for itself. It is, in effect, a relation rather than a geometric point. To be self-conscious means ultimately to make one's own identity objective or real by finitizing it within a subject-object dichotomy. This is the essential meaning of "externalization" (Entäusserung). And at the same time, this externalization entails a feeling of lack or want, which impels self-consciousness to reappropriate its objectivized being.

According to Hegel, the consumption of objects does not secure genuine self-consciousness but only a "sentiment of self" (*Selbstgefühl*) to the appetitive "I." The concept of self-consciousness requires that the subject become objective to himself, which he can do only in a vague, unsatisfactory way in the chain of desire-consumption-satisfaction-renewed desire. To become objective to himself, he must have another self-consciousness as his object. It is vitally important to understand Hegel correctly here. We cannot picture a self-consciousness, complete and full-blown, hunting around for another self-consciousness that would act as a "mirror." What we have instead is the absolute, as pure activity, dirempting itself into two "I's" which become self-conscious in the full sense only within its relationship. Only when self-consciousness has another self-consciousness as its object does it begin to transcend its primordial biological determination and become genuinely human.

The implications of this doctrine are far reaching. "Atomistic" individualism and the kind of natural rights theories frequently associated with it (e.g., those of Hobbes and Locke) seem much less tenable if one accepts Hegel's argument. The self is less a discrete unit than it is a continuum or relationship that spans both the individual self-consciousness and its other. Outside of this relationship, man is simply not the same creature we ordinarily take him to be in a social setting. Or to put this another way, selfhood is more truly the result of the relationships between individual human beings than it is a precondition for such a relationship, however much this kind of claim violates our ordinary way of thinking. Even in this most simple and primitive encounter between self-conscious beings we find a paradoxical, speculative relationship which cannot be grasped by the categories of the understanding:

> At first, and in respect to their immediate relationship, there is a self-consciousness for a self-consciousness such that each is an "other" to the first. I see in him myself as an "I," but I also see something immediately and empirically existing, another object quite independent of my ego. . . . In this determination there lies an enormous contradiction. "I" is something entirely *universal*, absolutely *permeable, not interrupted by any limit* and an *essence common to all men*. Both selves, here standing in relation to one another, constitute *one* identity, *one* light as it were, and yet they are at the same time *two*, each existing in completely *rigid isolation*, each introreflected, completely *distinct from* and *impervious against* the other.[12]

Universal self-consciousness or mutual recognition is not simply "given" in the confrontation of two self-consciousnesses. Although the continuum of identity-in-difference is implicitly present it must be made explicit in a struggle for recognition. This is the famous life-and-death battle of the *Phenomenology*. In this confrontation, each self-consciousness is certain of itself and demands to be recognized as self-certain by the other. The other stands before me both as another self-consciousness and as a discrete material thing. He demands that I acknowledge his being-for-itself, his power over and ability to abstract from his own material existence. But he must prove this power to me, as I am forced to prove it to him. To do so, we must both risk our lives in order to demonstrate that we might deserve to be comprehended as self-consciousness and not as mere being: "The absolute equality of the 'I' with itself is essentially not an immediate equality, but rather of the sort that it makes itself into what it is by annulling [aufheben] sensuous immediacy and, by so doing, makes itself free and independent of the sensuous, even for another. Thus it proves itself to be in conformity with its concept and must be recognized, because it gives reality to the 'I.'"[13]

However, if the life-and-death struggle actually terminates in the death of one of the antagonists, then it has not succeeded in creating a nexus of recognition. The loser has indeed proved his freedom from the sensuous, but only in an "abstract" or "negative" way.[14] And the survivor has still not achieved his purpose, recognition as a self-conscious being. The only "positive" outcome of the life-and-death struggle must be the submission of one antagonist. The winner (now a master) has the satisfaction of seeing his independence constantly confirmed and recognized. The loser (the servant) must learn to discipline his natural will and carry out the commands of another.

The resolution of the life-and-death struggle in mastership and servitude has some crucially important consequences for political philosophy. First, Hegel takes the master-servant relationship as a prototype for the earliest forms of the state. But he simultaneously rejects the view that force and domination should be construed as a principle of legitimacy, as rational grounds for obedience on the part of those who are dominated. The origin of states is not coterminous with their philosophical principle of justification. Like Rousseau, Hegel cannot accept the adage that "might makes right."

But even more important, the master-servant relationship makes possible a new understanding of freedom. The freedom from sensuous existence that the master displayed to a greater degree than his eventual servant is, at bottom, negative freedom. The master has proved that he is not a thing, and forces the servant to recognize this, but he gets no further than independence. His identity is mediated through the things he consumes and through the servant who obeys, in the end, only the master's "natural" will. Thus the actuality of the master's self-consciousness, his intuition of himself in other-being, does not conform to its concept.[15]

The master's freedom has no positive content, no reflection in empirical existence. Everywhere he looks, he finds only thinghood or human beings who have become like things (servants). What he lacks is the intuition of the Kantian principle that other people ought to be treated as ends in themselves rather than as means. This is the basis of a continuum of human identity that would allow the master to transcend his merely natural will and recognize an injury to the other as an injury to himself, his innermost core of self-identity. "There is one moment lacking for there to be genuine recognition: What the master does to the other he should also have to do to himself, and what the servant does to himself he should also have to do to the other. Thus, for lack of this moment, a one-sided and unequal recognition has arisen."[16] For this reason, Hegel declares that the master can never be completely free until the servant is.[17]

The servant, by contrast, has the potential for further self-development. He cannot so easily relapse into a merely natural will, because he must constantly execute the will of another. His will is disciplined by the absolute fear of death, which instills a dread and trembling in his whole being. By becoming acutely aware of his own mortality, the servant also comes to see the vanity and relative insignificance of his own particular will. He learns to grasp the possibility of acting not simply for himself but on behalf of a will that is not immediately his own. Clearly, moral freedom as understood by Hegel (who in this respect is still very close to Kant) requires that I distinguish my private, egotistical will from the moral will and that I subordinate the former to the latter. Although the master's commands are anything but moral, they at least accustom the servant to act at the behest of a will other than what immediate natural impulse would dictate. Moreover, because he must labor and form (bilden) objects for the master's use, the servant has found a medium in which he can intuit the unity of self and other-being, an intuition denied the master.[18]

Hegel, as Riedel observes,[19] has implicitly rejected one of the cardinal tenets of classical political philosophy by putting a higher value on *poiesis* than on *praxis*. Praxis, or action, was supposed to have primacy over poiesis, making or producing, because the former had its end within itself, while the latter resulted in an object different from the activities that brought it into being. Praxis was relatively self-sufficient and independent, while poiesis had to graft form onto an alien, external matter.

Hegel, in his various discussions of mastery and servitude, unfailingly regards the lack of objectification which defines praxis as a shortcoming. In his view, form is not something eternal and stable (as it was in some measure for the Greeks). Rather it is only the finite expression of negative activity. That is, form or determinate being is essentially negation (in the Spinozistic sense of *omnis determinatio negatio est*). This becomes a palpable fact to the laborer, who thus acquires a far deeper insight into the nature of the "I" or being-for-itself than does the master. He sees in the negative activity of formation a close approximation to the negative activity that consciousness (or the concept) in fact is. Hence he intuits himself (his concept) in other-being.[20]

In sum, a new, positive conception of freedom is made possible by the servant's labor and self-abnegation. To be free, it is not enough to be prepared to risk one's life in order to demonstrate independence from sensuous existence. Freedom requires a permanent transformation of the self (suppression of particular will) and a "spiritualizing" of desire by its refinement and objectification in labor. Hegel gives expression to these requirements as early as his Jena lectures on *Realphilosophie*:

> Recognition is immediate actuality, and in its element the person first comes to be as *being-for-itself* in general. The person enjoys and labors. Here for the first time desire has the *right* to make its appearance, for it is actual; i.e., it itself has a universal, a spiritual being. The labor *of* all and *for* all, and enjoyment, the enjoyment of all. Each serves the others and gives them help. Or, the individual [*Individuum*] has here for the first time an individual [*einzelnes*] existence. Previously he was something abstract and untrue.[21]

In the *Encyclopedia*, Hegel calls this achieved state of mutual recognition "universal self-consciousness." Only now has the relationship of spirit that we encountered in the initial confrontation of two appetitive self-consciousnesses become actual. The individuals are no longer self-external, as they would be qua "natural" beings. Instead, by suppressing their natural existence, they have created a continuum of self-consciousness in which the identity of each individual is a function of the spiritual whole to which he belongs. And at the same time, that spiritual whole is not a "beyond," an overarching totality outside individual self-consciousness, but rather a case of the true, "immanent" infinity of the *Logic*. In the *Encyclopedia*, Hegel describes it as follows:

> *Universal self-consciousness* is the affirmative knowledge of oneself in the other self, such that each has *absolute independence* as free

> singularity. However, by virtue of the negation of his immediacy or desire, each does not distinguish himself from the other, and thus each is universal [self-consciousness; L. H.] and objective. Real universality or mutuality is present in such a way that each self-consciousness knows itself in the other, who is free, and knows this by recognizing the other and knowing him as free.[22]

Freedom thus signifies the transcendence of limitation, but not in the Hobbesian sense of a "right to all things" or an absence of physical impediments to the satisfaction of desire. Rather it connotes the interpenetration of self-consciousness in such a way that each is no longer an external barrier to the other but an expansion and deepening of his identity. True freedom "consists in the identity of myself with the other, so that I am only truly free when the other is free also and recognized by me as free. This freedom of the *one* in *the other* unites men in an internal fashion, whereas need and necessity [*Not*] only bring them together in an external way. Men must therefore want to rediscover themselves in one another."[23] Similarly, in the *Philosophy of Right,* Hegel argues that freedom is essentially the same relation as love or friendship.[24] And sometimes Hegel goes even further and explicitly identifies universal self-consciousness with every important interpersonal relationship: "This universal reappearance of self-consciousness, the concept which knows itself, in its objectivity, as self-identical subjectivity and thus as universal, is the form of consciousness of the *substance* of every essential spirituality, of the family, the fatherland, the state, as well as of all virtues, love, friendship, bravery, honor, and fame."[25]

The unity of the concept and actuality or of the subjective and objective in universal self-consciousness brings us back to the *Philosophy of Right.* We now have at our disposal the "concept of right" that Hegel had developed in the *Encyclopedia* but also in his Jena years. The individuals who figure in the *Philosophy of Right* are already "denatured" to some extent. They do not enter upon the threshold of objective right as natural, desiring "atoms" but as participants in at least a rudimentary common life, for it is the common life (universal self-consciousness) that first gives them a definite, singular self-consciousness as opposed to the vague Selbstgefühl of desire and consumption. "Right" thus refers to all the forms and institutions of this common life that promote and actualize freedom in the speculative sense outlined above; right "is not to be taken only in the sense of limited, juristic right, but as encompassing the existence of all the determination of freedom."[26] The struggle for recognition has provided us with the phenomenal origin of political associations. In the *Philosophy of Right*, Hegel will attempt to find a rational ground of political life.

RIGHT AS AN EXPRESSION OF FREE WILL. Like Rousseau in the *Contrat Social*, Hegel argues that the state must be regarded as a construction of the will, and specifically of the free will. Against the background of his critique of the Enlightenment and French Revolution, Hegel's recourse to the will is especially striking. It was precisely the abstract, "negative" general will that paralyzed the French Revolutionary state. And this abstract freedom of the will is also the red thread running through the German Enlightenment from Kant to the deedless, pietistic "beautiful soul." If Hegel is to avoid these undesirable conclusions, he must try to demonstrate that the will, correctly understood (or *comprehended*), would generate a rich institutional life and a stable basis of authority solely out of itself.

In the case of the will, according to Hegel, we are dealing only with a variant of the subject-object structure of the "I." He maintains that theoretical and practical "attitudes" are not two different faculties, but in fact are always present together in any act of willing or presentation.[27] The will, like the "I" generally, possesses three moments: pure indeterminacy (equivalent to the first premise of Fichte's *Wissenschaftslehre*, the "I" = "I"); differentiation, determination or opposition ("I" ≠ not-"I"); and singularity, introreflection or self-identity (which Fichte did not conceive of, since he remained a dualist).

The first moment of will simply designates the unity of self-consciousness, the fact that the "I" is not anything in particular since it can abstract from all content. Hegel associates this abstract identity with the volonté générale of Rousseau and the Terror as well as with German moral philosophy. The second moment, differentiation or determinacy, is equivalent to the self-diremption by which the "I" becomes actual. Identity is unthinkable without difference, just as a will is unthinkable unless it wills something. For Hegel, the point is to show that this "finitizing" of the pure will ("I" = "I") within a subject-object structure is part of its very concept, not something superadded.

The third moment of the will cannot be conceived by the understanding because it is "the true and speculative (and everything true, insofar as it has been comprehended, can only be thought speculatively)."[28] It is absolute negative activity or the true infinite. As singular, the "I" is identical to itself within its diremption into pure will and specific content. As such it is "actually nothing other than the concept itself."[29] In other words, the concept of the will is really the same as the concept as such, as defined in the *Logic*. Free will is not something simply given, a mode of *being*. It is instead a return-into-self from other-being (namely, its content).

The discrepancy between free will once as abstract, empty, and unactual self-identity and again as determinate content is the engine of development in the *Philosophy of Right*. As in the *Phenomenology*, the free will cannot be "satisfied" or truly self-identical until its moments are fully objectified. The concept qua subjective must be able to contemplate the concept in re as objective spirit. This is what Hegel calls "concrete freedom,"[30] and it expresses the same notion as universal self-consciousness: other-being (here the content or actualization of free will) must be thought of as expanding and deepening our identity, not limiting it. The free will exists only in its concept or implicitly (an sich) as long as it has not established, by externalizing itself, institutional structures within which it can be permanently actual.

In a more specific context, Hegel is certainly willing to grant that the first moment of the will, its capacity to abstract from all determination, is a sine qua non of freedom. But since an actual will requires that we do determine ourselves, the question inevitably arises: what shall be the content of our will? If, Hegel argues, the content is not itself rationalized, or brought into accord with the concept of freedom, then free will must degenerate into arbitrary choice or Willkür. Hegel even goes so far as to point out the relative justification of determinism, for, as he reads it, this doctrine merely confronts formal freedom with the necessity of choosing *some* content, some end not contained in its pure abstraction.

In a way, Hegel is simply restating Kant's argument that freedom can mean nothing but autonomy or obeying a self-imposed law. To the extent that natural impulses dictate the content of my will, I am acting heteronomously. But since the Kantian moral law lacks any definite content, it is as open to the criticisms of determinism as any other theory of abstract freedom.[31]

For this reason, Hegel adopts a quite different and highly original theory of the will's freedom. He argues that the more or less natural, idiosyncratic impulses which at first determine the will must be purged of their immediacy and become themselves ethical or sittlich. On this interpretation, man could no longer be understood as a dual being, irrevocably divided into abstract, arbitrary caprice confronting a chaos of amoral or immoral natural impulses. Instead, the free man would willingly and unreflectively do the right thing, because his inclinations would have been spiritualized and formed by objective ethical institutions. Just as we intuit a unity of form and content in a work of art, so too must freedom and nature be harmonized in the free, ethical individual:

> When I will what is rational, I don't act as a particular individual, but rather according to the concepts of ethics in general. In an ethical action I make the matter at issue the primary concern, not myself. But in doing something perverse, man makes his particularity especially noticeable. The rational is the highway which everyone travels and where no one is conspicuous. When great artists complete a work, one can say: It must be *thus* and not otherwise. This means that the artist's particularity has completely disappeared so that no *mannerism* appears in his work. . . . But the worse the artist is, the more he himself, in all his particularity and caprice, comes into view.[32]

Accordingly Hegel does not discern any contradiction between freedom and necessity, provided necessity is understood in a speculative sense and not as causality.[33] Precisely because the free man thinks and acts as spirit, and not as a finite, idiosyncratic self, he sees in the constraints of political and social existence only the objective expression of what he himself is, namely, the concept:

> The ethical man is conscious of the content of his action as necessary and valid in and for itself. But he suffers no attrition of his freedom on this account; rather this freedom acquires a content and becomes actual only by virtue of this consciousness, as distinct from caprice, a contentless and merely potential freedom. . . . In general it is man's supreme independence, to know himself as determined through and through by the absolute idea. Spinoza designated this consciousness and comportment as *amor intellectualis Dei*.[34]

However, the vision of the unity of oneself and other-being (in this case of the will and inclinations) is not easily attained. To Hegel, it requires not only a subjugation of our impulses, or even their harmonization with a view to happiness. Rather the free will must come to the stage of thinking of itself as free so that freedom, and not nature or happiness, may be its object. Only in this way is the will's content adequate to its form. Hence Hegel defines the "abstract concept of the idea of will" as "*the free will willing the free will*."[35]

If this definition is the abstract formula for the *Philosophy of Right*, we may still wonder how Hegel can avoid the theoretical and practical conclusions of Rousseau's volonté générale. After all, Rousseau could certainly argue that his own contract theory is based on a "free will willing itself." Yet it would be apparent now that there are at least three closely related, but distinct, differences between Rousseau's general will and Hegel's free will, differences that lie at the heart of Hegel's critique of the Enlightenment and liberal political philosophy.

First, as we saw earlier, Hegel insists upon the continuity of history. Freedom is at least as old as the Greek polis, and its seeming demise in the Roman Empire only succeeded in deepening it and extending it to all human beings. So for the free will to will itself it cannot make tabula rasa of existing institutions, whether in a revolution or in the figurative sense of constructing a contract theory on the basis of a state of nature. Since the free will is the free will of spirit, and since spirit is essentially historical, it cannot will itself and simultaneously repudiate the historical objectifications of past willing. The French Revolution with its attempt to ground all legitimacy on thought was the "nodal point" in a long development and not a hiatus in history or a thoroughgoing rejection of spirit's essential continuity.

Second, analysis has shown that "free will" does not mean simply the will's first moment, its empty self-identity or capacity to abstract from all definite content. Instead the will, as the practical aspect of the "I," has a specific structure which we know to be the concept. Thus if free will is to will itself, it must will the actuality of the concept. That is, it must will that reality have the same articulated identity-in-difference that is the hallmark of the free will in its subjective aspect, self-consciousness.

When we combine this principle with the premise of historical continuity, we can easily see the trend of Hegel's thought. The old European institutions such as hereditary monarchy, estates, and corporations cannot derive their legitimacy from historical continuity alone. This would violate the demand that the will think itself as free, or that the legitimacy of institutions be grounded upon thought. However, will as thought is not incompatible with the continued existence of traditional structures provided that this will should be concrete and speculative thought, and not Verstand. The old institutions, as emanations of historical spirit, need not be discarded but only reinterpreted as moments of the concept objectified in actuality.

Third, the struggle for recognition and its outcome, universal self-consciousness, sharply distinguish Hegel's theory of the state from all varieties of liberalism, including even Rousseau's version. In his Jena lectures, Hegel formulates this difference as a priority of the universal over singular wills:

> The universal will is the will of each and all, but as will it is absolute only in this self, the deed of the universal as a unity. The universal will must gather itself into this unity. It first has to constitute itself as universal out of the wills of individuals, so that the universal appears as the principle and element [this is the outcome of the discipline imposed by mastership; L. H.]. But on the other hand, *it* is what is primary and essential. The individuals have to make themselves out of its negation, through externalization and education. The universal is earlier than they are and it exists as absolute for them. But they are in no way absolute for it.[36]

Hegel believes that the priority of the universal over singular wills is obscured by Rousseau's theory, even though the latter does distinguish the volonté générale from the volonté de tous. The fiction of a contract, to which all individuals must consent *as* individuals, makes it appear as though political associations were only a compound, or as though "the will . . . as a will of the singular person in his idiosyncratic caprice ought to be the substantial basis and first principle."[37] Consistently enough, he rejects any derivation of right such as Rousseau's which would deny the assertion that right, and political association generally, flow from the "rational will, existing in and for itself" or from "*true* spirit."[38]

Since the universal (as true spirit, universal self-consciousness or will in-and-for-itself) is logically prior to singular wills, Hegel's political philosophy obviously does not need to concern itself with how a collection of individuals might be able to form a state, or even with the Rousseauian problem of how factions can be suppressed and the volonté générale be made to shine forth. What Hegel must accomplish is the demonstration of how an inchoate and amorphous universal will can be institutionalized and given an objective form commensurate with the modern principle of self-conscious freedom.

This demonstration will be equivalent, in the political sphere, to the transformation of substance into subject (the *Phenomenology*) or of being into the concept (the *Logic*). From the viewpoint of finite self-consciousness, the individuals will gradually come to understand their profound identity with one another. Their common life will become an increasingly manifest object of the will and consciousness. Simultaneously, from the perspective of spirit, "substance" will develop from an unconscious nexus of recognition into the self-conscious subject which it implicitly is, namely, the state in its narrow and specific sense.

Abstract Right

Hegel defines abstract right as the sphere in which the free will is still immediate, or in the form of being.[39] To elucidate his meaning, a comparison with the *Logic* may not be amiss. In both cases we begin with the postulate of an abstract self-identity that is supposedly capable of being thought without difference. Being is being, the free will is a free will, or as Hegel says, "still this being-within-oneself [*Insichsein*] which lacks an opposite."[40] But it is apparent that this "indeterminacy"—an identity not definitely distinguished from anything else—is determinate in its own way. In the *Logic*, being transforms itself into nonbeing or Nichts. In the *Philosophy of Right*, the indeterminacy of the will excludes an "external world which it finds in an immediate, preexisting form [vorfinden]".[41]

The hallmark of the sphere of being or immediacy is the rigid exclusivity of finite, determinate entities. This is expressed in the *Philosophy of Right* by the term "person." Each person is self-identical and excludes all others. Also, personality is rigidly opposed both to natural desires and to the world of objects it confronts. In this sense it is tantamount to the first moment of free will. However, Hegel is careful to distinguish the person as abstract self-identity from the appetitive consciousness that must still pass through a struggle for recognition.[42]

This distinction must be kept in mind because the "I" of personhood does exist in a continuum of mutual recognition. Even though each person is sharply distinct from all others, legal personality would be unthinkable if each person did not possess a formal, recognized status independent of his natural being, desires, and physical attributes. Hegel makes this point explicit when he suggests that legal persons, who appear to be "islands unto themselves," are in fact radically dependent on the law as such: "By means of the externalization of right, I am a pure person, but I am only such as the law. *My meant existence is the law, i.e., I wholly depend on it.*"[43] In fact, abstract right must eventually yield to other categories because it cannot give a satisfactory account of the deeper, more complex bonds of unity in society which words like personhood only imperfectly express.

The rigid self-identity of legal personality, its incapacity to include mediation or negativity, constitutes its most serious flaw. As Hegel says, "it is the highest expression of humanity to be a person, but in spite of this the mere abstraction of personality connotes scorn in its very expression."[44] As in the *Phenomenology*, the "mask" of personality is a superficial status that only enjoins us to be persons and respect other persons.[45] This leaves a welter of natural impulses and inclinations that supply the content of our will, insofar as we act only as persons (and not under the aegis of a higher category such as morality). Freedom thus has a very restricted scope and meaning within legal status. It is little more than the "negative freedom" of liberalism, in which we have a right to pursue our self-interest unmolested unless we violate the same right in another.

Still, Hegel is far from disparaging this sphere of personhood, despite its limitations. In fact, he contends that he has outdone even the Enlightenment in his defense of property rights. Against utilitarianism, he argues that private property should not be justified solely as an expedient means for satisfying our physical needs and instincts. Man is not, in respect to law, a merely biological being. He is first of all a *person* possessing free will. Thus private property must be justified as the actualization of free will, the empirical existence of legal personality.[46] To Hegel, private property is a necessary moment of free will, since abstract freedom (the "I" = "I") must become objective to itself in order to acquire actuality. In this respect, it is the first expression of reason in the *Philosophy of Right*.[47] By reason, Hegel means that the identity of being and thinking is present at least on a rudimentary level. The same negative activity of spirit that allows me to be a person at all sanctions the existence of property as the complement and counterpart of personality. Property, then, has the same significance in being or objectivity as personality does in respect to thinking or subjectivity. Hence property and personality are not contingently joined. They are inseparable because they are merely expressions of the very same concept in two different forms.

On the other hand, Hegel asserts that possession cannot be transformed into property simply by means of an individual appropriation (as is in some ways the case with Locke). To externalize my will into some object (or, for that matter, to "mix my labor" with it) and exclaim, "This is now mine," does not turn that object into private property except within a nexus of mutual recognition in which legal personality and property are already institutionalized. This is because the free will is essentially a continuum of free wills, not an expression of private, idiosyncratic desire. When I appropriate, I do so as a person, and personhood is not a "biological" status but an expression of objective spirit.

> Possession, in the whole of a people, comes to be in its individuality a universal. It remains the possession of this individual, but only insofar as it is posited as such through the universal consciousness, or insofar as in it everyone else equally possesses what is *his*, i.e., possession comes to be *property*. . . . The security of my possession is the security of everyone's possession; in my property, everyone has his property. My possession has obtained the form of consciousness. It is determined as my possession. But as property it is not related to me alone; rather it is universal.[48]

But in property ownership, the nexus of recognition is only indirectly apparent. What I own is a thing. Even though the adjective "mine" implies a relationship to other persons who acknowledge and support my rights as their own, I have not yet entered into a direct relationship to other persons. As on the more primitive level of self-consciousness, I need another self as my object to gain any insight into the full significance of my freedom. This is the logical function of contracts in the *Philosophy of Right*.

Just as in the case of property, contracts are a necessity of reason; they actualize the identity of being and thinking because they make objective and transparent the nexus of recognition within which we are persons and not contingent, empirical beings:

> Even if, in respect to the consciousness [of the contracting parties; L. H.], it is need, benevolence, utility, etc. that lead them to make contracts, still it is implicitly [an sich] reason, namely, the idea of the real [i.e., present in the will; L. H.] empirical existence of the free personality which leads them to do so. A contract presupposes that those who enter into it *recognize* each other as persons and property-owners. Since a contract is a relationship of objective spirit, the moment of recognition is already contained and presupposed by it.[49]

The very act of contracting involves the express consent of at least two wills, or more precisely the Willkür of two individuals since what they contract to do is not specified by the rational will. The rational will says only that contracts should exist, not what their content should be.

However, contractual agreement commits the parties to perform certain acts no matter what they might wish to do once the contract has been signed. Thus a contract represents what Hegel calls a "common will" [*gemeinsamer Wille*] which, even though its origin may be found in caprice, still binds the contracting parties. When both parties sign the contract it is complete and objective. The actual performance of its provisions is not subsequently a matter of merely moral obligation. By stipulating, the parties have in effect created a new will (the common will) that is different from and binding upon their private, subjective wills. And this new will can be the source of legitimate coercion against the party who tries to violate the terms of the agreement.[50]

Contracts are thus the first step toward the creation of an objective will, imbedded in institutions and relatively independent of individual caprice. In contractual agreement, we can see more specifically what Hegel means by a free will existing in and for itself, distinct from what we may will or desire at any given moment. However, contracts still represent only a common will, not a general or universal will, since they rest on the consent of each individual as an individual. For this reason Hegel contends that the category of contract may not legitimately be applied to institutions such as marriage and still less to the state.[51]

Because contracts involve a distinction between my will as a recognized legal person and as momentary caprice, they open up the possibility of wrong (Unrecht): "In the relationship between two immediate persons as such, their will is not only *implicitly identical* and posited *in common* [*gemeinsam*] by them *in* the contract, but also it is a *particular* will. . . . As a particular will *for itself, distinct* from the universal, it takes its stand against what is *implicitly* right, acting on the basis of caprice and the contingency of its own insight and volition. It is wrong [das Unrecht]."[52] Logically, the transition from contracts to wrong means that we have left behind the sphere of being and immediacy. Wrong is seeming or semblance (Schein),[53] a category belonging to the doctrine of essence in Hegel's *Logic*. The essence, "right in itself or the general will,"[54] must manifest itself in the particular wills of legal persons. That is, right is the identity or continuum of one self-consciousness and another, the nexus of mutual recognition, objective spirit. But human beings only exist as finite, as discrete and particular wills, so right cannot exist at all except through the will and action of specific legal persons. And this is tantamount to the statement that essence only is, insofar as it appears.

However, the difference between essence and appearance can (Hegel would say, must) be driven to the point where appearance no longer reveals essence but becomes detached from it and thereby negates it. This is another instance of dialectical reversal and is called "Schein" by Hegel: "Seeming is an empirical existence incommensurate to the essence. Here essence is divorced from itself in an empty fashion and posited in such a way that in each case [i.e., of essence itself and the seeming which was formerly its appearance; L. H.] difference exists as diversity [Verschiedenheit]."[55] The termination of this dialectic comes about when essence "recaptures" its own appearance (now become a seeming), infusing the latter with a more profound unity: "Seeming is hence something untrue which disappears by wanting to exist for itself. In its disappearance, essence has proved that it is essence, i.e., has proved its power over seeming."[56]

In the more limited context of the *Philosophy of Right*, the disjunction between essence and seeming means that the individual and private wills try to usurp the authority of right for themselves and in so doing negate its very core, which is the identity of self-consciousnesses, the freedom of one person in and through all others. In civil actions ("nonmalicious wrong"), the parties acknowledge the supremacy of right over individual will, but they attempt to bend the law to their own purposes by applying precedents and interpretations that support their respective cases. In fraud, the most obvious case of "seeming," individual will hides behind the smokescreen of formally correct legal procedures while actually subverting right. To the fraudulent will, right itself has become only a "seeming," while the individual will is the essence. Finally, in crime, right loses its universal character entirely and is, in effect, proclaimed to be nothing but the right of individual will. The complete negation of right (the detaching of individual appearance or seeming from its ground in essence) then evokes retribution on the part of the universal will in which it "proves its power over seeming" and restores the authority of right.

For Hegel, the ground of social unity (variously called right in itself, mutual recognition, and universal self-consciousness) must be brought to the forefront of human awareness. This cannot come about until universal and particular, essence and appearance are driven to antipodal positions (the inverted world). Crime performs this divisive function by evoking the power of society against the criminal. The legal persons come to realize that they are not merely property owners and contract makers, atomic individuals to whom law is simply a means for pursuing self-interest. This is so because the criminal takes the very principle of self-interest or individual will and carries it to its furthest extreme. As Hegel says, crime is a "retreat into individuality."[57] By absolutizing his particular will, the criminal simultaneously creates a general will (not merely a common will) over against him. Although this general will is still only "reactive" (toward the crime), and "negative" (posited by the wish to negate the crime), it anticipates the positive unity of the moral and ethical spheres.

Crime's role in defining and strengthening the underlying bonds of social unity becomes most apparent when we consider its relation to punishment. Hegel consistently makes the assertion that a crime is "void" (*nichtig*) and self-contradictory because it denies the existence of right as right.[58] To act rightfully means to respect others as persons, to accord them the same status that you yourself claim. But when a person acts wrongfully, he denies the very continuity or identity of self-conscious existence. He appears to claim a right which is his alone, an absurdity if the essence of right is necessarily social, or rooted in the formal identity and equality of legal persons. The criminal is alienated in the quite specific sense that he no longer recognizes in the other another self-consciousness, or the identity-in-difference which self-consciousness is.

Punishment, accordingly, only reasserts the fundamental continuity of free personality. The criminal learns that he cannot possibly act in a wholly arbitrary, idiosyncratic fashion as though his actions did not implicitly contain a universal principle: "A wrongful action is indeed a singular, irrational action. But because it has been performed by a rational being, it is something *rational* and universal, not of course in its content, but certainly in its *form*. Furthermore, it must be regarded as a principle or *law*. But at the same time it is, as a law, *only valid for the agent*, because only he recognizes it as such by his action, not the others."[59] Because his actions can be understood as implying a universal principle (generally speaking, it is coercion), then the criminal can justifiably be "subsumed" under his own law: "Thus the agent may be subsumed under the same mode of action that he adopted, and in this way equality, which had been compromised by him, is restored."[60]

Hegel's extraordinary view of crime and punishment provides a striking contrast to the various theories current in the Enlightenment. He insists that a careful distinction be made between just any "ill" (*Übel*) that befalls society and the specific nature of a crime. If crime is only an ill (like inflation, plagues, or earthquakes), then it makes no sense to inflict further ills on the criminal unless doing so would produce some foreseeable good for society. Accordingly, the various "enlightened" theories of punishment try to determine what exactly the good effects of punishment might be (such as deterrence and rehabilitation). Hegel rejects all these theories, despite their potential usefulness for setting specific penalties, because they do not answer the question "What does justice require?"[61]

In fact, there is a powerful current of Enlightenment thought whose naturalistic and empiricist bent tends to obscure what Hegel takes to be the essential issues surrounding right and justice. He assumes that concepts like "just" and "unjust" can have meaning only when they are applied to free, autonomous beings, because only the latter have a sense of the difference between acting for the sake of universal rules and acting exclusively in self-interested ways. A lion does not treat its prey unjustly since there is no nexus of mutual recognition, no sense of binding rules between predator and prey. But the criminal, however "beastly" his crimes may be, is still a rational being and a legal person, so he cannot truly will the abolition of right, because right expresses what he is *as* free and *as* rational. Thus punishment, far from inflicting further ills on the criminal, does him the honor of treating him as rational and free, making it plain to him that he cannot act as a singular, self-enclosed will: "The criminal is *honored* as a rational man to the extent that we regard him as having a *right* to his own punishment."[62] In other words, punishment is not intended to modify the criminal's or anyone else's behavior. It is a restoration of right.

There is no question that Hegel's theory of punishment comes close to institutionalizing vengeance. But Hegel distinguishes carefully between the retaliation of personal vengeance (as in a vendetta) and punishment as carried out by the community in an impersonal way. The latter he calls "retribution" (*Wiedervergeltung*). Vengeance as such degenerates into a "bad infinity" because retaliation carried out against the original perpetrator does not restore the equilibrium of an impersonal right, but instead appears as a new crime demanding further retaliation. This bad infinity only gives way to the true infinite when the original crime can be understood as the negation of an already existing and recognized legal order. The criminal in a modern state does not normally desire to avenge himself on the specific officers, judges and members of the jury who incarcerated him. He sees (or should see) that they are not acting as individuals in coercing him, but on behalf of the entire legal system as agents of "right in itself." Thus, punishment should not ordinarily evoke an endless chain of retaliation, since it is carried out under the aegis of an entire community whose members will it only as legal persons. Punishment in the context of modern systems of law takes the form of a negation of a negation, a restoration of right: "The deed of a crime is . . . not primary and positive such that punishment would be its negation; rather the deed is something negative so that punishment is only a negation of negation. Actual right is thus the annulment [Aufhebung] of what has injured it and, for this reason, it demonstrates its validity and proves itself to be a necessary, mediated existence."[63]

Hegel does his best to comprehend the retribution of criminal law on its own terms. He does not regard it as a residual category where (rational) civil law cannot properly be applied. Instead he considers the legal controversies of civil law a form of wrong in which the difference between universal and particular will has simply not yet reached the point of polar opposition. Crime and punishment are consequently not to be understood as throwbacks to prerational, primitive modes of thought. The intuition of social unity that is acquired mediately through punishment of the criminal actually gives freedom of will a deeper significance than it possessed when defined only in terms of property ownership and free contracts.

Moreover, by treating crime as an integral part of abstract right, Hegel is trying to indicate the limitations of the latter as a means of defining political associations. Since abstract right constitutes only a formal, superficial principle of unity among the legal persons, it is not hard to understand why many would want to take a "shortcut" to the acquisition of property. They are not deterred from crime by conscience and morality and still less by any unreflective sense of ethical unity (Sittlichkeit), for these aspects of political life are foreign to abstract right as such. Thus, abstract right cannot be regarded as the whole of the state, the very foundation upon which it is built (as is the case in most variants of liberalism). Rather it is a subordinate moment that must eventually yield to other dimensions of right that more clearly embody the concept of free will. The first of these Hegel entitles "morality," and it addresses itself to the inwardness (*Innerlichkeit*) of the will.

MORALITY

Abstract right began with the definition of free will as being or immediacy. In morality, the will is introreflected[64] and so corresponds roughly to the "doctrine of essence" in the *Logic*. As we recall, introreflection refers to cases where the same thing, event, or person is seen twice in the light of paired terms which obviously imply each other (as in cause and effect, ground and consequent, substance and accident). In the context of objective spirit, morality represents just such an introreflection because it encompasses deeds as such, in their external existence, and again insofar as they embody the subjectivity of the doer, e.g., as intention, purpose, or culpability.

Legal status had contained an ambiguity in the definition of free will because the legal person could easily imagine that there is no conflict between fulfilling his obligations to others and simultaneously actualizing his acquisitive inclinations in property and contracts. Crime precipitates a struggle between the universal and particular moments of will because the criminal acts as though only the latter were real and the former a mere Schein. Punishment reasserts the predominance of the universal by showing the criminal that he is *essentially* a social being, that he cannot act in a purely private way. He is first of all a person, and only on the basis of personality (which is right-in-itself or mutual recognition) may he realize his particularistic desires. Punishment as negation of negation thus makes personality as such—and not property, contracts, or any other external, more or less immediate reflections of personality—into the will's new object. This is the beginning of morality: "Henceforth the will has as its object its very *personality*, which was its sole mode of being in abstract right. The infinite subjectivity of freedom, thus become for-itself, constitutes the principle of the *moral standpoint*."[65]

In morality, there can be no illusion that the will's particularity and self-interested inclinations dovetail with its universal aspect, the sphere of its obligations to others. As a morally responsible individual (what Hegel calls a "subject" as distinct from a legal person), my duties to others go far deeper than a mere laissez-faire attitude. I must concern myself with the whole person and his well-being. I cannot be a moral subject simply by respecting the property of others and honoring my contractual obligations. In morality, the whole of my comportment comes under scrutiny, even where no laws regulate it. And simultaneously my inwardness becomes the focus of interest because a good act must not merely have beneficial consequences, it must also have a motive commensurate with these moral principles. Hegel sums up these distinctions by contrasting the "negative" freedom of abstract right with the "positive" relation between one will and another in morality:

> Apropos of formal right, I said that it only contains prohibitions and that a strictly rightful action thus has only a negative deter-

> mination in regard to the will of others. In the moral sphere, by contrast, the determination of my will in respect to the will of others is positive; that is, the subjective will, in whatever it effects, internalizes [*als ein Innerliches haben*] the will-in-itself. . . . the welfare of others is at issue, and this positive relationship cannot put in an appearance until the moral standpoint is attained.[66]

It should be readily apparent that "morality" in the *Philosophy of Right* roughly corresponds to the section on "spirit certain of itself" in the *Phenomenology*. Hegel addresses himself again to the inner world of Protestantism that had been given philosophical expression in the works of Kant and Fichte. Both Kant and Fichte insist upon the equation of morality and freedom, and Hegel never denies this equation. He merely asserts that morality (and hence freedom) remains an empty formalism as long as the will has not been comprehended as self-differentiating, capable of giving itself objective content. Therefore, any doctrine of natural right (such as Lockean empiricism or utilitarianism) which has not attained the standpoint of Kant's moral imperative cannot comprehend the modern state as an actualization of free will. Defined as a property owner, man must necessarily regard the state merely as a means to safeguard or further his private ends; for him the universal will exist for the sake of the particular. Only from the Kantian outlook does the universal (the moral law which is also the law of freedom) begin to acquire the status of an end in itself.

In Hegel's view, the deficiency of empiricist doctrines of natural right (and the importance of the moral standpoint) become apparent even when we examine certain legal issues. By and large, the empiricist tradition—roughly equivalent to "abstract right"—assumes that the act, not the man, is being judged by the law. This is indeed a corollary of the position that man's inner life is either inaccessible to scientific thought or else simply an illusion, as in the Humean doctrine that there is no such thing as a "self." But Hegel asks, what is an act? Must we not inquire into the inner state, the purposes of the actor, if we are to determine anything as simple, even, as legal culpability? Hegel pursues the complex issues involved in determining the nature of a person's act. On one level, we can distinguish the purpose (*Vorsatz*) of the act simply as its intended, foreseeable consequences. But in many cases we must also inquire into the intention (Absicht) of the agent in order to determine what he in fact meant to effect and even whether he knew the difference between right and wrong. The inner sphere of moral choice necessarily makes its appearance in any legal code that does not simply judge the agent by the consequences of his act but also inquires into the degree of culpability.

The problem of legal responsibility leads Hegel to consider motives, the general conditions of all action. Even though an act may be given the general designation of murder or arson, when we ask why the person did it, we are normally not satisfied with the explanation that he acted out of a desire to kill or to set fires. We assume that some specific interest or inclination led him to perform the deed. In other words, we assume that human actions are means to some end intended by the agent. Because the law must often take motives into account, the scope and meaning of intention is expanded and deepened. Now the whole of a person's life becomes an issue, because even the proximate motives of an action (e.g., a desire for wealth or fame) are themselves only a means to a more encompassing end, happiness or welfare (*Wohl*).

The gradual transition from purpose to happiness and welfare seems designed to show that right cannot be seen only in terms of procedural justice. It must ultimately take into account the welfare of the individual. But Hegel does not conclude, as a utilitarian would, that the whole purpose of right is to promote the happiness of all as individuals. Right has its source in free will, and specifically in a self-differentiating general or universal will. For this reason, the demands of right as right may conflict with the welfare of some or even many individuals.

For Hegel it is *the good* that represents the unity of right and welfare. It combines the principle of the will's freedom (the sphere of abstract right) with individual subjectivity, now developed to include private happiness. The good, as a moral-legal principle, has already appeared in Kant's attempt to reconcile the purely formal aspect of autonomy with individual well-being. But because we are still dealing with the introreflected sphere of morality, the good is not yet actual; it is seen as an "ought" which has not penetrated individual will to become a "second nature" of the latter (as will be the case in ethical life).

If liberalism, especially its Lockean variant, can be thought of as the political philosophy par excellence of abstract right, then it is certainly Fichte's theory of the state that plays that role for morality. We recall from chapter 1 that Fichte conceived of the "I" as subject-object, an identity which becomes for-itself only insofar as it is a finite "I" confronting a not-"I" that is also posited by the primary, nonobjectifiable "I." The Wissenschaftslehre consists mostly of a series of syntheses in which the finite "I" tries to reappropriate the sphere of not-"I" and, by so doing, become self-identical. Its main strategy is moral action (obedience to the the categorical imperative) in which the "I" exercises causality upon the not-"I."

As a corollary of Fichte's rigid opposition between "I" and not-"I," nature, both internal and external, appears as something to be dominated. Fichte allows us only two alternatives. Either nature tyrannizes over us, or vice versa. In his approach to natural right, this opposition sets the tone. Each person appears to every other in a twofold guise: as a rational being and again as mere matter, capable of being treated as a thing. The purpose of political association is to repress nature so far as this is possible, and such repression is contingent on each citizen's willingness to legislate the limitation of his own freedom.

Fichte is so concerned that nature might reassert its dominance over morality that he advocates the adoption of what we would call police-state measures. The state must not merely punish crime; it must try to forestall it by preventing situations from arising in which nature might get the better of the moral law. As Hegel says, the state applies the rules of discursive understanding, reasoning from consequences to possible causes, to the point where

> there is . . . simply no action in which the consistent understanding of this state could not calculate the possibility of harm to others. . . . In this ideal of the state there is no action, not even the slightest stirring, which must not necessarily be subjected to some law, put under immediate supervision and observed by the police and other governing officials. Thus, in a state set up in accordance with this principle, the police know pretty much where every citizen is at any hour of the day and what he is doing.[67]

When Hegel objects to this proto-totalitarian scheme, it is not primarily for the same reasons a liberal would. He is not concerned that the state as such is too powerful, or that it is exercising its authority in a way not commensurate with its presumed mandate to protect life and property. Rather, he fears that the consistent moral state would atomize its citizens and make any spontaneous ties among them impossible. Freedom is not limited by community but first made actual therein. The tyranny of the "I" over nature finds its logical extension in the tyranny of the state over the "modifiable matter" of its citizens. The peculiar failing of the moral state, as opposed to liberal abstract right, lies in its fanatical adherence to the moral law in all its ramifications, no matter what the consequences for individual and collective welfare.

"Moral tyranny" represents one horn of the dilemma inherent in the subjective idealism of Kant and Fichte. The other, which Hegel explores in the *Philosophy of Right*, is the empty formalism[68] of the moral law. Whether the moral standpoint appears in the guise of pure duty (as in Kant) or of conscience (the ultimate principle of Fichte's *Vocation of Man*), it cannot tell us concretely what the good is. Hegel here repeats many of the arguments he made in the *Phenomenology*. Any principle, he asserts, is compatible with the moral law, since the latter supposedly only requires that a principle be noncontradictory.

As in the *Phenomenology*, Hegel treats conscience (in its Fichtean form as a will that aims only at what is good in and for itself) as a higher principle than duty. Conscience can generate specific purposes because it knows intuitively that they are good. But conscience becomes ensnared in the perplexities of trying to decide whether its actions spring from a genuinely universal will or only from its particularity. As universal, it is good, while as particular it is evil. But conscience, as a form of self-consciousness generally, includes both moments within itself; good and evil are in fact inseparable from the very nature of human identity. "I" means both the absolute identity of all self-conscious beings and their discrete existence as specific, differentiated selves. And it is this ambiguity that finds expression in the problem of good and evil.

Up until now, there has been an increasing discrepancy between the will of individual persons (or moral subjects) and the system of obligations and imperatives that embodies their common life. It appears that the persons cannot assert their rights to individual choice and action without putting themselves at loggerheads with the whole community. For this reason, right was "inverted" into wrong, and conscientious adherence to the good turned out, with equal justification, to be stubborn, self-centered evil. This antagonism between universal and particular represents just another phase in the Cartesian dualism of being and thinking. And, as in Hegel's other works, the resolution of dualism requires that its elements be driven to their most extreme alienation. Thinking, here in the form of conscientious subjectivity, turns out to be an activity of judgment devoid of all concrete standards of good and evil. Being, now defined as the good, turns out to be equally abstract and empty, a substance not yet truly become subject. Once both aspects of the dualism of right have been purged of all contingent matter, they prove to be identical in their differentiation. This new identity is the basis of ethical life or Sittlichkeit:

> Since both of them [i.e., conscientious subjectivity and the good; L. H.] have been elevated to totalities in their own right, they become indeterminate entities which *ought* to be determined. But the integration of both relative totalities to absolute identity has already *implicitly* been accomplished. This very subjectivity of pure *self-certainty*, suspended in its own vanity, is *identical* with the *abstract universality* of the good. Thus the consequently *concrete* identity of good and subjective will, the truth of both, is *ethical life*.[69]

ETHICAL LIFE

8

THUS FAR, Hegel in the *Philosophy of Right* has merely tried to work out a speculative justification for the two great achievements of modern enlightened self-consciousness: the abstract right of French and English liberalism and the moral standpoint of Protestantism and critical philosophy. These represent respectively the immediate identity of universal will and individual self-interest and its diremption into a rigid opposition between the moral will and natural impulses. Only in ethical life do we encounter the *concept* of the will in its completeness. From now on, Hegel will discuss those aspects of our social and political life in which universality of will penetrates and mediates private existence. There is no longer a necessary antagonism between the requirements of a common, civilized life and the promptings of self-interest of the sort we encountered in morality. But neither does the universal appear as a means to safeguard the pursuit of private ends, as in abstract right.

Ethical Life in Its Speculative and Historical Significance

Taken in its speculative significance, ethical life can now be understood as the concept of unity of subjectivity and the good.[1] The "I" in its practical aspect of free will must be seen as activity or mediation through the institutions of a common life (the good). In order to acquire a concrete identity, the individual must internalize the pregiven roles and institutions of his own state, replacing his immediate natural inclinations with a "second nature" of civic loyalty. By the same token, the good is no longer a mere hazy ideal, an abstract substance identical to itself and incommensurate with its concrete manifestations in individual action. Rather, it must imbue and inform individual self-consciousness in order to be actual, i.e., to exist at all. For this reason Hegel remarks that the ethical is a "subjective disposition [Gesinnung], but oriented to right in-itself."[2] Ethical life is not a "third thing" outside individual self-consciousness and communal existence; rather, as the true infinite, it differentiates itself into subjective and objective aspects, each of which, when completely analyzed, yields the other.

The concept of modern ethical life represents an important aspect, though not the whole, of Hegel's "solution" to the disintegrative and dualistic features of the Enlightenment. The problem Hegel poses may be summarized in the following way. Ethical life in the ancient world depended upon the unself-conscious performance of duty and close identification with polis law on the part of ancient citizens. But the modern Enlightenment is, in its very essence, a movement toward self-consciousness and critical thought. To be "enlightened" means at a minimum no longer to take at face value traditional patterns of authority, but to judge for oneself and act on the basis of one's own rightly understood self-interest. How then can ethical life be possible in the modern world? Can it be conceived in such a way that it would include, and not suppress, modern subjectivity?

Hegel's solution to the ethical life problem depends very much on the philosophic categories through which he analyzes it. In his view, it is one more facet of the global project of self-consciousness to know itself, i.e., to find an adequate external embodiment or reflection of its own peculiar nature. Now we have already noted that self-consciousness has the same structure of identity-in-difference as the concept; indeed the concept is a paradigm that Hegel derived from the experiential referent of self-consciousness. According to Hegel, then, the self should be "satisfied" and reconciled to its social and political environment when the latter displays the full development of the concept in re. Political reality must perfectly display the moments of (immediate) identity, difference, and return-into-self that are the defining characteristics of the "I," free will, and the concept. Thus ethical life, in the modern state, must consist of articulations (institutions) that embody the concept and in which the individual can therefore discover himself and achieve satisfaction.[3]

It is crucial to see what Hegel has actually gained by introducing the concept of ethical life at this juncture. From now on, ethical issues no longer focus on the individual as an individual. Rather, they imply a relationship between him and the institutions of the state. The science of ethics as morality, strictly speaking, has been transcended, since the individual can no longer fancy himself the ultimate arbiter of moral decisions. He cannot ask "What should I do?" and expect an answer whose content flows from pure reason, utility, or any other "abstract" principle.

Instead, the *concept* of free will must generate a series of institutions and laws that allow the individual to discover and intuit his very nature (the concept) in actual states. To retreat from these actualizations of free will into the ultimately arbitrary and abstract standpoint of morality—i.e., ethics from an individual perspective—would amount to a retrogression, a loss of freedom. One would have mistaken the empty, undifferentiated identity of the "I" (its "first moment" in the *Philosophy of Right*) for the "I" in its totality as a self-differentiating or negative activity that defines itself in and through otherness. Thus the locus of ethical concern shifts from subjective to objective institutions.[4]

What Hegel neglects to consider in his portrayal of ethical life is the dimension of political or public freedom that did so much to create an identity of individual and collective purpose in the ancient polis. His model of Greek ethical life is borrowed from Plato's *Republic*, of which he remarks: "Plato has in fact portrayed Greek ethical life according to its substantial mode of being. Greek political life constitutes the true content of the Platonic *Republic*."[5] By treating the *Republic* as the definitive statement of Sittlichkeit, it is easy for Hegel to represent his own version of the modern state as a paradise of subjective freedom. He attacks Platonic ethical life for trying to establish an immediate unity of individual and universal, for example in the prohibition of family life and private property among the guardians and the assignment of individuals to classes regardless of their own preferences.[6] He insists that a modern state must allow the private sphere to flourish so that universal ends will be reached only by way of mediation through subjective will and intentions. But he consistently restricts the exercise of such subjective choice to private matters. When it comes to affairs of state, public life as such, Hegel is always adamant that the individual may not participate in it as an individual, but only through various mediate agencies.

The question must therefore be asked: can subjective freedom ever be made compatible with Sittlichkeit if the individual cannot exercise this freedom in a public forum? Or, to put this differently, is it not possible that the disintegrative tendencies of enlightenment have their root precisely in the fragmentation and functionalization of human life? Where the individual cannot act as a whole person and accept responsibility for the entirety of public life, how can he be expected to regard political institutions as an actualization of his free will? The concept, Hegel's most crucial category, expresses a perfect identity of universal and particular, in this case of public life and individual will. But such an identity would not seem to be present so long as the conscious volition of the individual is directed only toward limited, private ends devoid of political significance.

The difficulties of Hegel's organic or Platonic interpretation of ethical life surface immediately when one considers its broad outlines. We find the family as an institution of immediate ethical unity and the state as its rational and conscious moment. But sandwiched in between these two (roughly equivalent to Aristotle's *oikos* and *polis*) we find civil society, an element alien to the traditional *philosophia practica*, at least in the form and meaning given to it by Hegel. Hegel clearly wants to find a place, albeit a subordinate one, for the modern system of labor and production (as well as its demands for subjective freedom) within a reinterpreted ethical life. But civil society poses intractable problems for any such facile disposition. It is above all a dynamic system constantly threatening to engulf the family at its base and the state at its apex. Hegel must try to demonstrate the possibility—indeed the necessity—for civil society to stay within its boundaries and avoid encroaching on the other moments of ethical life.

The Family

Hegel defines the family as an association based on love rather than production. It is the immediate and natural moment of ethical life because the affinity of its members for one another depends on natural affection and blood ties rather than on any explicit system of rights and duties. The family does have an objective existence in the "family fortune" (*das Vermögen*) and in this respect functions as a legal person. But internally, it is an ethical institution that imposes responsibilities on its members transcending not only abstract right, but even moral obligation.

Hegel attributes extraordinary importance to the family. For him, it is the one institution that helps to form and educate (bilden) the individual to lead a universal, ethical life. As family members, individuals learn that freedom is not incompatible with the relinquishing of rigid, exclusive self-identity, and that one's self-limitation in an ethical community can signalize a broadening and deepening of one's identity. In terms of speculative philosophy, they come to realize that the "I" is not merely abstract identity but an activity of self-externalization and return-into-self: "In love, an individual has the consciousness of himself in the consciousness of the other. He has externalized himself and in this mutual externalization has gained possession of himself."[7] Consequently, the state must acknowledge its enormous debt to the family, since the latter provides it with ethical citizens rather than simply persons.

Because of the family's importance in combatting atomization, Hegel consistently criticizes legal philosophies that portray it as a contract (e.g., Kant's Rechtslehre) as well as the Roman law tradition that treats wife and children as a husband's chattels. In neither case is the special ethical character of the family accorded adequate recognition. But the family has never been immune from pressure exerted by civil society and enlightenment in general. Hegel's attempts to justify and safeguard its special position appear in retrospect to have been relatively futile. For example, he offers arguments in support of arranged marriages (in some cases), advocates tough restrictions on divorce, and insists on confining women to hearth and home. Yet once marriage and family life have been understood as love relationships, these retrictions on voluntary choice appear anachronistic and even contradictory. The principle of subjective freedom must eventually penetrate the family too and transform it into the relatively loose association it has increasingly become. The point, of course, is not to indict Hegel for having failed to foresee future developments. Rather, one wonders why Hegel thought that an institution already so deeply affected by social change could be arrested in midcourse and frozen into a pattern partly based upon voluntary, emotional affinity and partly upon traditional or legal "authoritarian" elements. It would have been more in keeping with Hegel's philosophical principles to portray the tension between romantic love aspirations and the demands of objective ethical life.

In philosophical terms the family, as immediate ethical unity, must yield to civil society because only the latter can provide the individual with his identity as a specific person. Civil society supersedes the family because it has taken over so many of the family's traditional economic and "welfare" functions, thereby reducing it to its substantial basis in love alone. Hegel summarizes the eclipse of the family by civil society in a perspicacious and oft-quoted passage: "Of course, the family must make sure that the individual has bread on his table. But in civil society it is a subordinate moment and only lays the foundation. Its effective competence is not as encompassing as it once was. Civil society is instead the enormous power which draws man to itself and demands of him that he work for it, that he owe his whole existence to it, and that his actions should all be mediated through it."[8] In short, the individual is now the "son of *civil society*."[9]

Civil Society

Civil society for Hegel is the sphere of difference.[10] The will, as the practical side of self-consciousness, is not only immediate identity, but also self-differentiation. Of course, the will intended here is not merely individual human will, but the will "in itself," which is refracted into a series of finite wills. The immediate and natural identity of self-consciousness, objectified in the family whose members are not discrete persons, gives way to the sphere of difference in which the individual more or less consciously pursues his private ends, thereby acquiring a definite personal identity. The "substantial" identity of will or consciousness, however, does not vanish altogether; instead it is henceforth mediated through the various systems of mutual interdependence that make up the subject matter of Hegel's section on civil society.

But Hegel has yet another reason for considering civil society the sphere of difference. It acts to differentiate sharply and clearly, for the first time in history, the moments of the idea of ethical life. Hegel's reading of modern political economy convinced him that the medieval idea of society as a household ruled by a king combined in one notion elements that had in reality begun to diverge. The expansion of the market economy created a system of interactions among private individuals based mainly on contracts and exchange. At the same time, this new, apolitical civil society gave rise to the state in its specifically modern form as an institution designed to regulate and control the activities of civil society. In other words, state and civil society in their modern meanings presuppose and imply each other (they are "introreflected" in Hegelian parlance) because they are differentiae of the very same activity of distinction and separation. Civil society precipitates the differentiation of itself from the state (and also the family), thereby displaying the moments of the ethical idea in their full clarity and distinctness. The modern citizen alone can find all the moments of his ethical nature embodied in actuality because only now have his public, private, and domestic lives been completely distinguished.

Hegel's discussion of civil society here recalls to mind an issue that we considered earlier (see chapter 5): the historical significance of the French Revolution. In the *Phenomenology* Hegel stressed principally the "negative work" of the Revolution, its destruction of the old patterns of authority and social organization. But now, from the viewpoint of the *Philosophy of Right*, we can attain a different perspective on the whole matter. Essentially, the Revolution performed a positive, historically necessary operation; it separated civil society from the state, assigning to each its proper sphere and function. From now on the state would be freed from its patrimonial and particularistic feudal remnants. It could become a true republic, a *res publica* embodying the general will of the citizenry. Civil society, on the other hand, could be emancipated from a condition in which there was not as yet a clear dividing line between the king's private coffers and the economic resources of his realm, or between the feudal estate and the individual holdings of its tenants. Thus the Revolution brought to fruition a long development that culminated in the full explication of the moments of ethical life. The thought of the modern Enlightenment only appears to be ahistorical. In fact, its preoccupation with abstract rights, states of nature, and utility actually reflected a profound (but incomplete) insight into a thoroughgoing historical transformation of man and society. Hegel points out that "man," as a distinct object of our perceptions, first appears in modern civil society.[11] We can now form an idea of the abstraction "man" because, as a member of civil society, man is finally distinct from estates, family, occupation, and whatever other institutions or roles might claim his loyalty and define his identity.

Even though we can readily appreciate the importance of civil society, as a sphere of difference, in elaborating the moments of ethical life, we must still ask why civil society itself is ethical. Upon a cursory examination, the characteristic attitude of the bourgeois appears anything but ethical: "In civil society, each individual is his own purpose. Nothing else counts for him."[12] Moreover, Hegel portrays the transition from family life to civil society as a breakdown of Sittlichkeit: "However, in the following stage [i.e., civil society; L. H.], we can see the loss of genuine ethical life and substantial unity: the family dissolves and the members relate themselves to each other as independent units, while the only bond holding them together is mutual need."[13]

Yet Hegel soon retracts his indictment of civil society, arguing that ethical unity only seems to be absent from it.[14] This seeming arises because civil society separates universal and particular after the fashion of Adam Smith's "invisible hand." The universal (the common interest) is achieved through the mediation of thousands of self-interested transactions. Thus civil society does not merely rest upon self-interest. The universal is likewise essential to it, a fact that leads Hegel to broaden the concept of civil society far beyond the limits envisaged in English political economy:

> *One* of the principles of civil society is the concrete person who makes himself into his own end *qua particular*, as an ensemble of needs and a mélange of natural necessity and caprice. But the particular person [figures in civil society] as essentially *related* to other such particulars so that each satisfies himself and advances his claims to personal worth through the *mediation* of the others. And at the same time he does so purely and simply through the mediation of the form of *universality, the other principle* of civil society.[15]

The peculiar characteristic of life in civil society is thus the necessary illusion that we are entirely independent and pursuing ends of benefit only to ourselves, while in fact we are entirely dependent on the universal system of production and exchange. In Hegelian terms, one could say that ethical life is present in the whole system, but not present from the standpoint of finite self-consciousness. From the latter perspective, relationships within bourgeois society are contingent and accidental, and other persons remain quite external to us. The universal, the whole, and the ethical recede behind a vast field of finite relations. To the extent that civil society furnishes us the categories for thinking about political life, we necessarily interpret the state as a means to insure private welfare and security: "One can regard this system for now as the *external state*—a state based upon *physical necessity and the understanding* [*ein Not-und Verstandesstaat*]."[16] Civil society is thus the real ground of liberal and utilitarian political thought whose doctrines employ the categories of abstract right.

Particular interest first appears within civil society as *need* that must be satisfied by means of objects produced by the labor of others. This dependence gives rise to a "system of needs" in which not only the satisfaction of needs but their very nature depends on the possibilities of social production. The diversification and refinement of needs does not, as Rousseau had argued in his *Discourse on Inequality*, signify a loss of freedom. Rather it liberates man from his merely brutal tastes and wants, helping to acculturate him and provide him with a social existence. However, the system of needs degenerates into a bad infinity since there is no inherent limit to the quantity and quality of things men need. Civil society's system of needs liberates man from his merely natural existence, but in providing luxury it inflicts upon him an equally infinite increase in "dependence and want."[17]

The multiplication of needs simultaneously evokes a more and more complex division of labor. Eventually the immediate relationship between individual labor and needs is almost completely effaced. A worker produces not for his own needs, but, as we would say today, for the market: "Universal labor is . . . a *division of labor*, it is labor-saving. . . . Hence each individual, because he is an individual, labors for *one* need. The content of his labor goes beyond *his* needs. He labors for the needs of many, and everyone else does likewise."[18]

It is in the modern labor system that the problem of ethical life becomes especially acute. On one hand, the division of labor is a necessary and rational element in civil society. It promotes practical training and the acquisition of skills on the part of the worker. Moreover, from the standpoint of speculative philosophy, it is an essential moment in the development of self-consciousness toward spirit. As we saw in the dialectic of master and servant, labor initiates a process in which man, by making himself into a thing, arrives at an intuition of himself as negative activity. Even though labor is originally directed toward nature (its transformation and subjugation for the sake of natural, physical needs), it has a spiritual function. It is a "way of spirit," "not an instinct but a rational quality."[19] In other words, even though its origins may be found in the physical needs of man, labor simultaneously transforms human self-consciousness. Also, it infuses human life with universality, since the system of needs, the division of labor, and the market economy all conspire to spin a web of tight mutual interdependence (the universal in civil society) that carries man far beyond any simple, natural determination.

On the other hand, the modern division of labor entails consequences that deeply disturbed Hegel because they threatened the entire identification of objective ethical life (institutional articulation according to the concept) with subjective ethical attitudes, which is the very essence of Sittlichkeit. The core of the problem is the one-sidedness and abstractness of labor and its increasingly repetitive, mechanical character. There is a disparity between the totality which ethical life is intended to represent and the fragmentation and one-sidedness of the individual brought on and intensified by the division of labor:

> But through the abstraction of his labor [man] . . . becomes mechanical, enervated [*abgestumpft*], spiritless. The spiritual element, this fulfilled self-conscious life, becomes an empty doing. The capacity of a self consists in the rich compass of its activity. But now this is lost. Man can freely leave some labor to the machine; but thereby his own doing becomes all the more formal. His truncated [abgestumpft] labor limits him to one point, and his labor is all the more perfect the more one-sided it is.[20]

> Labor becomes all the more dead, it comes to be machine labor, the skill of the individual becomes the more infinitely limited, and the consciousness of the factory worker declines to the last extreme of dullness.[21]

Difference, the philosophical principle of civil society, is driven to the point of complete fragmentation in the modern labor system. Far from acquiring a richer, more encompassing identity in the activity of laboring, the worker suffers a loss of himself. The wealth and progress of civil society thus stem not simply from mediation through subjective freedom and particular ends; instead they are acquired at the expense of individual integrity. The concept would require that the wholeness of ethical life be mediated through individuals who are each a totality in their own right. But this is not the case under modern conditions where totality (the universal system of production and need) rests upon individual fragmentation.

Hegel is not unaware of these difficulties, but he seeks their resolution in the self-organizing capacity of civil society, a most unusual and problematic step. He insists from the outset that universality (here the integration of particularity into at least a relative totality) is as much a determining feature of civil society as private interest. Accordingly, he devotes the remainder of his discussion of civil society to the elaboration of articulations and organizational forms designed to make the universal a conscious object and hence to pave the way for the state. In other words, Hegel believes that civil society possesses something like a self-corrective force, or even telos, always working to counteract its atomizing, disintegrative tendencies.

Consequently, Hegel's concept of civil society begins to diverge from the descriptions of it found in political economy and liberal philosophy. Instead of treating it solely as a contractual nexus based upon the market, Hegel discovers in civil society the outlines of a common life, anticipations of the state. It is, in the final analysis, a detached, only apparently independent moment that must somehow return into the ethical matrix from which it had emerged.[22] The issues of production and distribution first occasion the coalescence of the atomized members of civil society into distinct spheres. Civil society's labor system generates wealth in general ("das Vermögen," a word Hegel uses in roughly the same sense as Smith's "wealth" of nations), which must somehow be allocated to individuals. This distribution takes place through estates that in addition assume responsibility for specific modes of production. Hegel uses the term "estate" (*Stand*) to indicate that the organization of production and distribution implicitly contains elements transcending economics per se. In estates, civil society is already implicitly political or ethical. The estates have a definite, recognized status within the state.[23]

Hegel's estates recapitulate the larger tripartite scheme of ethical life. The agricultural estate resembles the family in its immediate relationship to nature and its attitude of "trust." The reflecting or business estate (with three subdivisions of its own) represents civil society in its narrow meaning of a system of production and exchange. Finally, the universal class (civil servants) is eo ipso political since its members are state officials. There are at least two points worthy of note in Hegel's account of estates. First, we see again that civil society for Hegel means more than simply the market economy, as the case of the "universal estate" clearly shows. Second, as in his discussion of the family, Hegel fails completely to take account of the dynamic quality of civil society.

He distinguishes the agricultural estate from the business class by means of qualities that, even in his time, were becoming obsolete. Civil society cannot help but invade agriculture and transform lords and peasants into entrepreneurs and laborers precisely because its system of needs and production will draw the manor into the modern economic system. Hegel depicts agriculture in patriarchal, quasi-feudal terms, asserting that its "actual" character is a simple attitude of trust in God, nature's bounty, and the lord of the manor. This is rather astonishing in view of scattered remarks that indicate Hegel's recognition that agriculture was already big business.[24] It is also disturbing because it implies the absorption of the individual into his social function to the extent that he is not even a "self" any more.[25] Hegel seems to jettison the principles of subjective freedom that he always claimed to champion. His discussion of agriculture shows that he has not really reconciled ethical life and enlightenment, but merely allocated them to different estates.

Problems are likewise inherent in any neat division between state officials and the business and agricultural estates. Hegel is correct in insisting that the "private vices, public virtues" argument cannot reasonably be applied to the state. The latter probably could not maintain itself as a state (rather than as, say, a giant protection racket) without officials willing to curb their acquisitive impulses for the sake of the "universal." On the other hand, it is not so obvious that civil servants can maintain themselves as an exclusive estate with special privileges, esprit de corps, and a distinctive life style against the leveling and homogenizing tendencies of civil society. Again it seems that Hegel is trying to conjure up and stabilize "articulations" by fiat, rather than by scrutinizing the developmental tendencies of civil society itself.

From estates, Hegel turns to more explicit forms of self-organization in civil society. In all these—the administration of justice, the police, and the corporations—we will note that the universal has become an increasingly conscious object of will. Indeed, the dividing line between state and society is not immediately obvious in any of these administrative organs since all of them exercise political functions.

In his section on the court system, Hegel argues forcefully in favor of a written, codified law, public judicial proceedings, and jury trials. From a speculative viewpoint, the meaning of these institutions can be traced back to the issues we encountered in crime and punishment (cf. chapter 7). There, Hegel made the point that the criminal was simply being compelled to acknowledge his universal will as paramount. He was supposed to see that his punishment was an externalized version of himself—his own action—so that the punishment would no longer seem to be an alien "other" to his will. The rational and public legal proceedings that Hegel now advocates are an extension of the same principle. Ethical life requires that the individual identify himself with the institutions that regulate his conduct. But, in the case of justice, he can feel such affinity only if he knows what the law is and knows that it is administered fairly. Unwritten laws, star chambers, and unlimited judicial discretion turn the law into an inscrutable, alien power that one can only submit to but not really comprehend.

Hegel had maintained previously (cf. chapter 7: "Morality") that the good is a unity of right and welfare. Now he reintroduces that argument to show why right alone (which acquires empirical existence or Dasein in the courts) is incapable of actualizing the good within civil society. Right considers only the abstract question of justice. The judge in principle decides only whether a given particular case ought to be subsumed under a general rule of right. In order to make that decision he must ignore the character and life circumstances of the parties to a legal action. Nevertheless, since the good, in order to become actual within ethical life, requires that the welfare of the individual also be considered, other institutions are necessary to supplement the administration of justice. In this context, Hegel intends to revive his criticism of Fichte, as discussed above, for the latter's supposed endorsement of the maxim "*Fiat justitia, pereat mundus*."

The first of the institutions designed to promote individual welfare in civil society is the police. Hegel does not mean primarily the internal armies deployed by present-day states and municipalities. Rather he is thinking of those more general "police powers" (including consumer protection, public works, health agencies, a system of public education, and poor relief) that permit the state to exercise coercion against individuals when the public interest requires it. The idea behind Hegel's *Polizei* seems to be this: civil society treats individuals as legal persons who have a right to complete discretion and independence in their private affairs so long as they do not violate this same right in others. But this legalistic viewpoint, for all its merit, overlooks the degree to which the "system of needs" has rendered the individual dependent upon the society as a whole and indeed helpless in the face of impersonal market forces. Thus, some institutions have to be established that will consciously promote the universal when it simply cannot be actualized through the interplay of self-interested motivations.

It is the problem of poverty that evokes the most concern and perplexity on Hegel's part. Here we find his famous assertion that "despite its *excess of riches*, civil society is *not rich enough*, i.e., the wealth it has been singularly able to accumulate does not suffice to control the excess of poverty and the creation of a rabble."[26] The problem of poverty is especially intractable in modern societies for two reasons. First, if the state tries to alleviate it by creating jobs for the unemployed, then the crisis of overproduction that led to unemployment in the first place will only be worsened. On the other hand, if some sort of public subsidies for the poor are approved, then the state will be violating the very principle of civil society, the equation between work and subsistence. But even more serious, in Hegel's view, would be the loss of self-esteem and a sense of independence on the part of the recipients of poor relief as they began to develop vested rights in their subsidies. They would become something like wards of the state and yet resent their dependency and relative helplessness. This is the characteristic attitude, in Hegel's view, of a "rabble":

> Poverty in itself does not lead to the creation of a rabble. The latter only comes into being by virtue of a certain mentality which is connected to poverty, an inner outrage against the rich, society, the government, etc. . . . Thus there is born in the rabble the evil of lacking enough self-respect to have worked for its own subsistence and yet at the same time of claiming to receive subsistence as its right. No man can assert his rights against nature, but in society poverty immediately takes on the form of a wrong done to this or that class. The important issue of how poverty might be alleviated particularly torments and unsettles modern societies.[27]

The political implications of poverty worry Hegel greatly. He fears it will drive a wedge between citizens and undermine the ethical foundations of the state. Hegel was so strongly influenced by liberal political economy that he could not conceive of a solution to the poverty problem which would not eventually throttle the wealth-producing capacities of civil society. But if one cannot abolish the curse of poverty, at least one can make it bearable by helping the individual actualize his ethical nature in a well-organized state.

The police powers described by Hegel could not in and of themselves do much about poverty, much less check the disintegrative tendencies of civil society. The most they could accomplish would be to assist individuals or groups victimized by the random shifts in economic forces. For this reason Hegel calls the police "an external order"[28] and a merely "relative unification" of the universal and subjective particularity.[29] The expression "external order" means that police actions do not correspond to or embody a clear-cut rational principle with which citizens could identify. Police actions involve individual discretion and more or less arbitrary decisions that do not possess the immanent rationality (in Hegel's sense) of Sittlichkeit, but rather display the character of the "*infinity of the understanding*."[30]

Thus the individual cannot identify himself with the police; instead the latter is likely to acquire the "odium"[31] of being an arbitrary and oppressive meddler in the life of the individual. Furthermore, the police authority constitutes only a relative unification of universal and particular precisely because its power is exercised in a contingent manner and does not aim at integrating the whole person, the totality of his existence, into an ethical unity that is informed by universal ends. It is the corporation alone that can accomplish this latter purpose, albeit in a limited way.

The corporation is the only institution of civil society besides estates upon which Hegel unqualifiedly bestows the epithet "sittlich." Ethical life, previously lost in the myriad finite and self-interested transactions of civil society, "*returns* into civil society as an *immanent* principle; this constitutes the determination of the *corporation*."[32] We can understand the position of corporations most clearly if we see them as Hegel's solution to the problem of the second, business estate, i.e., the special domain of civil society in its modern sense as a market economy: "The concrete universal is an immediate living experience for the *agricultural estate* in the substantiality of its family life and closeness to nature. The *universal estate* has the universal explicitly as its purpose and basis in its very vocation. The mean term between them, the business estate, is essentially oriented toward the *particular* and for this reason the corporation is especially appropriate to this estate."[33]

Corporations can help check the division of civil society into hostile classes in a number of ways. First they can, to some extent, protect the individual against the contingencies of the market and, of course, teach him a skill he can use to earn a living. But even more important, they can impart a code of honor based upon one's estate (*Standesehre*) that counteracts the influence of amorphous public opinion. In Hegel's view, private accumulation of wealth in itself is not so galling to the have-nots as is its display in what Veblen was later to call "conspicuous consumption." But the latter is a direct result of a success ethic that equates an extravagant life style with personal status and accomplishment. If, however, the individual belongs to a recognized corporation, he will already have a stable, respected status in his community. His Standesehre will dictate a life style in conformity with the code of his corporation and remove the temptation for flashy display appropriate only in an anonymous mass society where recognition cannot be obtained in any other way.[34]

Corporations also take some of the sting and humiliation out of poverty. However poor a tradesman might become, the honor and recognition of corporation membership, in Hegel's opinion, prevent him from falling into the "rabble mentality" discussed above. Moreover, the sense of mutual responsibility that corporations instill leads Hegel to believe that the wealthier members would be willing to help support the poorer ones, especially since the former should feel no need of extravagant displays and luxurious living. Generally, the corporation is designed to eliminate the sort of patron-client relationship typified by Rameau's nephew and indeed by all of pre-Revolutionary France: "In the corporation aid received by the impoverished loses its contingent character and also the humiliating overtones which are unjustly associated with it. Likewise, wealth, dispensed out of a sense of duty toward one's association, no longer entails arrogance on the part of the wealthy man nor does it excite envy in the recipient."[35]

But it is the political role of the corporations that above all else lends them an ethical character. Hegel emphasizes the crucial function of the corporation in giving the ordinary person a sense of responsibility for affairs transcending the narrow concerns of private welfare:

> In our modern states, citizens have only a limited share in the universal affairs of state. But it is necessary to grant to the ethical man a universal activity apart from his private ends. This universal, which the modern state does not always provide him, he finds in the corporation. We saw before that the individual in civil society by taking care of himself also acts in others' behalf. But this unconscious necessity is not enough. It only becomes a conscious and thoughtful ethical life within the corporation.[36]

At last we come upon a tacit admission by Hegel that ethical life goes beyond the essentially Platonic identification of the individual with his social function. Hegel concedes that the individual must somehow direct his attention away from himself and focus upon matters of universal concern. But instead of expanding this insight into more general conclusions about the relationship between ethical life and public freedom, Hegel limits such universal activities to the internal affairs of corporations. Unlike Tocqueville, who regards corps intermédiares as means of developing a taste for liberty and the knowledge of how to exercise it in a larger arena, Hegel practically restricts civic participation to these bodies alone. And even here, he adds that corporations must be subject to the "higher supervision of the state."[37]

When one surveys Hegel's account of family and civil society in its entirety, the overwhelming impression arises that he has come nowhere near reconciling ethical life and subjective freedom. Instead of a true synthesis between Sittlichkeit and enlightenment, Hegel presents us with a scheme very suggestive of the more modern *Gemeinschaft-Gesellschaft* dichotomy. He makes it seem as though unconscious submersion in a group were the only alternative to the individual's isolation as an abstract Cartesian ego without any concrete ties to others except physical need, utility, and self-seeking. In this case, Hegel's theory of freedom and self-consciousness is better than its application to the circumstances of civil society. However, we cannot pass judgment on Hegel's project in the *Philosophy of Right* until we see what he has to say about the state, an institution in which freedom acquires an overly political dimension.

The State

To begin with, the state is a specific institution, separate from the family and civil society, that possesses its own internal structure (the internal form of right), carries on foreign policy and war, and has a definite role in world history. However, the state is not simply identical to the objective institutions that constitute it, what we in America would call the government. Hegel says it is the "*rational* in and for itself."[38] By this he means that it is an instance of the identity of being and thinking. It therefore encompasses not only objective institutions, but also the attitudes of its citizens toward those institutions (something like what political scientists call "political culture"). As the ethical institution par excellence, the state represents the unity in difference of subjective will and objective "articulations" of political life.

In respect to its origin, Hegel says that the state has a twofold ethical root in the family and the corporation.[39] In other words, the "elements" that enter into the composition of the state are already ethical. The state does not arise in any arbitrary fashion (e.g., in a contract) out of civil society. Rather, civil society gradually takes on an increasingly organized and articulated character of its own accord until it reproduces the ethical unity typical of the family and the corporations in their "estate-honor."

From this perspective, the state may be interpreted with equal justification as the logical ground and origin of the family and civil society even though these precede it in the order of development.[40] The development of civil society makes possible the emergence of the *modern* state with its characteristic division between private and public spheres by attacking and undermining the premodern state's patrimonial character. Yet the state as a totality of all spheres of civic life precedes civil society both logically and historically. The state simply "diremptsˮ itself into civil society and the (nuclear) family, thus giving itself, qua totality, a more highly developed and articulated character. It is both a moment of the whole (in its capacity as government) and the whole itself (as the universal present in family and civil society).

The primacy of the state over all other moments of ethical, moral, and legal existence has profound consequences. Hegel can demonstrate that the selfish "natural" men inhabiting civil society in liberal political philosophy are impoverished and shadowy abstractions who possess concrete existence only as members of the state. The state embodies the determination of individuals to transcend their narrow self-interest and lead a "universal life"[41] to a much greater degree than the family or the corporation. The family actualizes the universal only as sentiment, universal trust, and personal loyalty oriented to specific individuals. Corporations are built around the conscious principle that members of the same trade ought to help one another on account of their shared interests, but to those who do not belong the individual still has no ties other than what abstract right and morality would impose.

The state corrects these shortcomings. The relationship among citizens of a state is regulated by publicly promulgated laws and may be formulated in terms of rights and duties, an impossibility for the family if the latter is to preserve its special ethical character. In this respect the state resembles corporations more than the family. Yet, unlike the former, the state is not an association of narrow self-interest. As we have seen, Hegel regards the political union as such as an end in itself that includes and promotes private welfare but is not simply equivalent to the sum total of individual interests. The various ways in which Hegel has so far characterized the state (e.g., as embodiment of reason, as the self-conscious universal, and so on) converge in one point at least: the state is, for Hegel, the fullest expression of human freedom.

Few of Hegel's arguments have evoked such widespread protest and debate as this one. Ironically, though, it does follow if one grants to Hegel the conception of freedom that we have discussed already and taken as given throughout this book. If freedom means that one's personal identity is not hemmed in, but enhanced and enriched, by one's relationship to a social and natural context, then the state really does promote our freedom. At least in the modern state, we see every day the value and importance attached to human dignity, the general welfare, and access to an impartial system of justice, all of which indicate that right is held in high esteem. If we were members of a nomadic desert tribe, or belonged to a caste in old India, we would not see such categories embodied in the laws and institutions around us. Hence, in Hegel's view, our self-knowledge would be faulty and incomplete. We would not know ourselves as free (and therefore be free) since freedom would not yet have become an explicit part of our objective and subjective world. The state is, in other words, the unfolding of the concept in its objective form, corresponding to the concept as it exists subjectively, in self-consciousness. Hegel accordingly regards the state as a resolution of necessity and freedom.[42] It must develop and unfold in certain ways and not others, but those ways all conspire to confirm and actualize freedom.

What Hegel calls the internal right of the state (*das innere Staatsrecht*) or its constitution provides the immediate field of freedom's realization. As we have already seen, the state displays immanent rationality; it embraces both subject (individual will) and object (the will in itself). Hegel now proceeds to define these aspects more concretely as political disposition (Gesinnung) and constitution.[43]

The subjective and objective moments of the state's internal order are naturally very closely related. The proper disposition of citizens Hegel calls patriotism. By this he does not mean modern nationalism or chauvinism, which left him cold. He thinks of patriotism as an attitude of trust or confidence (*Zutrauen*) in the close identification of one's own interests with the good of the whole to which the political state attends. This "quiet" patriotism cannot develop among citizens unless the institutions of the political state are rational, i.e., unless they appear to the citizen as a confirmation of his own ethical nature.[44] If this is the case, then patriotism will become a habit that expresses itself more in a constant concern for the public welfare than in extraordinary acts of heroism.

According to Hegel, the modern state cannot hope to generate this sort of habitual patriotism among its citizens unless it possesses an organic constitution. Hegel uses the term "organic" to express the self-diremption and return-into-self of the concept. Or rather, he thinks that the concept allows us to comprehend how organic bodies can remain self-identical despite (and because of) the fact that the unity of life is dispersed into the various organs of the body, omnipresent and yet not located in any specific place:

> [The patriotic] disposition acquires its specific, determinate *content* from the diverse aspects of the organism of the state. This *organism* is the development of the idea into its differences and objective actuality. These different aspects are thus the *diverse powers* and their affairs and competencies. By virtue of their activity the universal constantly *produces* itself in a *necessary* fashion and precisely so that it is determined by the *nature of the concept*; and, to the extent that the universal is presupposed in its production, it also *preserves* itself. This organism is the *political* constitution.[45]

Hegel uses the idea of an organic constitution to criticize those who would make religion superior to the state. To be sure, Hegel does not want to exclude religion from the modern state. He thinks that a religious, especially Lutheran, conscience is an indispensable subjective element in a well-ordered state (as we recall from chapter 5). Nevertheless, no religion should exercise direct control over the affairs of the state. Just as civil society needed to be disentangled from the family and the organs of government, so too the sphere of religion must be differentiated from that of politics. Political authority cannot be based on religion in any direct way. Each sphere has its own principles and peculiar form of truth.[46]

However, the difference between state and church cannot degenerate into an opposition, for this would destroy the identity-in-difference that must characterize the two spheres. The state is not merely a finite, mechanical system designed to promote security. It also partakes of infinity since it is objective spirit, the same spirit that is honored as God in religion. Hence, the attitude typified by the beautiful soul or other protagonists of romantic religion rests upon a fundamental misconception. These religions of the heart can only retreat into the inwardness of conscience because they deny the state the divine quality that Hegel believes it possesses as an actualization of spirit. Likewise, they misconstrue the character of religion and indeed of spirit by confining it to an abstract, unactual inwardness. Hegel has short patience with empty pietism that, after the fashion of the beautiful soul, takes arrogant pride in an impeccability that is possible only because it never acts.

Ironically, Hegel's arguments in favor of the divinity of the state are precisely intended to safeguard its secular responsibilities and prevent any sort of veiled theocracy from arising. In this sense his aims are entirely consonant with those of the Enlightenment even though the arguments he uses are quite different. The Aufklärer thought they could promote a secular state by breaking the hold of religion upon the popular mind. Accordingly, they tried to equate religion with morality or turn it into a noncommittal deism. As far as Hegel is concerned, this strategy only made religious faith more obscurantist and fanatical by severing all its links with the rational doctrines of the Bible and by absolving religion of coresponsibility for the political attitudes and conduct of citizens. As we have already noted, Hegel regards the romantic religious revolt against reason as a necessary outcome of the Enlightenment's identification of reason with finitude and the understanding. Under these circumstances, he contends that the dignity and responsibility of the secular state must be safeguarded not by downgrading religion but by portraying the state as a coordinate moment in the same divine activity.

Apart from the difference that the state posits between itself and religion, it must also develop an internal organic structure, a system of differences that nevertheless constitutes its unity or self-identity. This system is the well-known "division of powers," which acquires an entirely new meaning and rationale in Hegel's political philosophy. The constitutional division of powers must be organic or derived from the concept, which means that each moment must itself be the whole: "The constitution is rational to the extent that the state *differentiates* and determines its effective power internally *according to the nature of the concept*. More specifically, *each* of these powers is intrinsically the *totality* [of the constitution; L. H.] since it contains within itself the other moments and permits them to work through it."[47]

For this reason, Hegel rejects the arguments, typified by Madison's *Federalist* No. 51, that constitutional powers must be kept separate in order to check and balance each other. This view, so Hegel suggests, rests upon the application of categories to the state that are not appropriate to it: mechanical analogies like equilibrium, or else a posteriori, utilitarian considerations. His point is that the internal structure of the state rests upon a principle (the concept) that simply expresses what the will, self-consciousness, the "I," and finally man as such, are in their very essence. To derive the division of powers from any other principle would mean to stand outside it, as a sort of abstract observer, and treat it as a means to some arbitrarily concocted end. But since the state is the actual form of freedom, the reasoning of Madison and other modern liberals seems to Hegel the work of "negative Understanding" bespeaking the mentality of a "rabble."[48] To objections that the state might become tyrannical if internal checks are not built into it, Hegel would simply reply that a tyrannical state would not be actual. Moreover, such a suspicious attitude would be incompatible with the subjective disposition of patriotism that is an essential moment of the actual state.

The division of powers, since it is the concept, corresponds precisely to the moments of the free will outlined before. The monarchical power, the power of ultimate decision, presents the will in its singular immediacy. The governmental or administrative power puts decisions into practice by relating their general content to particular cases. And, finally, the legislative power is the self-conscious universal.

The monarch, embodying all the moments of the concept as a totality, is especially designed to mediate the ambiguity of singular self-consciousness. The "I" is both immediate personal identity and pure self-certainty, the negative activity of self-positing which is identical in every "I." Likewise, the monarch is a specific person who holds his royal power on the basis of a natural principle of succession. Yet he also embodies the very idea of sovereignty and in this capacity the universality of his self-consciousness comes into clear focus. The citizen is "reconciled" to monarchy because it embodies a moment of his free will and ethical nature.

The monarch is a "knot" that ties the whole together, but only an "empty knot" since his personal qualities and preferences are not supposed to influence policy-making under ordinary circumstances.[49] He is supposed to "say yes" to legislative proposals and "dot the i" of laws,[50] no more than this. But the monarchy should not be treated as something that must be justified on utilitarian grounds. Hegel insists that the monarchy must be present in an organic state because the idea of free will, our starting point, has yielded it as one of its essential moments. Monarchy is not *derived* from free will; it *is* free will in one of its most important actualizations.[51]

Hegel's concept of the monarchy also leads him to adopt a unique position on the question of where the sovereign power of a state resides. He rejects the view, characteristic of modern enlightened and liberal thought, that the whole people is sovereign rather than the monarch. This can be a reasonable position only if one has abstracted the people from the organic or articulated constitutional forms in which, historically, its political life has been carried on. The notion of popular sovereignty is thus tantamount to the assertion that the atomized individuals who, taken together, make up civil society, would exercise sovereign power. In this "liberal" sense of the expression, popular sovereignty is a meaningless abstraction for Hegel. But if one thinks of the people as having already been articulated into corporations, estates, families, and the like, then one can speak of popular sovereignty because one is now referring to the state as a whole, including the monarch.

To Hegel, a mass society, the people abstracted from its concrete and multifaceted life context, is not a state. And once the people does form a state, then the monarch will be included as embodying an essential moment of the concept of free will. So the abstract question of where sovereignty is located is for Hegel's "pseudoproblem" raised by the understanding:

> [T]aken *without* its monarch and the *articulation* which necessarily and immediately accompanies monarchy, *the* people is a formless mass that is no longer a state. Thus *none* of the determinations accrue to it that are present only in an *internally formed* whole—sovereignty, government, courts, administrative hierarchy, estates, and whatever else. As soon as these moments, which exist only in relation to an organization, the life of the state, take shape in a people, the latter ceases to be an indeterminate abstraction, which, when imagined in a quite general way, is called "the people."[52]

The monarch incorporates the power of ultimate decision in the will. Hegel considers political decisions in some sense "existential" acts because no amount of reasoning and discussion will provide absolute certainty about the wisdom and rationality of a proposed policy. At some point, debate must be broken off and a decision taken whose ultimate ground is unfathomable. But once the decision has been made, the monarch's responsibility comes to an end and the governmental or administrative organs step in. It is their responsibility to apply decisions as well as existing laws and ordinances to the particular cases which arise in civil society.

In examining the responsibilities of the governmental power, which also include the police and courts, we again encounter the central issue that plagues civil society: namely, how the latter can be made ethical and the self-encapsulated individual be given a more universal existence. For this reason Hegel is extremely concerned, in this entire discussion, to strike a balance between the state's interest in particular affairs of civil society and the latter's legitimate claims to autonomy and self-government. In the corporation, which Hegel here considers together with local government, the state must have some influence upon personnel decisions. He notes that "In general these positions [i.e., administrative positions in the corporations; L. H.] must be filled through a combination of popular election by the interested parties and appointment and confirmation on the part of higher authorities."[53]

We can now see what Hegel meant when he remarked, apropos of the corporations, that these had to be subject to "higher supervision by the state." The presence of government officials in the corporations, and their attempts to play a mediating role between the state and civil society, gives the corporations a quasi-public character. The corporation members are supposed to be made aware that their chartered status and special privileges depend upon the active interest of the state in their continued existence and well-being. Thus, their esprit de corps will begin to transcend the narrow limits of mutual interest and shade over into a more universal, patriotic disposition.[54]

On the other hand, Hegel is quite serious about permitting at least a modicum of internal democracy in the corporations and in local communities. He is sharply critical of the highly centralized French administrative system that attempts to regulate local affairs down to the smallest detail. But Hegel's reasons for opposing excessive administrative centralization again suggest the difficulties of his entire project of resurrecting some form of Sittlichkeit under modern conditions. He points out that

> Recently, there has been a tendency to organize everything from the top down. This organizing has been the main concern while the lower echelons, the mass aspect of the whole, has easily been left in a more or less unorganic state. And yet it is extremely important that the mass become organic, for only in this way can it exercise effective power and control. Otherwise it is only a heap, a quantity of fragmented atoms. Legitimate power is present only in the organic condition of the particular spheres.[55]

Hegel has essentially repeated his polemic against Fichte's police state made in the "Differenzschrift." Excessive state supervision and administrative hierarchy impose a machine-like rigidity upon the "vital" organic integrity of local and corporate entities, thereby transforming them into an atomized mass. But internal democracy does not have an intrinsic value for Hegel. He portrays it as an arena for caprice and subjective opinion that, in spite of their relative justification as an expression of subjective freedom, are mainly exercised in deciding trivial matters without much significance for the state as a whole:

> The administration of corporation affairs by the corporations' own directors . . . will frequently be inept. . . . But we can regard this special sphere as having been left to the moment of *formal freedom*. Here the individual's own knowledge, decision, and execution as well as his petty passions and conceits have a playground where they can be given free rein. This is particularly so as the state's more universal interest in the affairs under consideration decreases and there is less and less reason for concern when these affairs are bungled or handled in a less satisfactory or more laborious fashion. And the state can likewise grant more latitude here, the more the laborious or foolish handling of such trivial affairs bears a direct relationship to the satisfaction and self-esteem which is derived from them.[56]

Given these limitations on internal democracy, one has to ask how the citizens could ever think of the state as more than a vast tutelary power. It could not be lost on them that they are being treated like children, allowed to participate in political affairs only when they are trivial and insignificant. The source of the problem is that Hegel equates subjective freedom with Willkür (arbitrary choice or caprice), and accordingly tries to confine it to affairs of private or only local and transitory significance. Even though he makes a kowtow to subjective freedom as the great principle of the modern world, he is not willing to see it interpreted as public or political freedom in which the individual would participate in those decisions of the highest importance to his life. Subjective freedom in Hegel's eyes concerns only the private and personal side of our lives, what in philosophy is called contingency. Unlike Plato, Hegel does energetically champion the right of the individual to decide for himself such contingent matters as what career to pursue or whom to marry. But precisely because subjective freedom is for him equivalent to contingency, Hegel does not see why it should be extended to important political matters that concern necessary, rational principles of right. The rational, as he puts it, is a highway where no one is conspicuous as an individual. And the organization of the state, in particular, displays the moments of the rational will, i.e., what each individual would explicitly will if he understood free will speculatively. The state is only his own nature as a rational being writ large.

Still, we ought to ask whether Hegel's dichotomy of subjective freedom and rational will is consistent with his philosophy as a whole and with our own political experience. I suggest that Hegel often ascribes to rational will a meaning that it cannot have according to his own reasoning. The rational will at best can will what is universal and necessary, for example a constitution that sets down the formal structure of political authority according to the concept. But it cannot specify which individuals are best suited to make important decisions, nor can it determine what policies are the correct ones. When Hegel argues that such decisions must be made by civil servants or by representatives of major economic interests, he tacitly identifies the rational will with a model of politics that he has certainly not proven to be the correct one: namely, the view that politics is essentially administration of the affairs of civil society. If this were the case, then one could safely assume that the most competent and knowledgeable individuals should be appointed as decision makers.

But Hegel's account of the origin of right and much that he says about freedom and ethical life would entitle us to frame a quite different theory of politics. We could argue that politics is the sphere in which mutual recognition finds its most complete expression. Hegel often asserts that mutual recognition involves at least the minimal acknowledgment that the other is a person, an "I," and deserving of respect for that very reason. But recent history has taught us that mutual recognition in Hegel's sense is probably the exception rather than the rule, and that one cannot rely on a highly trained administration to protect basic rights if their sacrosanctness is not recognized by the general population. Thus mutual recognition must be constituted in some way other than by government fiat.

My suggestion is that the attitudes Hegel would assign to a trans-individual Geist must be formed and worked out in the logos, the reasoning and speaking, of ordinary citizens. The dialogic character of politics requires that citizens be able to transcend the press of their private affairs (exactly the sphere where Hegel locates subjective freedom) and address themselves to the most important questions of political life. In political life, once-isolated and impotent individuals can coalesce by acknowledging their common identity and by finding a common language to express their situation. The product of their coalescence is power, and political power is the surest way for those who have been denied recognition to acquire it.

Had Hegel developed his dialectic of mutual recognition in this direction, he might have seen "subjective freedom" in a new light. Instead of equating it with the rights of contingency, he could have interpreted it as the focal point of the process in which speech and reason work to create a shared identity among citizens and a recognition by them of their responsibility for one another and for the whole of their society. This would have led him to rethink the relationship between the governmental power and popular participation in politics and perhaps to arrive at a more successful resolution of the problems posed by the Enlightenment. But Hegel never took this step, probably because he assumed that any public, political exercise of subjective freedom would only raise the specter of a new Terror.

Thus, for all his concessions to local and corporate self-determination, Hegel regards governmental power mainly as an affair of salaried public employees with tenured rights to office. The government can only help the citizen lead a "universal life" or make him ethical in the political sense by impressing upon him the state's concern with his private (essentially economic) interests. In the legislative power, on the other hand, we might expect to see a much closer connection between subjective freedom and the universal ends of the state.

The constitutional status of the legislature again raises the issue of the relationship between state and civil society. The experiences of the French Revolution led Hegel to reject any legislative power claiming to represent "the people" as individuals and certainly any political theory that tended to turn the legislature into a sovereign power. As we saw in the case of the monarchy, sovereignty cannot be said to reside in an unorganized mass of individuals. And once the people are organized into an organic system, every branch of the state could in a way be said to embody the popular will, not just the legislature.

Furthermore, Hegel opposes the standard Enlightenment arguments in favor of legislative supremacy. He sees no reason to imagine that the people (or its representatives) have any more knowledge of or insight into affairs of state than the monarch or the government. In fact he avers that the government should be presumed to possess a greater knowledge of the public good than the legislative branch, as well as a greater skill in effecting it. Likewise, Hegel does not believe that legislators are any more likely to will the common good than civil servants or kings. Indeed, they might be less likely to, given the pressure exerted on them by special interests.

The only remaining justification for retaining a legislature is that "the subjective moment of universal freedom, one's own insight and will"[57] must be given real existence within the state. Specifically, Hegel argues that civil society must have a means of communicating its grievances to the government and of checking abuses of power or maladministration on the part of low-level civil servants. The government may have a general idea of civil society's needs, but it requires a detailed picture of grass-roots problems that only those directly involved can provide. And since it is primarily interest, rather than opinions or political principles, that must be represented in the legislature, Hegel retains the traditional European estate system as the basis of political representation.

Hegel's "Platonic" tendency to equate the individual with his social or economic function emerges nowhere more clearly than in his theory of the estates. The very expression "estate" connotes both a political body and a division of civil society into economic or occupational groups possessing distinctive privileges and lifestyles. While Hegel recognizes the dualism of state and civil society as a necessary moment of the modern state (in its capacity as a totality of all spheres), he wishes to "mediate" this dualism. That is, the state must extend down into civil society and thus politicize it by asserting its right to name or confirm corporation directors and by admitting individuals into political life only insofar as they are organized in estates. And, by the same token, civil society is given a definite place in the state because its great interests are directly represented. Thus, the estates act as a transmission belt between state and civil society: "When they are regarded as a *mediating* organ, the estates stand between the government as such on one hand and the people on the other, insofar as the latter is resolved into its component spheres and individuals. The determination of the estates requires them not only to promote the *interests* of *particular* groups and of *individuals* but also, in equal measure, to develop a *sense* of the purposes of *state* and *government* and a corresponding *disposition*."[58]

Just as the corporations help forestall the development of "rabble" mentality by bestowing a certain dignity and honor on the individual, the estates prevent him from turning the totality of his life into a political issue. They canalize political activity into the articulation and aggregation of specific interests related to the individual's occupation and corporate concerns. Hence the individual does not appear in the state as a whole person making sweeping "ideological" demands. Instead, only certain problems of his entire life situation become salient—those for which the state can reasonably expect to find solutions. The qualitative distinctions that the estates institutionalize prevent the people, in Hegel's words, from dissolving into a "quantity" or "heap" of atoms whose volition and opinion would be "unorganic" and which would apply "mass power" against the state.[59]

The fact that the legislative power represents interests and not opinions or *Weltanschauungen* has important consequences for the internal organization of the estates. First of all, Hegel suggests that voting for deputies is not really necessary. He remarks of his theory of estates that

> it runs counter to another current notion—that the private estate must appear in the guise of *singular individuals* when it is admitted to participation in general affairs in the legislative branch. Individual participation, under this current notion, may mean that representatives are elected for this function, or even that every person should exercise the franchise. This atomistic, abstract viewpoint has already disappeared in the family as well as in civil society where the individual makes his appearance only as a member of a universal.[60]

In the first estate, that devoted to agriculture, representation is confined to those who own entailed estates. These landowners do not select deputies, but attend the sessions of their estate in person, forming a House of Lords. Here again Hegel is seduced by the romantic image of closeness to nature that leads him to gloss over the ongoing transformation of agriculture into a business and the consequent deterioration in the position of peasants and farm laborers. By fiat, Hegel declares that a complete community of interest and viewpoint must prevail among all individuals engaged in agriculture, a bit of legerdemain that does violence to the notion of actuality. As usual in Hegel's account of the agricultural estate, the Platonic side of Sittlichkeit, the identification of what one is with what one does, overshadows the principles of subjectivity and of public freedom.

In the second estate, it is the corporations and local governments that organize and articulate individual life. Hegel even slips into the language of scholasticism to describe the complete absorption of the individual into the functional "spheres" of civil society: "The individual is *genus*, but his *immanent*, universal activity is the *genus proximus* [*nächste Gattung*]. Hence he at first fulfills his actual and vital determination on behalf of the *universal* in the sphere of his corporation, local government, etc."[61] In other words, the individual as a citizen or human being is for Hegel a mere abstraction. He must belong to a corporation or a unit of local government (*Gemeinde*) to be recognized as a member of the state in any concrete sense.

But even within the corporations and local governments, representation does not signify that the deputy bears a specific mandate. Hegel distinguishes representation in the sense of acting in lieu of another person from representation as embodiment. It is the latter, he argues, that deputies to the estates must understand as their proper role; otherwise they would simply be agents for a mass of discrete individuals: "When the deputies are regarded as *representatives*, this has an organic, rational meaning only if they are *representatives* of one of the essential *spheres* of society, representatives of its great interests and not of singular *individuals* brought together in an aggregate. Representation thus no longer means that one person is acting *in another's stead*. Rather the interest itself is *actually present* in its representative."[62] Since the deputy is practically reduced to an embodiment of coal mining, banking, textiles, and so forth, Hegel sees no real reason to have him stand for election: "Voting is either quite superfluous or else it is reduced to a trivial game of opinion and caprice."[63] Hegel does not say how the deputies would be designated if there were no elections. Perhaps the state would name certain individuals who enjoy the confidence of their peers[64] and who have had previous experience in public administration and thus a "sense of the state."[65]

Hegel does indeed adopt some of the demands current in the Enlightenment: public sessions of the estates, freedom of the press, and the need for a well-informed public opinion. But his reasons for defending these positions are revealing. Public trials, for instance, are necessary to acquaint citizens with the law so it will not appear to be an alien "other." And open legislative sessions are useful because they further the Bildung of ordinary people, proving to them that the legislators are wiser and more competent than they are and hence forestalling any vain overestimation of their own political acumen. Hegel's discussion of the state thus shows him to be far closer to Platonic Sittlichkeit than to the tradition of political liberty and subjective freedom. His answer to the problem of the Enlightenment is to reinvigorate ethical life, understood only as the convergence of individual identity and social function. Civil society and the state are made organic by absorbing the individual into a panoply of partial and essentially private associations. However, there is reason to doubt whether Hegel himself was satisfied with this solution.

In his Jena lectures of 1805–6, Hegel is less optimistic about the reconciliation of enlightened subjectivity and ethical life. There he argues that neither morality nor civic life provides satisfaction for the individual as a whole person: "Every self has a limited purpose and an equally limited doing. The knowledge of oneself as essence in right and in duty is, as pure essence and pure knowledge, empty; as fulfilled, it is a limited manifold and the immediate actuality of something equally individual."[66]

Hegel, in this early essay, did believe that the government of the modern state overcomes the dualistic tendencies of the Enlightenment.[67] Yet the government is not the individual. It is a totality of which the individual is still only an insignificant moment. Hence Hegel asserts that the individual needs religion. Only in it can he overcome the dualism of being and thinking or of self-conscious subjectivity (certainty) and objectivity (truth), because in religion he is a whole person and not a one-sided member of a corporation, a peasant, a factory worker, etc.: "In religion each elevates himself to this intuition of himself as universal self. His nature, his social position falls away like a dream, like an island at the fringe of the horizon, appearing as no more than a little cloud of mist. He is equal to the prince. Before God he counts for as much as any other man. This is the externalization of his whole sphere, of his whole existent world."[68]

Yet religion, too, is ultimately unsatisfactory since it still contains the dualism of the here-and-now and the beyond. It is essentially an unhappy consciousness as the beautiful soul, its extreme form, revealed most clearly: "[I]n this way the two realms of heaven and earth come to lie apart from one another: only *beyond* this world, and not in the present, is spirit reconciled with itself. Even if it is satisfied here, it is still not spirit elevating itself above its existence."[69]

Now it could be argued that Hegel altered his views about political life in the modern state after his Jena period. But even in his lectures on the *History of Philosophy*, he sounds the same note. In comparing life in the ancient polis to the fragmentation and dualism of modern life, he remarks:

> In no individual do we actually find either consciousness or activity for the whole. The individual acts so as to sustain the whole, but he does not know how; he is concerned only with safeguarding his singular existence. It is divided activity of which each individual gets only a piece, just as in a factory where no one makes a whole product, only a part, since he lacks the skills the others possess. Only a few individuals know how to as-

> semble all the parts. Free peoples have a consciousness and activity oriented toward the whole. But modern peoples are, as individuals, unfree—*civil* [*bürgerliche*] freedom means precisely dispensing with the universal. It is a principle of isolation.[70]

Here the paradox of modern political life emerges most clearly. The modern state as a whole is "a great architectonic edifice . . . a hieroglyph of reason."[71] But as individuals, modern citizens are unfree; the exercise of subjective freedom (opinion and caprice) is allowed in private or trivial matters, but in important affairs, even in representation, subjective will must yield to the necessities of the organic state. This is an almost complete reversal of the priorities of the ancient polis. There the private sphere was devoted to physical and biological necessity. Freedom had no place in the household order because its members were not equal. Only in the public sphere, in the state, could freedom make its appearance, for this was the forum in which reason and speech could unfold their potentialities. Among equals, persuasion and logic had to replace brute force and command.

In effect, Hegel accepts Plato's argument that the life of the polis was too undifferentiated. Both assert that the state must be organized into sharply distinct moments that reflect the aspects of the individual soul (Hegel would say the concept of will). And it is for this reason that Hegel can call his modern state a complete actualization of freedom and rationality—not because the individual is an integrated self, an all-sided person. In this sense, Hegel's political philosophy is only a reconciliation in thought of the dualisms of modern life. From the philosopher's (or God's) vantage point, the state perfectly embodies the concept and hence fully satisfies the demands of free will. But from the nonphilosophic viewpoint (the finite self-consciousness of the individual), the "unhappy consciousness" of an internally fragmented life persists. The individual cannot lead a "universal life" (to use Hegel's expression) because his political existence is entirely absorbed into the occupational or estate interests of which the organic state is composed.

Measured by the lofty aspirations that Hegel set for it, the modern state of the *Philosophy of Right* is almost certainly a failure. Many of its crucial arguments depend upon some very selective and short-sighted readings of the political and economic trends of nineteenth-century Europe. Hegel's remarks on the family, estates, corporations, and popular sovereignty strike us as especially anachronistic in this regard. Moreover, if the analysis of the last several pages is sound, freedom even as Hegel conceived it does not receive its full due in the state sketched out in the *Philosophy of Right*. Still, to paraphrase Hegel himself, it is much easier to find fault with things than it is to uncover whatever truth is contained in them. In the concluding chapter, I shall survey Hegel's critique of the Enlightenment and point out what seem to me its most promising and instructive features.

HEGEL AND THE ENLIGHTENMENT: THE DEBATE IN CONTEMPORARY PERSPECTIVE

9

Up to this point we have attempted to reconstruct Hegel's critique of the Enlightenment within its proper historical context. In this essentially backward-looking inquiry, the main task all along has been to see the connections among different levels of thought and action, especially including philosophy, politics, science, economics, and culture. As we observed at the very outset, Hegel wanted to bring to light the predominant forms of consciousness that reappeared in all of these facets of the Enlightenment: the dualism and self-alienation that he traced all the way back to Descartes.

Even though this work has been mainly an essay in the history of political philosophy, we should not overlook the hidden and overt links between the Enlightenment of Hegel's day and the political and philosophical situation of the twentieth century. Hegel may not speak directly to our problems any more. But his critique of the Enlightenment, with some shifts of emphasis and context, can be brought to bear in an illuminating way on certain prominent features of contemporary life and thought. To some extent, these links have already been noted, particularly in the first three and last two chapters. In the remaining pages I would like to mention a few areas where Hegel's critique of the Enlightenment strikes me as still extremely relevant to our modern concerns.

The Philosophy of Self-Consciousness and Its Critics

In Hegel's view, the philosophers and men of letters associated with the Enlightenment hewed out one great foundation stone of modern thought, the concept of the "I" as "negative," as self-positing, self-recognizing, and self-forming. But, with the partial exception of the German Aufklärung, this—their practical insight—clashed decisively with their own empiricist preconceptions, which scarcely left room for such a bizarre and ineffable reality as the "I." Part of Hegel's confidence in the power of his own philosophic synthesis can be attributed to his conviction that he had demonstrated conclusively how the "I" could be both negative and self-forming and still capable of concrete articulations not necessarily antithetical to a stable social order.

But Hegel's confidence was misplaced. The Kantian and Fichtean idea that the thinking "I" posed structures of its own that made experience possible—the transcendental synthesis—has not proved as durable as Hegel thought it would. Rather, the Enlightenment's objectifying naturalism, which would either deny the distinctive character of the "I" or treat it as an illusion altogether, has outlasted its rival, transcendental philosophy. The influence of the Enlightenment's approach to human existence can be seen most decisively in the mainstream social sciences of the twentieth century that have adopted (although in a modified way) many of the methodological assumptions of the Enlightenment as well as its aspirations toward political efficacy and social control.

However, one highly influential current of modern philosophy seems a partial exception to the triumph of Enlightenment modes of thought. Phenomenology and existentialism, along with the social-scientific approaches they have generated, do take their bearings from a "transcendental" perspective, and have tried to save the "I" from reification in empirical psychology.[1] But the single most prominent and radical of these thinkers, Martin Heidegger, has moved almost as far away from Hegel's "concept," the "I"-paradigm, as has mainstream social science, albeit in a different direction. In the very first sentence of *Being and Time*, Heidegger boldly asserts that the *Seinsfrage*, the question of what it means to be, has been "forgotten."

He points out that this question was still a vital one for Plato and Aristotle, but that their answers to it have long since degenerated into the tradition of substance metaphysics that obscures, rather than clarifies, the meaning of being. Surprisingly, he includes Hegel in this tradition and even uses Hegel's definition of being as the most egregious example of our inability to pose (let alone answer) the question of what it means to be. Hegel, he says, "keeps looking in the same direction as ancient ontology, except that he no longer pays heed to Aristotle's problem of the unity of Being as over against the multiplicity of 'categories' applicable to things."[2]

Heidegger traces this "forgetfulness of being" in modern philosophy especially to Descartes and his distinction between being and thinking, the "I" and the world it objectifies in thought. Accordingly, he cannot accept Hegel's account of the self-positing "I" as a paradigm for the structure of being generally. For Heidegger, the only true path leads beyond the "I," beyond self-consciousness to the ancient, pre-Socratic ontology in which the "I" had not yet crystallized as a self-conscious "pole" of experience and in which, therefore, there was as yet no sharp dichotomy between being and thinking.[3]

Oddly enough, both "enlightened" social science and its apparently most radical antagonist, Heidegger, dispense with the sort of analysis of self-consciousness that Hegel believed essential for any progress in philosophy. In fact, one can discern in both of these currents of thought a disturbing elevation in the ontological status of what is rudimentary, undeveloped and unreflective as against the central role of self-consciousness in Hegel.

Modern social science, in many respects like its Enlightenment predecessor, has tended to reduce the endless variety of cultural and social life to a range of fairly simple determinations (behavioral psychology and sociology are obvious examples) which lend themselves to the working out of lawlike generalizations. Even in complex theories, like those developed by Talcott Parsons, that ascribe decisive importance to "subjective" factors (e.g., values), the status of the key variables is the same as in any natural-scientific theory. Their validity has no relation at all to whether individual humans actually experience the world in terms of them or would employ them to describe their experiences.

In Heidegger, and as a parallel development, we find human existence refracted into a series of "modes of being," essentially various inflections of what it means to be (human). But there is no central focus, no "negative" moment amidst these modes such that we could step outside them and thereby achieve toward them a critical distance. And if I cannot "objectify" my relationships to the world and to other people, conceiving of them as in principle contingent and therefore open to change, then it is hard to imagine how I could ever be a free, self-determining being. From Hegel's vantage point, then, Heidegger's critique of substance metaphysics culminates in a repudiation of the entire modern concept of autonomy, grounded, as Hegel thinks it is, on the premise of the power of the "I" to negate and transform itself and its world.

If we have followed Hegel with a degree of sympathy thus far, we may suspect that the conflict between modern social science and phenomenology repeats, in a more sophisticated way, the struggle between the Enlightenment and faith, depicted in chapter 6. The former presses the demands for human rights, positive science and a more rational political order, yet it seems incapable of giving a clear account of the self that is to be the beneficiary of freedom and rationality. Like faith, phenomenology struggles against the reification of the self and the absorption of the human world into the objectivizing and perhaps trivializing perspective of modern science. But, at least in Heidegger's case, one cannot reject the objectivizing "ontic" approach of modern science (and its forebear, substance metaphysics) without also dispensing with the "subject," the pure self that is the metaphysical counterpart of the abstract object. Thus, in an ironic reversal, Heidegger's version of phenomenology ends up actually agreeing with the most consistent and uncompromising forms of modern social science in attacking all philosophy that in any way makes the "I" a first principle. We shall shortly return to the dialectic between enlightenment and faith in another context, that of modern culture.

One great benefit that may derive from reading Hegel is a certain skepticism in respect to both of the contemporary alternatives discussed above, insofar as either purports to offer a "true" or "complete" account of what it means to be human and to live in a society. We should at least raise the question, once again, of whether the German idealists may have been correct in the fundamental principles of their approach to philosophy. They hoped, of course, to show how experience depends on the positing of a definite, but alterable, relationship between the "I" and the not-"I." Moreover, they believed (Hegel especially) that the "I" has a primordial need, not reducible to any "material" need or desire, to find an adequate manifestation of itself and its own activity in its experiences of self and world. Whatever the weaknesses of Hegel's philosophy, he does provide a subtle, thought-provoking analysis of self-consciousness and shows us how it is related to the "objectifying" activity of scientific inquiry as well as to our experiences of freedom in a social setting.[4]

Culture and Personality in an Enlightened Age

Some contemporary philosophers who have written on Hegel, notably Charles Taylor, have shed a great deal of light on the romantic context of Hegel's ideas. Taylor sees Hegel's philosophy as a variation on a recurrent romantic theme: conceiving the self as expressive and autonomous, rather than as passive and mechanical. As true as this romantic characterization may be, we must guard against identifying Hegel too closely with the romantic movement and its offshoots. Indeed—and this is where Hegel's relevance to our own age becomes evident—one can easily read Hegel as a philosopher who criticized romanticism with almost as much vigor as he did the Enlightenment.

In his view (as I tried to bring out in chapters 4 through 6), the Enlightenment and various forms of romantic protest, including intense religious faith, have conditioned each other for centuries. The Enlightenment grapples with human experience by means of categories largely derived from "substance metaphysics" and the study of nature. This finite thought, or philosophy of reflection, as Hegel would call it, inevitably evokes protest. The Enlightenment seems to those who are romantically inclined to disparage and distort a very significant part of their experience, especially that which concerns symbolic truth, custom and tradition, and religious belief. But since the Enlightenment has a monopoly on the definition of rational thought, those who protest feel they must go beyond the limits of rationality altogether, toward a cult of sentiment, an immediate intuition, in the heart, of right and wrong, or even an invocation of the "law of the stronger" in organic nature (these last are the positions taken by two of Hegel's opponents, J. F. Fries and K. L. von Haller).[5] Whole areas of life formerly included under the canopy of theology—and hence amenable to rational inquiry—are now cast adrift, open to irrational caprice (Willkür) in Hegel's sense of the word.

The opposition between a critical, rigorous, but somewhat narrowly defined and reductionistic rationality (Enlightenment) on one hand and the self-expressive cults of faith and feeling on the other introduces the possibility of what Adorno and Horkheimer call the "dialectic of enlightenment."[6] Progress in eliminating "metaphysical remnants" from rational thought has been accompanied for some time now by a sort of return of the repressed, in which nonrigorous, even avowedly irrationalist and mythological thinking stages a comeback in political rhetoric and popular culture. Fascism provides one obvious example. But we could also point, in contemporary Western societies, to the proliferation of religious cults, pseudosciences, vaguely metaphysical nostrums, "humanistic" psychologies, and romantic political movements, all of which propose to address global human problems that have somehow fallen between the cracks of the academic and scientific establishments.

Hegel's solution to the dualism of authoritative but positivistically restricted reason on the one side, and the welter of romantic, half-metaphysical, half-mythological popular belief on the other, strikes me as profoundly relevant. We must find a more satisfactory answer, he thinks, to the problem of what it means to know oneself and even to *be* a self. We must appreciate the distorted and beclouded kernel of truth in the romantic protest: the objectifying, detached attitude of the Enlightenment and its contemporary offshoots cannot be mistaken for the only possible relationship of the "I" to the world. Indeed, to believe that it is will lead one, as it did Hume, to deny altogether the reality of the "I" in favor of an entirely objectifying and self-concealing outlook. The "problem" felt by romantics of all stripes is a real one; it is not just a failure of nerve or a regression to infantile, prescientific ways of thinking.

On the other hand, appreciating the limitations of rational thought as defined by the Enlightenment does not mean jettisoning rationality altogether. For Hegel, reason in its broad meaning is a part of the universalizing and formative activity that is the very essence of spirit. The rational man, the veteran of Hegel's *Phenomenology*, for example, is the enemy of any attempt to identify "self" with raw, unformed, and unmediated natural feelings. When Hegel insists that rationality is a broad highway where all travel and no one is conspicuous as an individual,[7] he really is reviving a classical rather than a romantic ideal. One must become a self by a process of self-creation that takes place partly on the level of individual acculturation (Bildung) and partly has already been achieved by history in raising the cultural level of whole nations and regimes. This process of becoming a self consists in the interpenetration of rational ideas (e.g., morality and freedom) with the very structure of human nature, such that the original, raw nature of the individual is molded and transformed into a second, social nature in accordance with, but only so as to actualize, the abstract ideas themselves.

In Hegel's notion of a rational personality one does see a great deal more than the Enlightenment, even in its Kantian-Fichtean variants, would have seen. The rational man must absorb and reflectively comprehend the crucial experiences of the ancient and modern worlds (as in the *Phenomenology*). But one also sees an uncompromising rejection of all versions of "narcissism," i.e., practical credos that picture self-fulfillment as inner-directed and without any necessary connection to the lives and well-being of others. Consequently, the human ideal in Hegel's philosophy is only "self-expressive" if we understand by "self" the fully mature and "mediated" personality which has identified itself with the predominant rational demands of its culture, such as freedom, morality, and science itself.

The Origins of Human Rights and the Struggle for Recognition

Nowadays the issues surrounding human rights are frequently debated, but the framework of the debate—a legitimate state and recognized legal persons—is ordinarily taken for granted. Hegel's approach to human rights, once one has pieced it together, is unusually intriguing, just because he does not take the above elements as given.[8] In Hegel's age, the proposition that men had rights simply by virtue of being human had only begun to make an imprint on political life, most notably in the American and French Revolutions. There were still powerful trends of thought, both secular and ecclesiastical, for which "human rights" were an empty abstraction. After all, the nations and regions of Europe had endured for several thousand years without incorporating into their laws and customs any such system of abstract right. Consequently, the burden of proof still lay on those philosophers who wanted to defend the idea of universal human rights. They needed to show why people have such rights, why it is impermissible to treat anyone, no matter what his birth and status, as though he were an inferior creature or a mere "thing."

Hegel's most detailed discussion of rights (and duties) appears of course in the *Philosophy of Right*. But I have advanced the argument (in chapter 7), doubtless a controversial one, that his account of rights makes sense only if we go beyond that work and examine his description of the struggle for recognition. Here we find a rough equivalent, mutatis mutandis, for the liberals' state-of-nature argument, an account of how men move from a nonsocial existence defined mainly by biological needs to a state of affairs where they can be treated as legal persons and recognize each other as having a right to such treatment. The *Philosophy of Right* seems to me to assume at least the rudimentary existence of the framework of recognition since it does after all begin with "abstract right" built around the concept of "legal personality."

Having already sketched out the essentials of Hegel's discussion of recognition, I would like simply to draw out a few of its implications here. There are at least two ways of establishing a connection between human nature (what men are like) and human rights (what claims they may make with justice on others). One can, like the liberal writers, construct a "natural man" with certain passions and desires, then ascribe to him a right (we would say today a liberty) to satisfy these without being impeded. The "right" is very close to being a de facto description (especially in Hobbes) of how human beings actually do behave, obeying the quasi-biological imperatives of the "laws of nature."[9]

Two points about the liberal rights construction need to be underlined. First, man, as he is in the state of nature, may be described largely as a creature of passion and desire. Moreover, this image of man changes hardly at all once the liberals go on to portray the characteristics of state and society. A commonwealth, in Hobbes, contains "natural men" in the sense that the fundamental passions of its citizens are no different than they would be in the state of nature. Even in a social setting we are still confronting stripped-down, simplified, atomized individuals devoid of any historically specific ties to one another (these latter having been "thought away" in the very articulation of the state of nature).

Second, the life, freedom, and satisfaction of a person, the most relevant subject matter of his rights, are conceived of in an entirely individualistic way. Society is brought in only as a more or less effective means to gratify his desires. Thus, in both Hobbes and Locke rights always appear as claims that the individual possesses in isolation from his membership in a collectivity, whether or not he must surrender any of these rights as the price of such membership.

Neither the image of human nature nor of the state in the liberals' rights construct would find many adherents today. Modern social science has stressed the tight integration of the individual into the collectivity in regard both to his self-image and his actual behavior. The modern state meanwhile has become in many respects a protector, rather than a potential opponent, of human rights, acting as a court of last resort for individuals whose rights are threatened by large private organizations or (as in this country) biased laws and institutions.

Hegel's account of the origins of human rights seems like a promising alternative because it calls into question precisely the two assumptions, mentioned above, that permeate the liberal rights construct: rights as functions of our "desiring" nature and extreme individualism. As we saw in chapter 7, Hegel tries to envision a scenario in some ways comparable to the liberals' state of nature, where man is defined predominantly by his biological desires. But he insists that the desire for physical satisfaction only masks a deeper, nascent wish, on the part of every human being, to be recognized as distinct from and superior to mere nature. The telos of the dialectic of recognition is twofold. First, both parties (master and servant) learn in different manners to repress or discipline their raw natural desires and transform themselves in conformity to nonnatural standards of conduct (either defiance of one's own fear of death or else the disciplining, formative activity of labor). Second, the apparent individualism with which the struggle for recognition begins culminates in the establishment of a new and higher awareness. The individual realizes (or should realize) that the very self in the name of which he claims rights is in decisive ways a social product, the result of being recognized and simultaneously extending recognition to others. The individual who becomes a member of society and occupies a legal status is only outwardly and biologically the same as "natural man." In terms of what really counts, his spiritual life as an "I," he is already a socialized being, whose "meant existence," as Hegel has commented, is actually the system of law that realizes and defines his role as citizen.[10]

For Hegel, then, it would be relatively easy to understand and endorse the transformations in the relationship between individual and society that have come about in the last few centuries. Hegel would surely be the first to support the view that the state is not inherently the foe of human rights, but should in principle be their strongest guarantor, a role it has begun to play more frequently since the advent of the civil rights movement and affirmative action programs in this country. Also, Hegel consistently upheld the position that human freedom makes sense only in the context of an established social and cultural milieu. This is why he sometimes criticized the Lockean contention that liberty exists prior to the establishment of a state and must be zealously guarded against its power.

To be sure, Hegel recognized that existing states commit injustices against their citizens with dismaying frequency. But the fact that they do so, he argued, should not lead us to see the collectivity as in principle an enemy of freedom. Hegel thought of freedom as a transcending of limits and boundaries among men, the expansion and enrichment of the self which comes from participation in a common enterprise. To be free meant, for Hegel, not so much the struggle to reduce one's tax payments or evade as many public responsibilities as one could for the sake of private concerns. Rather, living a free life meant finding the satisfaction of one's higher nature in acting for the sake of the public good, performing one's own duties as well as possible with the awareness of the contribution one was thereby making to a flourishing common life.

Again, although we may not agree with the details of Hegel's argument, we should see in it a clear and consistent alternative to the human rights tradition that has been bequeathed to us by the liberal writers. Hegel ties rights clearly to the nonnatural and nonbiological category of personhood. To be a person, in turn, is to be recognized, which entails a connection to all other persons. And recognition, finally, is attained by virtue of self-consciousness, the "I" that emerges at least partly in a struggle with natural desire and impulse and in a dialectic with another self. There can be no rigid opposition between individual and society here because the two terms were never originally distinct in the first place.

Hegel and the "Hamiltonian" State

Of all the elements in Hegel's system of philosophy, his theory of the state appears on initial reading the least relevant to contemporary problems. We find him "comprehending" and demonstrating the necessity of institutions that were becoming outmoded even in his own day: corporations resembling medieval guilds, estates, semifeudal class relationships in the countryside. The overall impression one gets from the *Philosophy of Right* is that Hegel seriously underestimated what he called "abstract freedom" as well as the democratization of society. As most writers on Hegel have pointed out, he misread the historical trends of his time, attaching far too much importance to social and political structures doomed to obsolescence and destruction.

However, if we wish to profit as much as possible from studying Hegel, we might try to take into account not simply the letter but also the spirit of his political thought. We may disregard for a moment the specific institutions that figure so prominently in the *Philosophy of Right* and ask what role, in general, he believed the state should play in modern life, and why.

As a way of answering that question, I would like to digress briefly and recall a distinction made in the early twentieth century by *The*

New Republic's editor, Herbert Croly. In analyzing the crisis of American democracy, Croly traced it back to a conflict between two fundamentally different visions of the proper relation between citizens and the state. The first, which he labelled "Jeffersonianism," placed unswerving trust in popular virtue and in the unconscious play of market forces. The Jeffersonians tended to hold that a well-ordered and reasonably egalitarian society would result only if the "aristocratic" and "monarchical" pretensions of the state were defeated and each citizen's individual talents and preferences were given ample scope. Hamilton and his ideological successors, on the other hand, pursued a general policy that Croly describes as "one of energetic and intelligent assertion of the national good. [Hamilton] knew that the only method whereby the good could prevail either in individual or social life was by persistently willing that it should prevail and by the adoption of intelligent means to that end."[11] However, the Hamiltonian doctrine evinced a suspicion of mass movements and usually supported measures to insulate the state from popular pressure wherever possible.

It seems to me that Hegel would qualify as an unyielding Hamiltonian on almost every count. And the strengths and weaknesses of his political philosophy are to some extent the same ones Croly associated with the Hamilton doctrine. We shall begin our analysis by identifying the strengths of Hegel's (and Hamilton's) position.

At least in the United States, the state and especially the executive branch of the federal government has frequently been a whipping boy for both the radical left and right. The right is suspicious of an effective and omnicompetent Hamiltonian state because it fears that such a state might become "socialistic" and try to redistribute wealth. The left, especially since the 1960s, has attacked "bureaucracy" in the name of participatory democracy and "power to the people." Ironically, both right and left are drawing on the same Jeffersonian tradition, especially in their common assumption that a harmony of individual and public interest would eventually result if the will of ordinary citizens were not constantly thwarted by a self-serving elite. They differ primarily over whether the popular will is expressed best by market outcomes or by conscious political decisions made at public meetings and the like.

But neither version of Jeffersonianism has made much headway in halting the burgeoning of the modern state. Hamilton's position (and by extension Hegel's) seems to be vindicated, to be the only "actual" or "rational" response that the collectivity could make to its citizens' demands for greater personal and economic security, environmental and health protection, public education, and similar services or benefits. If it is true that the obsolete and archaic aspects of Hegel's state have disappeared, so too has the idyllic Jeffersonian society been consigned to oblivion. Indeed, the principle Hegel defended—that we need and should have an effective state run by a professional, well-educated elite with wide powers to control civil society—was far more prescient and accurate than the Jeffersonians' faith in popular virtue and laissez-faire.

That the modern state has penetrated into every sphere of civil society is so obvious that we need not dwell on it. What I would emphasize instead is the underlying agreement between Hegel and certain neo-Hamiltonians of twentieth-century America (men like Croly himself, John Kenneth Galbraith, Theodore Lowi, and Lester Thurow)[12] on the fundamental "rationality" and appropriateness of the state's enhanced role in our lives. All argue that the public good will not come about of its own accord, or through the give and take of interest group politics. They insist on a vigorous public sector in which officials are charged with pursuing policies in the long-range public interest. Some of them—Lowi and Galbraith especially—hope to insulate the state from public pressure in certain very important ways.[13] Further, all of them are sharply critical of ideological attacks of the "Jeffersonian" stamp that assume that a large, bureaucratic state automatically threatens individual liberty or tends to impose mass conformity. The Hamiltonians (and here again Hegel fits the pattern) tend to see local and private-sector tyranny, the dominance of the strong over the weak, as at least as much of a threat to basic human rights and liberties as the power of a rationally organized and intelligently run state. And finally, they all have short patience with attacks on "elitism" and the unequal distribution of the power to make crucial decisions.

Without committing oneself heart and soul to the viewpoint described above, it is easy enough to see its plausibility. In the modern age there really is something quixotic and even dangerous in demands to "abolish the state" or "throw out the bureaucrats." Since in many cases real injustices and failings of civil society were the efficient causes of the bureaucracies' creation, to abolish them may frequently mean reinstating those same old injustices or at a minimum closing one's eyes to serious problems, thus allowing them to get worse and worse.

Even more disturbing is the underlying hypocrisy of the Jeffersonian position evoked in the midst of modern society. If we are honest with ourselves we know that the state cannot and will not wither away.

To employ the sort of rhetoric that implies that some such Aufhebung of the state is indeed possible is to indulge in a dangerous delusion. The attributes of state power that Hegel identified—law-making, decision, bureaucracy—will reassert themselves in one way or another, probably in a way far less amenable to rational control and articulation than if they were overtly recognized. One could argue, for example, that the Soviet political system became tyrannical to some extent because antistate rhetoric masked the rapid accumulation of power, first in the Politburo, then in the hands of Stalin himself. Since the Bolshevik leaders mostly thought of the division of powers as an outmoded bourgeois ideology, they saw no need to apply it to their own revolution, even as the need for such a division became ever more pressing.

Besides acknowledging the Hamiltonian-Hegelian brief in favor of a rational, effective state, we also noted the tendency of this position to mistrust interest-group politics and populist, antielitist arguments. Whatever the justification for this view, one can still see in it signs of a crippling weakness both in Hegel's political theory and in the more diverse stream of Hamiltonian democracy to which I have related Hegel.

The *Philosophy of Right*, as we recall from chapters 7 and 8, sketched out a state in which each individual was to find satisfaction in his assigned sphere in society. There was to be little opportunity for any thoroughgoing and sweeping critique of public affairs. Indeed, Hegel deliberately arranged things so that citizens could "let off steam" politically on the corporate and municipal levels, squabbling about who should hold which minor offices. The outspoken Croly defends a position similar to Hegel's (though far more democratic) in his own plea for Hamiltonian politics.[14]

It is surprising that a philosopher like Hegel, so acutely aware of the fragmentation of the self and the alienation of the citizen from "ethical life" in the ancient sense, could so readily acquiesce in this kind of divorce between the state and the individual citizen. As I suggested, Hegel apparently thought that the Protestant Reformation and the renewal of interest in philosophy had created an "inner space" in which the intellectual and religious life of the individual would compensate him for the loss of ethical unity. He could see the architectonic edifice of the modern state and of modern theology and in this vision find a sort of satisfaction. And, of course, he could do his very best to contribute to the public good through his professional activities.

Yet there is still something missing here. One must ask whether any state can flourish unless a substantial part of its citizen body shows an active, intense concern for public issues. As Tocqueville argued in his study of American democracy, the egoism and self-absorption characteristic of a modern democracy is the most fertile soil in which a despotism (however "soft" and reasonable-seeming) can take root. Tocqueville praised American local government not for Hegel's reason, that it kept citizens' interests riveted on parochial concerns, but for just the opposite reason, that it cultivated a "taste" for liberty and forged links between otherwise atomized, isolated people.[15]

In this respect, Tocqueville makes the proper Jeffersonian response to Hegel's Hamiltonianism. He suggests that the spirit, the ethos of a people (which Hegel always considered so important) cannot be sustained merely by private associations and contracts. It is not enough to leave politics to the salaried public officials, philosophers, and enlightened politicians. Somehow, individual citizens must be coaxed out of their Cartesian shells and made to see that they—and not the officials and bureaucrats—do have political power and judgment enough to make their own decisions about public issues.

If this does not happen, we might suspect, then, in a crisis the wholly privatized citizen whom Hegel praises will not feel that he has any true stake in the state, that it is on any level the expression of his will. The Weimar Republic in Germany offers an instructive example of the dangers at the heart of Hegel's vision of a rational state. The German people had been used to the principle that the monarch and his ministers should make most of the vital decisions. This had been common practice from Hegel's time up until the collapse of the Empire after World War I. During the Republic, the old behavior persisted. German citizens organized themselves into parties that were sometimes scarcely more than glorified interest groups. As governments rose and fell, the civil service (so important to Hegel) did in fact maintain the continuity of policy and public services. For many Germans, it *was* the state.

The Weimar Republic was, in other words, highly vulnerable to totalitarian movements partly because of the elements Hegel identified precisely as crucial to a rational state: a citizenry suspicious of and unaccustomed to political involvement, as well as a highly trained, professional corps of civil servants who often made policy when elected governments could not. Astonishingly few citizens in Weimar Germany, when the threat of Nazism became plain, were actually willing to defend their state (as opposed to their Volk). If we think of Tocqueville's analysis, we might venture the suggestion that many Germans simply did not view their society in political terms, as an association of citizens committed to defending certain political values, ideals, and aspirations toward justice. They defined themselves in religious, ethnic, or class terms, roles that tended to mark them off from their fellow citizens and efface the things that all of them, as citizens, would have shared.

In conclusion, then, it seems to me that Hegel's flaws as a political philosopher should not be attributed to any alleged "state worship." Hegel, like the Americans of a Hamiltonian persuasion, turned to the state because he saw the defects in other institutions designed to achieve the good—contracts, morality, even the family and civil society, which were really part of the state in its wider meaning. He should instead be criticized for failing to see clearly the link between a politically knowledgeable and critical citizenry, on one side, and on the other, an effective, secure state possessing a genuine mandate to try to achieve the public good. In a crisis, these citizens are the only hope and support for a "rational" state. Without them, it will degenerate into a mere machine of coercion or collapse like a house of cards.

NOTES

Introduction

1. G. W. F. Hegel, "Differenz des Fichteschen und Schellingschen Systems der Philosophie," in *Jenaer Schriften*, p. 22; hereafter cited as "Differenzschrift."

2. Hegel, "Die Einleitung nach den Vorlesungen Hegels von 1823 bis 1827/28," in *Einleitung in die Geschichte der Philosophie*, p. 151 (Haldane and Simpson trans., 1:366); hereafter cited as *Einl. G. Phil.*, "Vorlesungen, 1823–28."

3. Ibid., p. 153.

4. Hegel, *Die Geschichte der Philosophie*, 2:22 (Haldane, 1:366); hereafter cited as *G. Phil.*, 1, 2, or 3. Cf. also Hegel's illuminating summary of sophism in ancient Greece in Haldane, pp. 352–72.

5. *Einl. G. Phil.*, "Vorlesungen, 1823–28," p. 225.

6. *Grundlinien der Philosophie des Rechts oder Naturrecht und Staatswissenschaft im Grundrisse*, Zusatz ¶138, p. 260 (Knox trans. p. 254); hereafter cited as *P. R.*

7. Hegel, *Vorlesungen über die Philosophie der Geschichte*, p. 135 (Sibree trans., p. 104); hereafter cited as *P. Gesch.*

8. *Einl. G. Phil.*, "Vorlesungen, 1823–28," p. 151.

9. Hegel, *Einleitung in die Geschichte der Philosophie*, "Die Berliner Niederschrift," p. 61; hereafter cited as *Einl. G. Phil.*, "Berliner Niederschrift."

10. Hegel, *Enzyklopädie der philosophischen Wissenschaften*, 1:16 (not in Wallace trans.); hereafter cited as *Enz.* 1 or 3.

11. René Descartes, "Discourse on Method," in *Descartes: Philosophical Writings*, p. 131.

Chapter 1

1. Hegel, *Die Phänomenologie des Geistes*, p. 140 (Baillie trans., p. 227); hereafter cited as *Ph. G.*
2. Hegel, *Wissenschaft der Logik*, 2:253 (Johnston and Struthers trans., p. 217); hereafter cited as *Logik* 1 or 2.
3. Ibid., p. 549.
4. Hegel, *Einleitung in die Geschichte der Philosophie*, "Die Heidelberger Niederschrift," p. 27; hereafter cited as *Einl. G. Phil.*, "Heidelberger Niederschrift."
5. Ibid., p. 35.
6. *G. Phil.* 3:268 (Haldane, p. 160).
7. Ibid., p. 270 (Haldane, p. 161).
8. Ibid., p. 328 (Haldane, p. 217).
9. Ibid., p. 335 (Haldane, p. 224).
10. Ibid., pp. 328–29 (Haldane, p. 218).
11. *Enz.* 1, ¶64, p. 154 (Wallace trans., p. 127).
12. *G. Phil.* 3:338 (Haldane, pp. 226–27).
13. Ibid., p. 350 (Haldane, p. 237).
14. Ibid., pp. 339–40 (Haldane, p. 228).
15. Ibid., p. 344 (Haldane, p. 232).
16. Ibid., p. 340 (Haldane, p. 230).
17. Ibid., p. 367 (Haldane, pp. 261–62).
18. David Hume, *A Treatise of Human Nature*, p. 251.
19. Ibid., pp. 251–52.
20. *Ph. G.*, pp. 89–129 (Baillie, pp. 161–213).
21. Immanuel Kant, *Kritik der reinen Vernunft*, B134–35, p. 144b (Smith trans., p. 154); hereafter cited as *K. r. V.*
22. Ibid., B131–32, pp. 140–41b (Smith, pp. 152–53).
23. Ibid., B134, p. 144b (Smith, p. 154).
24. Ibid., A111, p. 162a (Smith, p. 138).
25. Ibid., A105, pp. 152–53a (Smith, p. 135).
26. Ibid., B139, p. 151b (Smith, p. 157).
27. Ibid., A125, p. 184a (Smith, p. 147).
28. Ibid., A126, p. 186a (Smith, p. 148).
29. Ibid., A89, p. 131 (Smith, p. 124).
30. Ibid., B134, footnote, p. 143b (Smith, p. 154).
31. *G. Phil.* 3:535 (Haldane, p. 408).
32. Hegel, "Glauben und Wissen oder Reflexionsphilosophie der Subjektivität in der Vollständigkeit ihrer Formen als Kantische, Jacobische und Fichtesche Philosophie," *Jenaer Schriften*, p. 304, hereafter cited as "G.W."; and *G. Phil.* 3:558–59.

33. "G.W.," p. 304.
34. Ibid., p. 306.
35. *Ph. G.*, p. 63 (Baillie, p. 131).
36. *G. Phil.* 3:555 (Haldane, p. 428).
37. *Ph. G.*, p. 65 (Baillie, p. 133).
38. *Enz.* 1:Zusatz ¶47, p. 126 (Wallace, p. 97).
39. *G. Phil.* 3:578 (Haldane, p. 447).
40. Ibid.
41. *K. r. V.*, B404/A346, p. 374 (Smith, p. 331).
42. *Logik* 2:490 (Johnston, pp. 418–19).
43. *G. Phil.* 3:568 (Haldane, p. 439).
44. Johann Gottlieb Fichte, "Erste Einleitung," *Erste und Zweite Einleitung in die Wissenschaftslehre und Versuch einer neuen Darstellung der Wissenschaftslehre*, p. 10 (Heath/Lachs trans., p. 6); hereafter cited as *Wiss. Ein.*
45. Ibid., p. 6 (Heath, p. 4).
46. Ibid.
47. Ibid., p. 12 (Heath, p. 9).
48. Ibid., p. 14 (Heath, p. 10).
49. Ibid., pp. 15–16 (Heath, p. 11). The resemblance of Fichte's "free act" to modern existentialist notions of the for-itself (Sartre) or "possible Existenz" (Jaspers) is unmistakable. A great deal of modern existentialist writing, both theoretical and literary, seems to aim precisely at the conception of the "I" as freely determinable. The similarity is hardly surprising since Husserl, the intellectual mentor of much of that school, studied Fichte carefully and derived the essentials of his own theory of the intentionality of consciousness from the latter's work.
50. Ibid., p. 21 (Heath, p. 16).
51. *Logik* 2:259 (Johnston, p. 222); my emphasis—L. H.
52. J. G. Fichte, "Zweite Einleitung," *Wiss. Ein.*, p. 40 (Heath, p. 30).
53. Ibid., p. 44 (Heath, p. 33).
54. "Erste Einleitung," *Wiss. Ein.*, p. 22 (Heath, p. 17).
55. *Enz.* 3:Zusatz ¶385, p. 33.
56. "Zweite Einleitung," *Wiss. Ein*, p. 45 (Heath, p. 34).
57. Fichte, "Versuch einer Neuen Darstellung der Wissenschaftslehre," *Wiss. Ein.*, p. 112.
58. "Zweite Einleitung," *Wiss. Ein.*, p. 48 (Heath, p. 37).
59. Fichte, *The Vocation of Man*, p. 66; hereafter cited as *Voc. Man.*
60. "Zweite Einleitung," *Wiss. Ein.*, p. 50 (Heath, p. 38).
61. "Versuch einer Neuen Darstellung der Wissenschaftslehre," *Wiss. Ein.*, p. 115.
62. Ibid.; my emphasis—L. H.
63. *Voc. Man.*, pp. 66–67; my emphasis—L. H.
64. *Science of Knowledge* (Heath trans.), p. 109; hereafter cited as *Sci. Knowl.*
65. Ibid., p. 103.
66. Ibid., p. 109.

67. Ibid., p. 224.
68. "Zweite Einleitung," *Wiss. Ein.*, p. 40 (Heath, p. 30).
69. *Logik* 1:16 (Johnston, p. 36).
70. *Enz.* 3:Zusatz ¶379, p. 14.
71. *Voc. Man.*, pp. 82–83.
72. *Sci. Knowl.*, p. 137.
73. Ibid., p. 137.
74. "Differenzschrift," p. 56.
75. *G. Phil.* 3:634 (Haldane, p. 499).
76. "Differenzschrift," p. 69.
77. Friedrich Wilhelm Joseph von Schelling, "Darstellung meines Systems der Philosophie," in *Werke* 3:10; hereafter cited as "Darstellung."
78. Ibid., p. 9.
79. "Bruno oder über das Göttliche und Natürliche Prinzip der Dinge. Ein Gespräch," in *Werke* 3:111; hereafter cited as "Bruno."
80. "G.W.," p. 410.
81. "Bruno," pp. 131–32.
82. Ibid., pp. 133–34.
83. "Darstellung," p. 22.
84. Ibid., p. 16.
85. *Ph. G.*, pp. 18–19 (Baillie, p. 79).
86. *G. Phil.* 3:377 (Haldane, p. 288).

Chapter 2

1. "Differenzschrift," p. 141.
2. Schelling, "Letter of November 2, 1807," cited in Kuno Fischer, *Geschichte der neueren Philosophie*, vol. 7, *Schellings Leben, Werke und Lehre*, p. 146.
3. *Logik* 1:76–77 (Johnston, p. 88).
4. Ibid., p. 76 (Johnston, p. 88).
5. *Ph. G.*, p. 18 (Baillie, p. 78); my emphasis—L. H.
6. "Differenzschrift," p. 106.
7. Stanley Rosen, *G. W. F. Hegel: An Introduction to the Science of Wisdom*, p. xviii.
8. Ibid., p. 42.
9. *Enz.* 3: ¶413, p. 199 (Wallace, p. 47).
10. *Ph. G.*, pp. 556–57 (Baillie, p. 798).
11. *Enz.* 3:Zusatz ¶413, p. 201.
12. Ibid., ¶415, p. 202 (Wallace, p. 48).
13. *Enz.* 1: ¶20, pp. 71–72 (Wallace, pp. 35–36). The term "universal-in-action" as a translation of *tätiges Allgemeine* was suggested to me, like much else in this chapter, by reading Stanley Rosen's excellent work on Hegel.
14. Ibid., Zusatz 1, ¶42, p. 118 (Wallace, pp. 88–89).
15. *Logik,* 2:253 (Johnston, p. 217).

16. *Enz.* 3: ¶412, p. 198.
17. *Einl. G. Phil.* "Vorlesungen, 1823–28," p. 97.
18. *Enz.* 1: Zusatz 1, ¶163, p. 312 (Wallace, p. 292).
19. *Ph. G.*, pp. 125–26 (Baillie, pp. 208–9).
20. Ibid., p. 19 (Baillie, p. 80).
21. Ibid., pp. 20–21 (Baillie, pp. 81–82).
22. Ibid., p. 23 (Baillie, p. 85).
23. Ibid., p. 21 (Baillie, p. 81).
24. Ibid. (Baillie, p. 82).
25. Ibid., p. 24 (Baillie, pp. 85–86).
26. "Verhältnis des Skeptizismus zur Philosophie. Darstellung seiner verschiedenen Modifikationen und Vergleichung des neuesten mit dem alten," in *Jenaer Schriften*, p. 246; hereafter cited as "Skeptizismus."
27. "Differenzschrift," p. 96.
28. *Logik* 1: 144–66 (Johnston, pp. 144–69).
29. Ibid., p. 175 (Johnston, p. 171).
30. Ibid., p. 49 (Johnston, pp. 64–65).
31. *Enz.* 1: Zusatz ¶88, p. 192 (Wallace, p. 167).
32. *Logik* 1: 175 (Johnston, p. 171).
33. *Enz.* 1: Zusatz ¶96, pp. 203–4 (Wallace, p. 179).
34. *G. Phil.* 1: 367–68 (Haldane, 1: 302–3).
35. Ibid., p. 368.
36. *Logik*, 2: 295 (Wallace, p. 252).
37. *Enz.* 1: Zusatz 2, ¶24, p. 86 (Wallace, p. 52).
38. Ibid., Zusatz 3, ¶24, p. 87 (Wallace, p. 53).
39. Ibid., Zusatz ¶112, p. 232 (Wallace, p. 208).
40. *Logik* 2: 24 (Johnston, p. 25).
41. Ibid., p. 24 (Johnston, p. 26).
42. Ibid., p. 188 (Johnston, p. 162).
43. *Enz.* 1: Zusatz ¶151, p. 297 (Wallace, p. 276).
44. *Logik* 2: 246 (Johnston, p. 212).
45. "Differenzschrift," p. 108.
46. *Enz.* 3: Zusatz ¶382, p. 26.
47. *Logik*, 2: 251 (Johnston, p. 216).
48. *Enz.* 1: Zusatz ¶158, pp. 303–4 (Wallace, p. 283).
49. *Logik* 2: 253 (Johnston, pp. 217–18).
50. *Einl. G. Phil.*, "Vorlesungen, 1823–28," pp. 98–99.
51. *Enz.* 1: ¶215, pp. 372–73 (Wallace, pp. 357–58).
52. Ibid., Zusatz ¶213, p. 369 (Wallace, p. 354).
53. *Logik* 2: 464 (Johnston, p. 396).
54. *Enz.* 1: ¶214, p. 370 (Wallace, p. 355).
55. *Logik* 2: 464 (Johnston, p. 396).
56. *Enz.* 1: ¶6, pp. 47–49 (Wallace, pp. 10–12).
57. Ibid., ¶236, p. 388 (Wallace, p. 374).
58. *Einl. G. Phil.*, "Vorlesungen, 1823–28," p. 238.

59. *Enz.* 3: Zusatz ¶381, p. 21.
60. Ibid., Zusatz ¶382, p. 26.
61. *P. Gesch.*, p. 76 (Sibree, p. 55).
62. *Enz.* 3: Zusatz ¶443, pp. 237–38.
63. *P. Gesch.*, p. 104 (Sibree, p. 78).
64. *Ph. G.*, p. 30 (Baillie, p. 93).
65. *Enz.* 3: Zusatz ¶385, p. 33.
66. *Enz.* 3: ¶383, p. 27 (Wallace, p. 7).
67. Ibid., Zusatz ¶381, p. 21.
68. *Ph. G.*, p. 140 (Baillie, p. 227).
69. Ibid., p. 258 (Baillie, p. 378).
70. *Einl. G. Phil.*, "Vorlesungen, 1823–28," p. 176.
71. *Enz.* 3: ¶382, p. 25 (Wallace, p. 6).
72. Ibid., Zusatz ¶382, p. 26.
73. *Enz.* 3: Zusatz ¶431, p. 220.
74. *Einl. G. Phil.*, "Berliner Niederschrift," pp. 36–37.
75. Ibid., pp. 227–28.
76. *P. Gesch.*, p. 240 (Sibree, p. 194).
77. *Enz.* 3: ¶568, p. 375 (Wallace, p. 178).
78. *Enz.* 1: ¶74, p. 163 (Wallace, p. 137).
79. *Enz.* 3: ¶564, p. 374 (Wallace, p. 176).
80. *Einl. G. Phil.*, "Vorlesungen, 1823–28," p. 174n2.
81. *Ph. G.*, p. 529 (Baillie, p. 760).
82. *Einl. G. Phil.*, "Vorlesungen, 1823–28," p. 177.
83. *Ph. G.*, pp. 32–33 (Baillie, pp. 96–97).

CHAPTER 3

1. *G. Phil.* 3: 269 (Haldane, p. 161).
2. *Logik* 1: 140 (Johnston, p. 142).
3. *Logik* 2: 286 (Johnston, p. 245).
4. *Ph. G.*, p. 29 (Baillie, p. 93).
5. *Enz.* 1: Zusatz ¶80, p. 169 (Wallace, p. 144).
6. Ibid.
7. *Ph. G.*, p. 29 (Baillie, p. 93).
8. *Logik* 2: 288 (Johnston, p. 246).
9. *Enz.* 1: ¶20, p. 73 (Wallace, p. 38).
10. *Logik* 1: 38 (Johnston, p. 56).
11. "Differenzschrift," pp. 95 and 98.
12. Ibid., p. 26.
13. *Enz.* 1: ¶7, p. 50 (Wallace, p. 13).
14. Ibid., ¶12, p. 57 (Wallace, pp. 21–22).
15. Ibid., ¶8, p. 51 (Wallace, p. 14).
16. *Ph. G.*, p. 17 (Baillie, pp. 76–77).

17. *Einl. G. Phil.*, "Vorlesungen, 1823–28," p. 159.
18. *Enz.* 1: ¶7, p. 49 (Wallace, p. 12).
19. Ibid., ¶38, p. 108 (Wallace, pp. 77–78).
20. Ibid., p. 47.
21. Emil L. Fackenheim, *The Religious Dimension in Hegel's Thought*, pp. 44–50, 116–215.
22. *G. Phil.* 3:421 (Haldane, p. 295).
23. Ibid., p. 423 (Haldane, p. 298).
24. Ibid., p. 427 (Haldane, p. 306).
25. Ibid., p. 429 (Haldane, p. 310).
26. Ibid., p. 424 (Haldane, p. 299).
27. *Logik* 2:260 (Johnston, p. 223). This indifference to speculative truth which distinguishes Locke's "genetic" approach to general concepts can be found, according to Hegel, even in the so-called idealism of Berkeley. Cf. *Logik* 1:173.
28. *G. Phil.* 3:417 (Haldane, p. 296).
29. *Enz.* 1: ¶21 and Zusatz, pp. 76–78 (Wallace, pp. 41–43).
30. Ibid., ¶22 (Wallace, p. 43).
31. *Logik* 1:26–27 (Johnston, p. 45).
32. *Enz.* 1: ¶8, p. 52 (Wallace, p. 15).
33. Ibid., Zusatz ¶227, p. 380 (Wallace, p. 365).
34. Hegel, "Über die wissenschaftlichen Behandlungsarten des Naturrechts, seine Stelle in der praktischen Philosophie und sein Verhältnis zu den positiven Rechtswissenschaften," *Jenaer Schriften*, p. 445; hereafter cited as "Naturrecht."
35. *Enz.* 1: ¶38, pp. 108–9 (Wallace, p. 78).
36. Ibid., ¶38, pp. 109–10 (Wallace, pp. 79–80). Although Hegel does not mention Hobbes in this context, the latter would provide a fine example of Hegel's point. When Hobbes proposes to treat a commonwealth like a watch, taking it apart to see how it works and putting it back together again, he assumes that society is essentially a mechanism. In mechanical relationships, the parts are each self-subsistent and may be examined in isolation from the whole to which they belong. In the *Philosophy of Right*, to be discussed in chapters 7 and 8, Hegel counters that a commonwealth is not a mechanism and that the Hobbesian commonwealth, reconstructed from supposedly elementary parts, would thus differ profoundly from the concrete commonwealth as it existed before Hobbes dissected it. Hegel does not object to analysis per se. He only objects to the claim that a society analyzed and reconstructed in a mechanical way bears any real resemblance to a living human association.
37. *Logik* 2:259–60 (Johnston, pp. 222–23).
38. *Enz.* 1: ¶38, p. 110 (Wallace, p. 80).
39. "G.W.," p. 371.
40. "Naturrecht," p. 445.
41. Ibid., p. 446.
42. *Logik* 2:259 (Johnston, p. 222).

43. "Naturrecht," p. 450.
44. *Einl. G. Phil.*, "Vorlesungen, 1823–28," p. 113.
45. *Einl. G. Phil.*, "Berliner Niederschrift," p. 66.
46. *Enz.* 3:Zusatz ¶381, pp. 24–25.
47. Ibid., ¶412, p. 197 (Wallace, pp. 45–46).
48. Ibid., Zusatz ¶412, p. 198.
49. "Skeptizismus," p. 259.
50. Ibid.
51. *Ph. G.*, p. 176 (Baillie, p. 273).
52. Ibid., p. 178 (Baillie, p. 276).
53. Ibid., p. 195 (Baillie, pp. 298–99).
54. Ibid., p. 223 (Baillie, p. 331).
55. Ibid., p. 224 (Baillie, p. 332).
56. Ibid., p. 225 (Baillie, p. 333).
57. *Enz.* 1:Zusatz ¶140, p. 277 (Wallace, p. 255).
58. Ibid., p. 278 (Wallace, p. 256).
59. Ibid., p. 277 (Wallace, p. 255).
60. Ibid., p. 278 (Wallace, p. 256).
61. *Ph. G.*, p. 226 (Baillie, pp. 334–35).
62. Ibid., p. 225 (Baillie, p. 334).
63. Ibid., p. 226 (Baillie, p. 335).
64. *Logik* 2:227–28 (Johnston, p. 195).
65. *Ph. G.*, p. 255 (Baillie, p. 374).
66. Ibid., p. 184 (Baillie, p. 282).
67. "Differenzschrift," p. 20.

Chapter 4

1. *Enz.* 1: ¶39, p. 111–12 (Wallace, p. 82).
2. Ibid., ¶22, p. 79 (Wallace, p. 44).
3. *Ph. G.*, p. 32 (Baillie, p. 96).
4. Ibid., p. 368 (Baillie, p. 538).
5. *P. Gesch.*, p. 57 (Sibree, pp. 39–40).
6. Ibid.
7. *P. R.*, ¶146, pp. 294–95 (Knox, pp. 105–6).
8. *Ph. G.*, pp. 320–21 (Baillie, p. 469).
9. Ibid., p. 321.
10. Ibid., p. 256 (Baillie, p. 375).
11. *Einl. G. Phil.*, "Vorlesungen, 1823–28," p. 234.
12. *P. R.*, ¶142, p. 292 (Knox, p. 105).
13. *Ph. G.*, p. 258 (Baillie, pp. 377–78).
14. *G. Phil.* 2:1 (Haldane, 1:350).
15. *Ph. G.*, p. 311 (Baillie, p. 452).
16. Ibid., pp. 344–45 (Baillie, pp. 503–4).

17. *Ph. G.*, p. 346 (Baillie, p. 504).
18. G. W. F. Hegel, "Die Positivität der christlichen Religion" (Zusätze), *Frühe Schriften*, pp. 202–17.
19. Ibid., pp. 211–12.
20. *P. Gesch.*, p. 496 (Sibree, p. 417).
21. *Enz.* 3: ¶387, p. 39 (Wallace, p. 11).
22. *Einl. G. Phil.*, "Berliner Niederschrift," pp. 41–42.
23. *Ph. G.*, p. 351 (Baillie, p. 515).
24. Jean-Jacques Rousseau, "Emile," in *Jean-Jacques Rousseau: His Educational Theories Selected from Emile, Julie, and Other Writings*, p. 59.
25. *G. Phil.* 3:527–29 (Haldane, pp. 401–2).
26. *Ph. G.*, p. 27 (Baillie, p. 90).
27. Ibid., p. 353 (Baillie, p. 517).
28. Ibid.
29. Ibid., p. 354 (Baillie, p. 519).
30. Ibid., p. 351 (Baillie, p. 515).
31. Ibid., p. 355 (Baillie, pp. 519–20).
32. Ibid. (Baillie, p. 520).
33. Ibid. (Baillie, p. 521).
34. Ibid., pp. 355–56 (Baillie, p. 521).
35. Ibid. (Baillie, p. 522).
36. Ibid., p. 357 (Baillie, p. 523).
37. Ibid. (Baillie, p. 523).
38. Ibid., p. 358 (Baillie, p. 524).
39. Ibid., p. 359 (Baillie, p. 525).
40. Ibid. This passage, like numerous others concerning culture, contains an allusion to Diderot's dialogue "Rameau's Nephew," written in the 1760s and first published in Germany in 1805, after having been translated by Goethe.
41. Ibid., p. 360 (Baillie, pp. 526–27).
42. Ibid. (Baillie, p. 527).
43. Ibid., p. 361 (Baillie, p. 528).
44. Ibid.
45. Ibid., pp. 361–62 (Baillie, p. 529).
46. Ibid. (Baillie, p. 530).
47. Ibid., p. 364 (Baillie, p. 533).
48. Jean Hyppolite, *Genesis and Structure of Hegel's Phenomenology of Spirit*, p. 405.
49. *Ph. G.*, p. 365 (Baillie, p. 534).
50. Ibid. (Baillie, p. 533).
51. Ibid. (Baillie, p. 534).
52. Ibid., p. 366 (Baillie, p. 534).
53. Ibid. (Baillie, pp. 535–36).
54. Ibid., pp. 367–68 (Baillie, p. 537).
55. Ibid., p. 368 (Baillie, pp. 537–38).

56. Denis Diderot, "Rameau's Nephew," in *Rameau's Nephew and Other Works*, p. 19.
57. Ibid., p. 34.
58. Ibid.
59. *Ph. G.*, p. 369 (Baillie, p. 539).
60. Ibid., p. 370 (Baillie, p. 540).
61. Ibid. (Baillie, p. 539).
62. Ibid., pp. 370–71 (Baillie, pp. 540–41).
63. "Rameau's Nephew," pp. 50–51.
64. *Ph. G.*, p. 372 (Baillie, p. 543).
65. *G. Phil.* 3:506 (Haldane, p. 380).
66. Ibid., p. 510 (Haldane, p. 384).
67. *Ph. G.*, p. 374 (Baillie, p. 545).
68. Ibid. (Baillie, p. 546).

Chapter 5

1. *Ph. G.*, p. 375 (Baillie, p. 547). I have translated this passage rather differently than Baillie did. He renders *Macht* as "state power" in accordance with a theme developed earlier in this section. But the Rameau passage makes it clear that, by this time, Hegel is concerned with power as such, and not exclusively with state power. Hence, I translate "Macht" simply as "power," which is its literal meaning.
2. Ibid., pp. 378–79 (Baillie, p. 553).
3. *G. Phil.* 2:469 (Haldane, p. 271). Hegel calls the Stoic sage "enlightened" because he rejects such taboos as cannibalism and incest as being merely natural, not rational.
4. *G. Phil.* 3:526 (Haldane, p. 398).
5. Ibid., p. 506 and p. 526 (Haldane, pp. 379, 390).
6. Ibid., p. 511 (Haldane, p. 385).
7. *Einl. G. Phil.*, "Vorlesungen, 1823–1828," p. 220.
8. *Ph. G.*, pp. 378–79 (Baillie, p. 552).
9. Ibid., p. 125 (Baillie, p. 208).
10. Ibid., p. 379 (Baillie, p. 553).
11. *Einl. G. Phil.*, "Vorlesungen, 1823–28," p. 169.
12. *Enz.* 1: ¶2, p. 42 (Wallace, p. 5).
13. The term "pure insight" (*reine Einsicht*) comes from the German *einsehen* which normally means "understand" or "see the point." Hegel uses it to suggest that we know or understand only that which we ourselves are or create. The term is also used sometimes by Fichte to indicate the psychological "leap" that one must make to become a genuine idealist in his sense, i.e., to grasp that "reality," the not-"I," is ultimately determined by the "I" in the way we have discussed already. This use is quite appropriate in the context we now have before us. See the *Science of Knowledge*, p. 250.

14. *Ph. G.*, p. 378 (Baillie, p. 552).
15. Ibid., p. 383 (Baillie, p. 560).
16. Ibid., pp. 384–86 (Baillie, pp. 560–62).
17. *Einl. G. Phil.*, "Berliner Niederschrift," p. 43.
18. *Ph. G.*, p. 390 (Baillie, p. 568).
19. Ibid., p. 391 (Baillie, p. 569).
20. *Einl. G. Phil.*, "Vorlesungen, 1823–28," p. 177.
21. *Ph. G.*, p. 391 (Baillie, p. 569).
22. Ibid., p. 392 (Baillie, p. 570).
23. Ibid., pp. 394–95 (Baillie, p. 573).
24. Ibid., p. 395 (Baillie, p. 573).
25. *Enz.* 3: ¶573, pp. 379–80 (Wallace, p. 183).
26. *Ph. G.*, p. 395 (Baillie, p. 574).
27. Ibid., p. 396 (Baillie, p. 574).
28. Ibid. (Baillie, p. 575).
29. "G.W.," p. 294.
30. *Ph. G.*, pp. 405–6 (Baillie, p. 588).
31. Ibid., pp. 406–7 (Baillie, p. 589).
32. Ibid., p. 397 (Baillie, p. 576).
33. Ibid. (Baillie, p. 577).
34. Ibid., p. 408 (Baillie, p. 592).
35. *Enz.* 3:Zusatz ¶384, p. 31.
36. *G. Phil.* 3:513 (Haldane, p. 387).
37. Ibid. The last clause is, however, not reproduced in Haldane in the same form.
38. *Ph. G.*, p. 410 (Baillie, p. 594).
39. Ibid., pp. 399–400 (Baillie, pp. 578–80).
40. Ibid., p. 399 (Baillie, p. 579).
41. Ibid., p. 400 (Baillie, p. 580). Baillie translates *Nutzen* as profitability, which seems to me less accurate than usefulness.
42. *Enz.* 1:Zusatz ¶24, pp. 90–91 (Wallace, p. 57).
43. *Einl. G. Phil.*, "Heidelberger Niederschrift," p. 13.
44. *Ph. G.*, p. 414 (Baillie, p. 599).
45. *P. Gesch.*, pp. 527–28 (Sibree, p. 446).
46. Ibid., pp. 527–28 (Sibree, p. 447).
47. Ibid., p. 52 (Sibree, p. 35).
48. Ibid., p. 51 (Sibree, pp. 34–35).
49. *Einl. G. Phil.*, "Vorlesungen, 1823–28," p. 234.
50. *Ph. G.*, p. 415 (Baillie, pp. 600–601).
51. Jean-Jacques Rousseau, *On the Social Contract*, p. 53.
52. *P. Gesch.*, p. 418 (Sibree, p. 346).
53. *G. Phil.* 3:528 (Haldane, p. 402).
54. *P. Gesch.*, p. 527 (Sibree, p. 446).
55. *G. Phil.* 3:529 (Haldane, p. 402).
56. *Ph. G.*, p. 416 (Baillie, p. 602).

57. Ibid., pp. 415–16 (Baillie, pp. 601–2).
58. Ibid., p. 416 (Baillie, pp. 601–2).
59. *P. Gesch.*, p. 525 (Sibree, p. 443).
60. *G. Phil.* 3:528 (Haldane, p. 402).
61. *Ph. G.*, p. 417 (Baillie, p. 603).
62. Ibid., p. 418 (Baillie, p. 604).
63. Ibid.
64. Ibid., p. 419 (Baillie, pp. 605–6).
65. Ibid. (Baillie, p. 606).
66. Ibid., p. 418 (Baillie, pp. 604–5).
67. Ibid. (Baillie, p. 604).
68. Ibid., pp. 418–19 (Baillie, p. 605).
69. Ibid., p. 420 (Baillie, p. 607).
70. *P. Gesch.*, p. 533 (Sibree, p. 451).
71. Ibid., p. 535 (Sibree, p. 452).
72. *Enz.* 3: ¶552, p. 360 (Wallace, p. 161).
73. *P. Gesch.*, p. 535 (Sibree, p. 453).
74. *Ph. G.*, p. 422 (Baillie, p. 609).
75. *P. Gesch.*, p. 523 (Sibree, pp. 441–42).
76. Ibid., p. 537 (Sibree, p. 454).
77. *G. Phil.* 3:515.

Chapter 6

1. I. Kant, "Beantwortung der Frage: Was ist Aufklärung?" in *Immanuel Kant: Politische Schriften*, p. 1 (Beck, p. 286).
2. *Sci. Knowl.*, p. 233.
3. *P. Gesch*, p. 526 (Sibree, p. 444).
4. "G.W," pp. 298–99.
5. Ibid., p. 432.
6. Kant, *Kritik der Praktischen Vernunft*, pp. 5–7 (Beck, pp. 118–21). Hereafter cited as *K. p. V.*
7. *K. r. V.*, A523/B561, p. 523 (Smith, p. 464).
8. Ibid., A546/B574, p. 533 (Smith, p. 472).
9. Kant, *Grundlegung zur Metaphysik der Sitten*, p. 103 (Beck, p. 101).
10. Ibid., p. 68 (Beck, p. 80).
11. Ibid., p. 86 (Beck, p. 91).
12. Ibid., p. 111 (Beck, p. 106).
13. Ibid., p. 87 (Beck, p. 92).
14. *Sci. Knowl.*, p. 232.
15. Ibid., p. 230.
16. Fichte is also treated in the next section on "Conscience," a principle he introduces in his *Vocation of Man*.
17. *K. p. V.*, p. 152 (Beck, p. 214).

18. *Ph. G.*, p. 425 (Baillie, p. 616).
19. Ibid., p. 426 (Baillie, p. 616).
20. *K. p. V.*, p. 34 (Beck, p. 136).
21. Ibid., p. 169 (Beck, p. 225).
22. *Ph. G.*, p. 428 (Baillie, p. 620).
23. Ibid., p. 430 (Baillie, p. 622).
24. *K. p. V.*, pp. 172–73 (Beck, pp. 227–28).
25. *Ph. G.*, p. 432 (Baillie, pp. 624–25).
26. *K. p. V.*, p. 172 (Beck, p. 227).
27. *Ph. G.*, p. 435 (Baillie, p. 630).
28. Ibid. (Baillie, p. 631).
29. Ibid., p. 436 (Baillie, p. 631).
30. Ibid., p. 439 (Baillie, p. 635).
31. Ibid., p. 440 (Baillie, p. 636).
32. *G. Phil.*, 3:595 (Haldane, p. 463).
33. "Konzept der Rede beim Antritt des philosophischen Lehramtes an der Universität Berlin" (Einleitung zur Enzyklopädie-Vorlesung; Okt. 1818), in *Enz.* 3:399.
34. "Positivität der Christlichen Religion," p. 105.
35. Ibid., Neufassung des Anfangs, p. 219.
36. *Logik* 1:267 (Johnston, p. 246).
37. "Positivität der Christlichen Religion," Neufassung des Anfangs, pp. 220–21.
38. "G.W.," pp. 287–88.
39. *Enz.* 3: ¶475, p. 298 (Wallace, p. 98).
40. *Ph. G.*, p. 444 (Baillie, p. 641).
41. Ibid., p. 445 (Baillie, p. 644).
42. *Voc. Man*, pp. 110–11.
43. Ibid., p. 111.
44. Ibid., p. 105.
45. *Ph. G.*, p. 444 (Baillie, p. 641).
46. Ibid., p. 447 (Baillie, p. 647).
47. Ibid., p. 449 (Baillie, p. 649).
48. Ibid., p. 450 (Baillie, p. 650).
49. Ibid.
50. Ibid., p. 457 (Baillie, p. 659).
51. Ibid., p. 458 (Baillie, p. 660).
52. Ibid. (Baillie, pp. 660–61).
53. Ibid., p. 457 (Baillie, p. 659).
54. Ibid., p. 458 (Baillie, p. 660).
55. Ibid., p. 459 (Baillie, p. 662).
56. Johann Wolfgang Goethe, *Wilhelm Meisters Lehrjahre*, p. 95.
57. Ibid., p. 126.
58. Ibid., pp. 130–31.
59. *Ph. G.*, p. 461 (Baillie, p. 664).

60. Ibid. (Baillie, pp. 664–65).
61. Ibid., pp. 462–63 (Baillie, pp. 666–67).
62. *Enz.* 1: ¶77, pp. 166–67 (Wallace, p. 140).
63. *Ph. G.*, p. 15 (Baillie, p. 74).
64. *Enz.* 1: ¶73, p. 163 (Wallace, p. 136).
65. Ibid., ¶63, p. 152 (Wallace, p. 125).
66. "G.W.," pp. 387–88.
67. *Ph. G.*, pp. 463–64 (Baillie, pp. 667–68).
68. Ibid., p. 464 (Baillie, p. 669).
69. *Enz.* 3: ¶511, p. 316 (Wallace, p. 117).
70. Ibid., ¶511, pp. 316–17 (Wallace, pp. 117–18).
71. *Ph. G.*, pp. 467–68 (Baillie, p. 673).
72. Ibid., p. 471 (Baillie, p. 677).
73. *Ph. G.*, p. 472 (Baillie, p. 679).

Chapter 7

1. *P. R.*, ¶5, p. 50 (Knox, p. 22).
2. Ibid., Zusatz ¶5, p. 52 (Knox, pp. 227–28).
3. *Enz.* 1:Zusatz ¶19, p. 71 (Wallace, pp. 34–35).
4. *P. R.*, pp. 12–13 (Knox, p. 2).
5. Ibid., p. 16n (Knox, p. 224).
6. Ibid., p. 24 (Knox, p. 10).
7. Ibid., p. 26 (Knox, p. 11).
8. For example, see Avineri, Taylor, and even Findlay, who is otherwise highly critical of Hegel's political philosophy. All of these commentators deny, in a more or less decisive way, that Hegel is a totalitarian "state-worshipper."
9. *P. R.*, ¶3, p. 36 (Knox, p. 17).
10. *P. Gesch.*, p. 535 (Sibree, p. 452).
11. *Ph. G.*, p. 139 (Baillie, p. 225).
12. *Enz.* 3: ¶430 and Zusatz, p. 219 (Wallace, p. 55, for paragraph alone).
13. G. W. F. Hegel, "Texte zur Philosophischen Propädeutik," *Nürnberger und Heidelberger Schriften 1808–1817*, p. 120; hereafter cited as "Philosophische Propädeutik."
14. *Enz.* 3:Zusatz ¶432, p. 221.
15. Ibid., ¶433 and ¶435 with Zusätze, pp. 222–25 (Wallace, pp. 56–57). See also *Ph. G.*, p. 147 (Baillie, pp. 236–37).
16. *Ph. G.*, p. 147 (Baillie, p. 236).
17. *Enz.* 3:Zusatz ¶436, p. 227.
18. *Ph. G.*, p. 149 (Baillie, p. 239).
19. Manfred Riedel, "Objektiver Geist und praktische Philosophie," *Studien zu Hegels Rechtsphilosophie*, pp. 29–33 et passim.
20. *Ph. G.*, p. 149 (Baillie, p. 239). In the rudimentary "philosophies" of master and servant we thus find adumbrations of the dichotomy between an-

cient and modern metaphysics. The nonlaboring classical master conceives of the world as a permanent nature or *physis* defined by teleological form. The modern laboring consciousness puts the emphasis on activity or form creation whose highest expression is the concept, or the absolute as formation process.

21. "Hegel's Social Philosophy in the Jena *Realphilosophie*, 1804–5," in "Hegel's Social Philosophy in the Jena Realphilosophie," ed. and trans. Allen Wood, p. 2; hereafter cited as "Realphilosophie (1804–5)."

22. *Enz.* 3: ¶436, p. 226 (Wallace, p. 57).

23. Ibid., Zusatz ¶431, p. 220.

24. *P. R.*, Zusatz ¶7, p. 57 (Knox, pp. 228–29).

25. *Enz.* 3: ¶436, p. 226 (Wallace, p. 57).

26. Ibid., ¶486, p. 304 (Wallace, p. 104).

27. *P. R.*, Zusatz ¶4, pp. 46–48 (Knox, pp. 225–27).

28. Ibid., ¶7, p. 55 (Knox, p. 24).

29. Ibid. (Knox, pp. 23–24).

30. Ibid., Zusatz ¶7, p. 57 (Knox, p. 228).

31. Ibid., ¶15, p. 67 (Knox, p. 28).

32. Ibid., Zusatz ¶15, pp. 67–68 (Knox, p. 230).

33. See my discussion of freedom and necessity in chapter 2.

34. *Enz.* 1:Zusatz ¶158, pp. 303–4 (Wallace, p. 283).

35. *P. R.*, ¶79 (Knox, p. 32). This is the counterpart, in practical philosophy, of the *Logic*'s culmination in thought thinking itself.

36. "Hegel, *Jenenser Realphilosophie: Philosophie des Geistes*, 1805–6," in "Realphilosophie (1805–6)," p. 3.

37. *P. R.*, ¶29, pp. 80–81 (Knox, p. 33).

38. Ibid., p. 80 (Knox, p. 33).

39. Ibid., pp. 92–93, Hegel's handwritten notes (not reproduced in Knox).

40. Ibid., Zusatz ¶34, p. 93 (Knox, p. 234).

41. Ibid., ¶34, p. 92 (Knox, p. 37).

42. Ibid., ¶35, p. 94 (Knox, p. 37).

43. "Realphilosophie (1804–5)," p. 19.

44. *P. R.*, Zusatz ¶35, p. 95 (Knox, p. 235).

45. Ibid.

46. Ibid., ¶45, p. 107 (Knox, p. 42).

47. Ibid., Zusatz ¶41, p. 102 (Knox, pp. 235–36).

48. "Society and Labor in Hegel's Realphilosophie, 1803–4," in "Realphilosophie (1803–4)," pp. 6–7.

49. *P. R.*, ¶71, p. 153 (Knox, p. 57).

50. "Realphilosophie (1804–5)," p. 6.

51. *P. R.*, ¶75, pp. 157–58 and Zusatz, pp. 158–59 (Knox, pp. 58–59, 242).

52. Ibid., ¶81, p. 169 (Knox, p. 64).

53. Ibid., ¶82, p. 172 (Knox, p. 64).

54. Ibid., Zusatz ¶82, p. 173 (Knox, p. 244).

55. Ibid.

56. Ibid.
57. "Realphilosophie (1804–5)," p. 9.
58. *P. R.*, Zusatz ¶97, p. 186 (Knox, p. 246).
59. "Philosophische Propädeutik," p. 244.
60. Ibid.
61. *P. R.*, p. 189, handwritten note to ¶99 (not reproduced in Knox).
62. Ibid., ¶100, p. 191 (Knox, p. 71).
63. *P. R.*, Zusatz ¶97, p. 186 (Knox, p. 246). I have attempted elsewhere to retrace the evolution of Hegel's thinking on the issue of crime and punishment and have discussed the relevant passages in the *Philosophy of Right* in greater detail. See my "Hegel's Theory of Crime and Punishment" in *The Review of Politics*.
64. *Enz.* 3: ¶503, p. 312 (Wallace, p. 113).
65. *P. R.*, ¶104, p. 198 (Knox, p. 74).
66. Ibid., Zusatz ¶112, pp. 210–11 (Knox, p. 249).
67. "Differenzschrift," pp. 84–85.
68. *P. R.*, ¶135, p. 252 (Knox, pp. 89–90).
69. Ibid., ¶141, p. 286 (Knox, p. 103).

Chapter 8

1. *P. R.*, ¶141, p. 287 (Knox, p. 103).
2. Ibid., (Knox, p. 104).
3. Ibid., ¶144, pp. 293–94 (Knox, p. 105).
4. Ibid., ¶148, p. 297 (Knox, pp. 106–7).
5. *G. Phil.* 2:275 (Haldane, p. 96).
6. Ibid., pp. 289–95 (Haldane, 109–15).
7. *P. Gesch.*, p. 60 (Sibree, p. 42).
8. *P. R.*, Zusatz ¶238, p. 386 (Knox, p. 276).
9. Ibid., ¶238 (Knox, p. 148).
10. Ibid., Zusatz ¶182, p. 339 (Knox, p. 266).
11. Ibid., ¶190, p. 348 (Knox, p. 127).
12. Ibid., Zusatz ¶116, p. 339 (Knox, p. 267).
13. Ibid., Zusatz ¶33, p. 91 (Knox, p. 234).
14. Ibid., Zusatz ¶181, pp. 338–39 (Knox, p. 266).
15. Ibid., ¶182, p. 339 (Knox, pp. 122–23).
16. Ibid., ¶183, p. 340 (Knox, p. 123).
17. Ibid., ¶195, p. 351 (Knox, p. 128).
18. "Realphilosophie (1804–5)," pp. 2–3.
19. "Realphilosophie (1803–4)," p. 4.
20. Ibid., p. 14.
21. Ibid., p. 6.
22. *P. R.*, Zusatz ¶181, p. 339 (Knox, p. 266).
23. Ibid., ¶201 and Zusatz, pp. 354–55 (Knox, pp. 130–31, 270).

24. Ibid., Zusatz ¶203, p. 356 (Knox, p. 270).
25. Ibid.
26. Ibid., ¶245, p. 390 (Knox, p. 150).
27. Ibid., Zusatz ¶244, pp. 389–90 (Knox, pp. 277–78).
28. Ibid., ¶249, p. 393 (Knox, p. 153).
29. Ibid., ¶229, p. 381 (Knox, p. 145).
30. Ibid., ¶234, p. 383 (Knox, p. 146).
31. Ibid., Zusatz ¶234, p. 383 (Knox, p. 276).
32. Ibid., ¶249, p. 393 (Knox, p. 151).
33. Ibid., ¶250, p. 393 (Knox, p. 152).
34. Ibid., ¶253, p. 395 (Knox, pp. 153–54).
35. Ibid., ¶253, p. 396 (Knox, p. 154).
36. Ibid., Zusatz ¶255, pp. 396–97 (Knox, p. 278).
37. Ibid., Zusatz ¶255, p. 397 (Knox, p. 278).
38. Ibid., ¶258, p. 399 (Knox, p. 155).
39. Ibid., ¶255, p. 396 (Knox, p. 154).
40. Ibid., ¶256, pp. 397–98 (Knox, p. 155).
41. Ibid., ¶258, p. 399 (Knox, p. 156).
42. Ibid., Zusatz ¶258, p. 403 (Knox, p. 279), ¶261, pp. 407–9 (Knox, pp. 161–62).
43. Ibid., ¶267, pp. 412–13 (Knox, p. 163).
44. Ibid., ¶268, p. 413 (Knox, p. 164).
45. Ibid., ¶269, p. 414 (Knox, p. 164).
46. Ibid., ¶270, p. 428 (Knox, p. 173).
47. Ibid. ¶272, p. 432 (Knox, p. 174).
48. Ibid., ¶272, p. 434 (Knox, p. 175).
49. "Realphilosophie (1805–6)," p. 9.
50. *P. R.*, Zusatz ¶280, p. 451 (Knox, p. 289).
51. Ibid., ¶279, p. 446 (Knox, p. 181).
52. Ibid., ¶279, p. 447 (Knox, p. 183).
53. Ibid., ¶288, p. 458 (Knox, p. 189).
54. Ibid., ¶289.
55. Ibid., Zusatz ¶290, p. 460 (Knox, pp. 290–91).
56. Ibid., ¶289, p. 459 (Knox, p. 190).
57. Ibid., ¶301, p. 471 (Knox, p. 196).
58. Ibid., ¶302, p. 471 (Knox, p. 197).
59. Ibid., ¶302, p. 472 (Knox, p. 197).
60. Ibid., ¶303, p. 473 (Knox, p. 198).
61. Ibid., ¶308, p. 477 (Knox, p. 201).
62. Ibid., ¶311, p. 480 (Knox, p. 202).
63. Ibid.
64. Ibid., Zusatz ¶309, p. 478 (Knox, p. 293).
65. Ibid., ¶310, p. 479 (Knox, p. 201).
66. "Realphilosophie (1805–6)," p. 23.
67. Ibid., p. 33.

68. Ibid., p. 23.
69. Ibid., p. 25.
70. *G. Phil.*, 2:400 (Haldane, p. 209).
71. *P. R.*, Zusatz ¶279, p. 449 (Knox, p. 288).

Chapter 9

1. Edmund Husserl's "Philosophy as a Rigorous Science" is still one of the most perspicacious defenses of the transcendental role of the "I" in cognition. His remarks on "naturalistic philosophy" explain his reasons for criticizing empirical psychology on this score. See *Phenomenology and the Crisis of Philosophy*, pp. 79–122.
2. Martin Heidegger, *Being and Time*, pp. 21–22.
3. Cf. Heidegger, *An Introduction to Metaphysics*.
4. Jürgen Habermas in his *Knowledge and Human Interests* has tried to revive at least some aspects of the German idealists' theory of consciousness and freedom in opposition both to modern positivism and to hermeneutics and phenomenology.
5. Hegel frequently takes issue with both of these writers in the *Philosophy of Right*. Note especially his remarks about Fries in the "Preface" and about Haller in the long footnote to ¶258.
6. Max Horkheimer and Theodor Adorno, *Dialektik der Aufklärung*.
7. *P. R.*, Zusatz ¶15, p. 67 (Knox, p. 230).
8. I discuss this theme much more thoroughly in an article entitled "The Origins of Human Rights: A Hegelian Perspective," in the *Western Political Quarterly*.
9. Locke's case is more complex, since his laws of nature are ordained, he says, by God. But I will follow two noted scholars who otherwise agree on very little, Leo Strauss and C. B. Macpherson, in supposing that Locke actually held much the same view as Hobbes on the issue at hand, i.e., that the laws of nature are actually general rules for attaining what, by our natural right to self-preservation, we all wish to have: peace, security, and physical safety. See Strauss, *Natural Right and History*, pp. 227–31, and Macpherson, *The Political Theory of Possessive Individualism*, p. 239 ("Locke, like Hobbes, held that men are moved primarily by appetite and aversion").
10. "Realphilosophie" (1804–5), p. 19.
11. Herbert Croly, *The Promise of American Life*, p. 41.
12. Cf. especially the following works: John Kenneth Galbraith, *The Affluent Society*, where the author laments the stark contrast between our private affluence and public poverty; Theodore J. Lowi, *The End of Liberalism*, who indicts "interest-group liberalism" for, among other things, frittering away sovereignty to "private satrapies" (p. 296); and Lester C. Thurow, *The Zero Sum Society*, who traces many of our economic problems to a diffuse political system where no one can be held responsible for failure and drift.

13. Galbraith, for example, wants to see education financed by sales taxes, which automatically rise with a growing economy, rather than by the general property tax, which can usually be increased only when voters approve bond issues. This is clearly an attempt to limit direct democracy for the sake of a long-term public good, a Hamiltonian measure. Lowi, although he rejects "a heavy Prussian system of hierarchical subordination," wants to promote "administrative centralization" by clear and detailed statutes that would limit the ability of interest groups to intervene and influence policy on the administrative level, in effect winning battles there that they had lost at the legislative stage (*End of Liberalism*, p. 304).

14. Croly, *Promise of American Life*, pp. 399–454.

15. Tocqueville, *Democracy in America*, vol. 2, bk. 4, chaps. 7 and 8.

SELECTED BIBLIOGRAPHY

Works by Hegel

Einleitung in die Geschichte der Philosophie. Edited by Johannes Hoffmeister. Philosophische Studientexte. Berlin (East): Akademie-Verlag, 1966.

Enzyklopädie der philosophischen Wissenschaften. Edited by Eva Moldenhauer and Karl Markus Michel. Vol. 8 (*Erster Teil: Wissenschaft der Logik*) and vol. 10 (*Dritter Teil: Philosophie des Geistes*). Theorie Werkausgabe. Frankfurt am Main: Suhrkamp Verlag, 1970. [English versions, *The Logic of Hegel* (*Lesser Logic*). Translated by William Wallace. Oxford: Clarendon Press, 1892. *Hegel's Philosophy of Mind.* Translated by William Wallace. Oxford: Clarendon Press, 1894.]

Frühe Schriften. Werke. Edited by Eva Moldenhauer and Karl Markus Michel. Vol. 1. Theorie Werkausgabe. Frankfurt am Main: Suhrkamp Verlag, 1971.

Grundlinien der Philosophie des Rechts. Werke. Edited by Eva Moldenhauer and Karl Markus Michel. Vol. 7. Theorie Werkausgabe. Frankfurt am Main: Suhrkamp Verlag, 1970. [English version, *Hegel's Philosophy of Right.* Translated by T. M. Knox. London: Oxford University Press, 1967.]

Jenaer Schriften 1801–1807. Werke. Edited by Eva Moldenhauer and Karl Markus Michel. Vol. 2. Theorie Werkausgabe. Frankfurt am Main: Suhrkamp Verlag, 1970.

Nürnberger und Heidelberger Schriften 1808–1817. Werke. Edited by Eva Moldenhauer and Karl Markus Michel. Vol. 4 Theorie Werkausgabe. Frankfurt am Main: Suhrkamp Verlag, 1970.

Phänomenologie des Geistes. Edited by Johannes Hoffmeister. Hamburg: Verlag von Felix Meiner, 1952. [English version, *The Phenomenology of Mind*. Translated by J. B. Baillie. New York and Evanston: Harper & Row, 1967.]

Politische Schriften. Edited by Karl Markus Michel. Theorie 1. Frankfurt am Main: Suhrkamp Verlag, 1966.

"Social Philosophy in the *Jena Realphilosophie*." Edited and translated by Allen Wood. Unpublished manuscript, 1973.

Vorlesungen über die Geschichte der Philosophie. Werke. Edited by Dr. Karl Ludwig Michelet. Vols. 13–15. Edition: Freunden des Verewigten. Hamburg: Verlag von Duncker und Humblot, 1833. [English version, *Hegel's Lectures on the History of Philosophy*. 3 vols. Translated by E. S. Haldane. New York: Humanities Press, 1955.]

Vorlesungen über die Philosophie der Geschichte. Werke. Edited by Eva Moldenhauer and Karl Markus Michel. Vol. 12. Theorie Werkausgabe. Frankfurt am Main: Suhrkamp Verlag, 1970. [English version, *The Philosophy of History*. Translated by J. Sibree. New York: Dover Publications, 1956.]

Wissenschaft der Logik. Werke. Edited by Eva Moldenhauer and Karl Markus Michel. Vols. 5 and 6. Theorie Werkausgabe. Frankfurt am Main: Suhrkamp Verlag, 1969. [English version, *Hegel's Science of Logic*. 2 vols. Translated by W. H. Johnston and L. G. Struthers. New York: Macmillan, 1929.]

Other Works

Adorno, Theodor W. *Drei Studien zu Hegel*. Frankfurt am Main: Suhrkamp Verlag, 1974.

———, and Horkheimer, Max. *Dialektik der Aufklärung*. Amsterdam: Querido Verlag N. V., 1944.

Aristotle. *The Politics*. Translated by Ernest Barker. London: Oxford University Press, 1958.

Avineri, Shlomo. *Hegel's Theory of the Modern State*. Cambridge Studies in the History and Theory of Politics. London and New York: Cambridge University Press, 1972.

Brockard, Hans. *Subjekt: Versuch zur Ontologie bei Hegel*. Epimeleia: Beiträge zur Philosophie, vol. 17. Munich and Salzburg: Verlag Anton Pustet, 1970.

Burke, Edmund. *Reflections on the Revolution in France and on the Proceedings in Certain Societies in London on that Event*. Edited by William B. Todd. New York: Holt, Rinehart, and Winston, 1959.

Croly, Herbert. *The Promise of American Life*. New York: E. P. Dutton, 1963.

D'Abbiero, Marcella. *"Alienazione" in Hegel: Usi e Significati di Entäusserung, Entfremdung, Veräusserung*. Rome: Edizioni dell' Antaneo, 1970.

Descartes, René. *Philosophical Writings*. Selected and translated by Norman

Kemp Smith. New York: Random House, by arrangements with St. Martin's Press, 1958.

Diderot, Denis. *Rameau's Nephew and Other Works*. Translated by Jacques Barzun and Ralph H. Bowen. Indianapolis and New York: Bobbs-Merrill, 1956.

Fackenheim, Emil L. *The Religious Dimensions in Hegel's Thought*. Bloomington: Indiana University Press, 1967.

Fichte, Johann Gottlieb. *Erste und Zweite Einleitung in die Wissenschaftslehre und Versuch einer neuen Darstellung der Wissenschaftslehre*. Edited by Fritz Medicus. 2d ed. Hamburg: Verlag von Felix Meiner, 1954.

———. *Science of Knowledge (Wissenschaftslehre), with the First and Second Introductions*. Edited and translated by Peter Heath and John Lachs. New York: Appleton-Century Crofts, 1970.

———. *The Vocation of Man*. Translated by William Smith. La Salle, Illinois: Open Court, 1965.

Findlay, John Niemeyer. *The Philosophy of Hegel: An Introduction and Reexamination*. New York: Collier, 1962.

Fischer, Kuno. *Geschichte der neueren Philosophie*. Vol. 7: *Schellings Leben, Werke und Lehre*. Heidelberg: Carl Winters Universitätsbuchhandlung, 1923.

Galbraith, John Kenneth. *The Affluent Society*. New York and Toronto: Mentor, 1958.

Goethe, Johann Wolfgang. *Wilhelm Meisters Lehrjahre*. Zweiter Teil. Munich: Deutscher Taschenbuch Verlag, 1967.

Haag, Karl Heinz. *Philosopher Idealismus*. Kritische Studien zur Philosophie. Frankfurt am Main: Europäische Verlagsanstalt, 1967.

Habermas, Jürgen. *Erkenntnis und Interesse*. Theorie 2. Frankfurt am Main: Suhrkamp Verlag, 1968.

———. "Hegels Kritik der Französischen Revolution." In *Theorie und Praxis*. Politica: Abhandlungen und Texte zur politischen Wissenschaft, Vol. 11. 2d ed. Neuwied am Rhein: Hermann Luchterhand Verlag, 1963.

Hartnack, Justus. *Kant's Theory of Knowledge*. Translated by M. Holmes Harshorne. New York: Harcourt, Brace, and World, 1967.

Heidegger, Martin. *Being and Time*. Translated by John Macquarrie and Edward Robinson. New York: Harper and Row, 1967.

———. *Hegel's Concept of Experience*. Translated by Kenley Royce Dove. New York: Harper and Row, 1970.

———. *An Introduction to Metaphysics*. Translated by Ralph Mannheim. Garden City, N.Y.: Anchor Books, 1961.

Hinchman, Lewis. "Hegel's Theory of Crime and Punishment." *The Review of Politics* 44 (1982):523–45.

———. "The Origins of Human Rights: A Hegelian Perspective." *Western Political Quarterly* (Spring, 1984).

Holborn, Hajo. *A History of Modern Germany 1649–1840*. New York: Alfred A. Knopf, 1969.

Hume, David. *A Treatise of Human Nature*. Edited by L. A. Selby-Bigge. London: Oxford University Press, at the Clarendon Press, 1967.

Husserl, Edmund. *Phenomenology and the Crisis of Philosophy*. Translated by Quentin Lauer. New York: Harper and Row, 1965.

Hyppolite, Jean. *Genesis and Structure of Hegel's Phenomenology of Spirit*. Translated by Samuel Cherniak and John Heckman. Evanston, Ill.: Northwestern University Press, 1974.

———. *Studies on Marx and Hegel*. Edited and translated by John O'Neill. New York: Harper & Row by arrangement with Basic Books, 1969.

Kant, Immanuel. *Grundlegung zur Metaphysik der Sitten*. Edited by Theodor Valentiner. 5th ed. Stuttgart: Philipp Reclam jun., 1963.

———. *Kritik der praktischen Vernunft*. Edited by Raymund Schmidt. Leipzig: Verlag Phillip Reclam jun., n.d. [English version, *Critique of Practical Reason*. Edited and translated by Lewis White Beck. Chicago: University of Chicago Press, 1949.]

———. *Kritik der reinen Vernunft*. Edited by Raymund Schmidt. 2d ed. Hamburg: Verlag von Felix Meiner, 1956. [English version, *Critique of Pure Reason*. Translated by Normal Kemp Smith. New York: Humanities Press, 1929.]

———. *Kritik der Urteilskraft*. Edited by Raymund Schmidt. Universalbibliothek. Leipzig: Verlag Philipp Reclam jun., n.d.

———. *Politische Schriften*. Edited by Otto Heinrich von der Gablenz. Klassiker der Politik. Vol. 1. Cologne and Opladen: Westdeutscher Verlag, 1965.

———. *Prolegomena to any Future Metaphysics*. Edited by Lewis White Beck. Indianapolis and New York: Bobbs-Merrill, 1950.

Kaufmann, Walter. *Hegel: A Reinterpretation*. Garden City, N.Y.: Doubleday, 1966.

Kojève, Alexandre. *Introduction to the Reading of Hegel: Lectures on the Phenomenology of Spirit*. Assembled by Raymond Queneau. Edited by Allan Bloom. Translated by James H. Nichols, Jr. New York and London: Basic Books, 1968.

Kuhn, Thomas. *The Structure of Scientific Revolutions*. International Encyclopedia of Unified Science, vol. 2, no. 2. Chicago: University of Chicago Press, 1962.

Lauer, Quentin, S. J. *A Reading of Hegel's Phenomenology of Spirit*. New York: Fordham University Press, 1976.

Löwith, Karl. *From Hegel to Nietzsche: The Revolution in Nineteenth-Century Thought*. Translated by David E. Green. Garden City, N.Y.: Doubleday, 1964.

———. *Weltgeschichte und Heilsgeschehen: Die theologischen Voraussetzungen der Geschichtsphilosophie*. Stuttgart: W. Kohlhammer Verlag, 1953.

Lowi, Theodore J. *The End of Liberalism*. 2d ed. New York and London: W. W. Norton, 1979.

Macpherson, C. B. *The Political Theory of Possessive Individualism: Hobbes to Locke*. London: Oxford University Press, 1962.

McTaggart, J. M. E. *A Commentary on Hegel's Logic*. London: Cambridge University Press, 1931.

Marcuse, Herbert. *Reason and Revolution: Hegel and the Rise of Social Theory*. Boston: Beacon Press by arrangement with Humanities Press, 1960.

Martin, Kingsley. *French Liberal Thought in the Eighteenth Century: A Study of Political Ideas from Bayle to Condorcet*. Edited by J. P. Mayer. 3d ed. New York: Harper and Row by arrangement with Phoenix House, London, 1962.

Marx, Karl. *Critique of Hegel's "Philosophy of Right."* Edited by Joseph O'Malley. Translated by Joseph O'Malley and Amette Jolin. London and New York: Cambridge University Press, 1970.

———. "Kritik der Hegelschen Dialektik und Philosophie überhaupt" (Nationalökonomie und Philosophie Mx. 6). In *Marx-Engels Studienausgabe*. Vol. 1. Edited by Irving Fetscher. Frankfurt am Main: Fischer Bücherei, 1966.

Mure, Geoffrey R. G. *An Introduction to Hegel*. London: Oxford University Press at the Clarendon Press, 1940.

———. *A Study of Hegel's Logic*. London: Oxford University Press at the Clarendon Press, 1950.

Norman, Richard. *Hegel's Phenomenology: A Philosophical Introduction*. New York: St. Martin's Press, 1976.

Plato. *The Republic*. Translated by Allan Bloom. London and New York: Basic Books, 1968.

Popper, Karl. "Was ist Dialektik?" Translated by Johanna and Gottfried Frenzel. *Logik der Sozialwissenschaften*. Neue Wissenschaftliche Bibliothek. Vol. 6. Cologne and Berlin: Verlag Kiepenheuer und Witsch., 1970.

Riedel, Manfred. *Studien zu Hegels Realphilosophie*. Frankfurt am Main: Suhrkamp Verlag, 1972.

Ritter, Joachim. *Hegel und die Französische Revolution*. Frankfurt am Main: Suhrkamp Verlag, 1972.

Rosen, Stanley. *G. W. F. Hegel: An Introduction to the Science of Wisdom*. New Haven and London: Yale University Press, 1974.

Rousseau, Jean-Jacques. *Jean-Jacques Rousseau: His Educational Theories Selected from Emile, Julie, and Other Writings*. Edited and translated by R. L. Archer. Woodbury, N.Y.: Barron's Educational Series, 1964.

———. *On the Social Contract with Geneva Manuscript and Political Economy*. Edited by Roger D. Masters. Translated by Judith R. Masters. New York: St. Martin's Press, 1978.

Schelling, Friedrich W. J. von. *Darstellung meines Systems der Philosophie* and *Bruno oder über das göttliche und natürliche Prinzip der Dinge. Ein Gespräch. Werke*. Edited by Manfred Schröter. Vol. 3: *Schriften zur Identitätsphilosophie 1801–1806*. Edition: Münchner Jubiläumsdruck. Munich: E. H. Beck and R. Oldenbourg, 1927.

———. *System des transzendentalen Idealismus. Werke*. Edited by Manfred Schröter. Vol. 2: *Schriften zur Naturphilosophie 1799–1801*. Munich: E. H. Beck und R. Oldenbourg, 1927.

Soll, Ivan. *An Introduction to Hegel's Metaphysics*. Chicago and London: University of Chicago Press, 1969.

Strauss, Leo. *Natural Right and History*. Chicago: University of Chicago Press, 1950.

Swing, Thomas K. *Kant's Transcendental Logic.*. New Haven and London: Yale University Press, 1969.

Taylor, Charles. *Hegel*. London: Cambridge University Press, 1975.

Thurow, Lester. *The Zero Sum Society*. New York: Penguin Books, 1981.

Tocqueville, Alexis de. *Democracy in America*. The Henry Reeve text as revised by Francis Bowen and edited and corrected by Phillips Bradley. Vol. 2. New York: Vintage Books, 1945.

Tucker, Robert. *Philosophy and Myth in Karl Marx*. 2d ed. London: Cambridge University Press, 1972.

Westpahl, Merold. *History and Truth in Hegel's "Phenomenology."* Atlantic Highlands, N. J.: Humanities Press, 1978.

Wolff, Robert Paul, ed. *Kant: A Collection of Critical Essays*. Garden City, N.Y.: Anchor Books, 1967.

INDEX